Religious C
and the Invention of Karma
in Theravāda Buddhism

Curzon Studies in Asian Religion

Curzon press publishes a Series specifically devoted to Asian Religion, considered from a variety of perspectives: those of theology, philosophy, anthropology, sociology, history, politics and literature. The primary objects of study will be all the religious traditions of the Indian sub-continent, Tibet, China, Japan, South-East Asia, Central Asia, and the Near and Middle East.

The methodology used in the works published in the Series is either comparative or one focused on (a feature of) a specific tradition. The level of readership ranges from undergraduates to specialist scholars. The type of book varies from the introductory textbook to the scholarly monograph.

Proposal or scripts for the Series will be welcomed by the Series Editor or by Jonathan Price, Chief Editor, Curzon Press.

Religious Giving and the Invention of Karma in Theravāda Buddhism

James R. Egge

Routledge
Taylor & Francis Group
LONDON AND NEW YORK

First Published in 2002
by Curzon Press

Published 2013 by Routledge
2 Park Square, Milton Park, Abingdon, Oxfordshire OX14 4RN
711 Third Avenue, New York, NY 10017

First issued in paperback 2014

Routledge is an imprint of the Taylor & Francis Group, an informa business

Typeset in Horley Old Style by LaserScript Ltd, Mitcham, Surrey

British Library Cataloguing in Publication Data
A catalogue record of this book is available from the British Library

Library of Congress Cataloguing in Publication Data
A catalogue record for this book has been requested

ISBN 978-0-700-71506-0 (hbk)
ISBN 978-1-138-86262-3 (pbk)

CONTENTS

ACKNOWLEDGEMENTS

I would like first to thank those who enabled me to write the doctoral dissertation upon which this book is based. Frank Reynolds introduced me to the study of Theravāda Buddhism, mentored me through my years in graduate school, and continually challenged me to think about the larger questions that my research might be answering. Wendy Doniger was a great source of advice, criticism, and encouragement, and was my primary guide to Vedic literature. Steve Collins taught me how to read Theravādin texts, both in English and in Pāli, suggested many paths of inquiry that ultimately proved fruitful, and offered invaluable critiques of my arguments and translations. I hope that readers will recognize his influence on the better parts of this book. Other teachers and colleagues at the University of Chicago, including Paul Griffiths, Matthew Kapstein, and Robert Yelle, listened to presentations of work in progress and made useful comments. Jon Walters kindly read an early attempt to formulate my argument and sent me back to the drawing board, and Maria Hibbets and Charles Hallisey shared their insights on giving and karma in Theravāda and other South Asian traditions.

During the process of writing this book, my colleagues in the Religion Department of Concordia College helped me to think about how to present my claims to a non-specialist audience. Sue Hamilton, Joseph Walser, and Jeff Shirkey read versions of the manuscript, and by following many of their suggestions I have improved it significantly; the shortcomings that remain are of course my own responsibility.

I owe a debt of gratitude to the editors and translators on whose work I have depended. When not otherwise indicated, for the sake of consistency I offer my own translations of Sanskrit and Pāli texts, but in most cases I do not think that my translations represent an improvement over those of my predecessors, and in every case I have benefited from consulting their work.

Most of all, I thank my family and friends whose loving support made it possible for me to carry out this project. I gratefully dedicate this book to the memory of my grandparents, Olav and Inger Olsen and Joseph and Blenda Egge.

ABBREVIATIONS

A	Aṅguttara Nikāya
AB	Aitareya Brāhmaṇa
ADhKBh	Abhidharmakośabhāṣya
Ap	Apadāna
ĀpDhS	Āpastambha Dharmasūtra
ĀpŚS	Āpastambha Śrautasūtra
ĀśvGS	Āśvalāyana Gṛhyasūtra
AV	Atharva Veda
Āyār	Āyāraṃga
BAp	Buddhāpadāna
BĀU	Bṛhadāraṇyaka Upaniṣad
BDhS	Baudhāyana Dharmasūtra
Bv	Buddhavaṃsa
ChU	Chāndogya Upaniṣad
Cp	Cariyāpiṭaka
CPD	Critical Pāli Dictionary
CS	Chaṭṭha Saṅgāyana
D	Dīgha Nikāya
Dasav	Dasaveyāliya
Dhp	Dhammapada
Dhp-a	Dhammapada-aṭṭhakathā
Dhs	Dhammasaṅgaṇī
GDhS	Gautama Dharmasūtra
It	Itivuttaka
It-a	Itivuttaka-aṭṭhakathā (Paramatthadīpanī II)
J	Jātaka
Ja	Jātaka-aṭṭhakathā (includes Jātaka text)
JB	Jaiminīya Brāhmaṇa
KapS	Kapiṣṭhala Saṃhitā
Khp	Khuddakapāṭha
KS	Kāṭhaka Saṃhitā

KṣU	Kauṣītaki Upaniṣad
Kv	Kathāvatthu
M	Majjhima Nikāya
Manu	Manusmṛti
MBh	Mahābhārata
Mil	Milindapañha
Mp	Manorathapūraṇī (Aṅguttara commentary)
MS	Maitrāyaṇī Saṃhitā
MuU	Muṇḍaka Upaniṣad
Nidd	Niddesa
Pd	Paramatthadīpanī
PED	Pali English Dictionary
Ps	Papañcasūdanī (Majjhima commentary)
PTS	Pali Text Society
Pv	Petavatthu
Pv-a	Petavatthu-aṭṭhakathā (Paramatthadīpanī IV)
ṚV	Ṛg Veda
S	Saṃyutta Nikāya
ŚB	Śatapatha Brāhmaṇa
Sīh	Sīhaḷavatthuppakaraṇa
Sn	Suttanipāta
Sp	Samantapāsādikā (Vinaya commentary)
Spk	Sāratthappakāsinī (Saṃyutta commentary)
Sūyag	Sūyagaḍaṃga
Sv	Sumaṅgalavilāsinī (Dīgha commentary)
TĀ	Taittirīya Āraṇyaka
TB	Taittirīya Brāhmaṇa
Thag	Theragāthā
Thīg	Therīgāthā
TS	Taittirīya Saṃhitā
Ud	Udāna
Utt	Uttarajjhāyā
VaDhS	Vasiṣṭha Dharmasūtra
Vin	Vinaya
Vism	Visuddhimagga
VJ	Vessantara Jātaka
Vv	Vimānavatthu
Vv-a	Vimānavatthu-aṭṭhakathā (Paramatthadīpanī III)

INTRODUCTION

Question and Method

Meritorious giving and mental purification: one path or two?

Theravādin Buddhists recognize two soteriological goals: the attainment of nirvāṇa (Pāli *nibbāna*), and the attainment of a good rebirth in the heavens or on earth. While the latter constitutes a continued existence within *saṃsāra*, the cycle of death and rebirth, the former consists in an escape from it. In order to reach these ends, Theravādins pursue different courses of action. Those seeking nirvāṇa typically cultivate *sīla*, or self-restraint,[1] and practice meditation. Those who desire rebirth as a deity or human being also observe *sīla*, but they especially practice *dāna*, or giving to religious recipients.[2] This situation raises the question of whether Theravādins conceptualize these two courses of action as two distinct ethics, or as two stages on the same path. In other words, do Buddhists who seek heaven and those who seek nirvāṇa understand their religious activities to be fundamentally the same or different in kind? One can find textual evidence to support either response; an adequate model of Theravādin ethics and soteriology will account for both views.[3]

A view of Buddhism as a unified ethics directed toward the ultimate goal of nirvāṇa is expressed well by Hammalawa Saddhatissa:

> . . . the ultimate ideal aim which may serve as the ultimate standard of right conduct, relates, according to Buddhist thought, to the supramundane or *lokuttara* state. The connection between the moralities of everyday life and this *lokuttara* state is entirely covered by the Buddha's teaching. This connection is, in fact, known to Buddhists as *mārga* or *magga*,

> the Path or the Road, along which each person must travel for himself, beginning with the practice of the common moralities up to the supramundane state beyond good and evil.[4]

Proponents of such an understanding of Buddhism recognize that the practice of a beginner intent on a pleasant rebirth will differ from that of an elder seeking nirvāṇa. Nonetheless, these scholars locate these different practices along a single continuum of *sīla*, *samādhi*, and *paññā* – right conduct, meditative concentration, and wisdom. In this interpretation, almsgiving, the primary means of making merit for most Theravādin laypeople, is seen primarily as an exercise in generosity and detachment, and its ethical significance lies in its being a means toward awakening.[5] As Bhikkhu Bodhi writes,

> [Giving] does not come at the apex of the path, as a factor constituent of the process of awakening, but rather it serves as a basis and preparation which underlies and quietly supports the entire endeavour to free the mind from the defilements.[6]

W. S. Karunatillake describes similarly the purpose of performing *puṇyakarma*s, good or meritorious deeds:

> The main aim of doing a *puṇyakarma* is the gradual attainment of mental purity and perfection, ultimately leading to the realization of *nibbāna*. This state is realized by the systematic training of the mind through the gradual eradication of the three mental 'black-outs,' the root-causes of all evil action, namely avarice (*lobha*), ill-will (*dosa*) and delusion (*moha*). An action qualifies to be a *puṇyakarma* only if it leads to the eradication of any one or more of these root-causes of evil. That alone leads to a better state of life hereafter.[7]

Action (Pāli *kamma*, Sanskrit *karma*) here provides the category in terms of which all ethically and soteriologically significant activity is described. By purifying the mind, good actions lead to good rebirths and, eventually, to the attainment of nirvāṇa.

Perhaps the best-known explanation of Theravāda as comprising two distinct soteriologies is Melford Spiro's distinction between "nibbanic" and "kammatic" Buddhism.[8] Spiro characterizes nibbanic Buddhism as the cultivation of morality and meditation in order to gain release from *saṃsāra*, and kammatic Buddhism as giving and practicing morality with the goal of improving one's position within *saṃsāra*. Nonetheless, he holds that kammatic Buddhism is based on the values of "normative" nibbanic Buddhism; these systems differ only because kammatic Buddhism is an accommodation to the needs of lay practitioners.[9] Consequently, he puzzles over his informants' view that factors extrinsic to the intention of the donor affect the merit produced through giving:

> Monks, who frequently preach on *dāna*, often remind their audience that the merit derived from giving depends on this pure intention, i.e., the spiritual quality of the benefactor. For the most part, however, the Burmese have reversed this relationship between donor and recipient. For them the merit deriving from *dāna* is proportional to *the spiritual quality of the recipient* rather than that of the donor.[10]

Richard Gombrich is troubled by similar beliefs in Sinhalese Buddhism:

> Here, however, Buddhism faces a difficulty. If generous intention is all that counts . . . why should people give to the Sangha rather than to anyone else? This problem seems to have been acute from the earliest time, for already in the canon we find the highly ambivalent doctrine of the *suitable recipient*.[11]

Although Gombrich sees an "acute" "difficulty" and "problem" for which the tradition provides only a "highly ambivalent" solution, he is unable to make his Buddhist informants share his concern. He tells that one monk answered his questions concerning this point by saying that a gift to a monk given out of respect will produce greater merit than a gift to a beggar given out of pity. Gombrich then adds, "[When I spoke up for the latter he showed no comprehension]."[12] Gombrich concludes that intentionality "has been compromised by the variant of the recipient."[13]

Spiro and Gombrich find the emphasis placed on the recipient problematic because they assume that *dāna* should be about detachment and generosity. I instead argue that Theravādin Buddhists, including Spiro and Gombrich's informants, attach importance to the qualities of the donee because they understand meritorious giving not only as an exercise of generosity, but also as an act of worship directed toward the recipient. Giving, thus understood, consists in outwardly directed acts of sacrifice performed with the goal of acquiring merit. This kind of meritorious giving may be distinguished from inwardly directed efforts to eliminate ignorance and desire. These two ethics provide two distinct sets of meanings that can inform an action: giving can be seen as an act of devotion leading to a good rebirth, or as an act of detachment leading to nirvāṇa. These sacrificial and purificatory soteriologies form a complementary pair, in that a monk's worthiness to receive offerings is determined by his mental purity, i.e. by his progress toward nirvāṇa.[14]

I designate meritorious giving as sacrificial because, as I show in chapter 1, the Buddhist texts themselves describe giving in terms of a discourse of sacrifice. This discourse is characterized by vocabulary appropriated from the Vedic tradition, including words derived from the roots $\sqrt{}$*yaj* (to sacrifice) and $\sqrt{}$*hu* (to offer an oblation) and by related terms including *dakṣiṇā* (Pāli *dakkhiṇā*, the gift given to the officiants at a sacrifice) and *puṇya* (Pāli *puñña*, merit). These terms connote an understanding of sacrifice as acts of making offerings, especially offerings of food, to a worthy recipient. Sacrifice so understood does not necessarily involve killing the thing offered; in Vedic ritual, plant and dairy products are common offerings. It is therefore appropriate to translate *yajña* (Pāli *yañña*) in Buddhist texts as 'sacrifice,' as students of Semitic, Greek, Roman, and other religions have similarly understood sacrifice as a meal offered to deities. This meal may be abandoned or destroyed, such as by being burnt by fire or eaten by priests, or the worshipers may consume part or all of it, but in either case sacrifice serves as a point of communion between worshiper and recipient.[15] I argue that when passages of the Pāli canon (or *Tipiṭaka*) identify giving to Buddhist monastics as sacrifice, they similarly understand sacrifice as a meal given to superior beings, one that differs from Vedic sacrifice in its form and in its recipients, but not in its basic character. By thus describing giving, the authors of these texts deliberately invoke a category central to the religious thought of ancient India in order to ascribe meaning and efficacy to the act of religious giving.

An important move toward articulating the distinction between sacrificial and purificatory soteriologies was made over two decades ago by P. D. Premasiri, who noted an important difference in meaning between the terms *puñña* (merit, meritorious) and *kusala* (good, wholesome) in the Pāli *suttas*:

> *Puñña* in its canonical use generally signified the actions etc. which conduce to a happy consequence to the agent in a future existence. This term was clearly borrowed from the earlier ethical terminology of the Brahmanic tradition. *Kusala*, on the other hand, generally signified that which conduces to spiritual bliss culminating in the attainment of the highest bliss of *nibbāna* which leaves no room for the fruition of any actions.[16]

As Premasiri acknowledges, this distinction is not consistently maintained even in the canonical texts, which in places use *puñña* and *kusala* synonymously.[17] Nonetheless, as I will show, this difference, which corresponds to the distinction I make between sacrifice and mental purification, is a crucial one for understanding not only the Pāli canonical texts, but also the overdetermined attitudes toward giving that Spiro and Gombrich identify.

Understandings of meritorious giving and mental purification as distinct ethical practices play an important role in the Theravādin textual tradition, but so do understandings of them as two aspects of a single path. Ideas of a unitary ethics are most frequently expressed in terms of karma (*kamma*),[18] a category that embraces acts of meritorious giving as well as acts of mental purification. That is, meritorious and purificatory acts are both understood as forms of good karma. I call this way of talking about soteriology karmic discourse, while I refer to those passages that distinguish between two soteriologies as sacrificial-purificatory discourse. Karmic and sacrificial-purificatory discourses can be distinguished by the terms they use to describe action, by their understandings of how acts produce their effects, and by how they represent the effects of action. In this book, I argue that sacrificial and karmic discourses both play prominent roles in Theravāda from the canonical texts to contemporary practice.

Sacrifice and karma in the *suttas* and in history

Recognizing different discourses within the tradition is valuable because doing so allows us to see conversations and even arguments going on within the tradition at large and within individual texts. The Pāli canonical texts took shape over the course of hundreds of years, and our understanding of this remarkable collection of literature is only increased when we recognize it as the product of a number of historically situated authors speaking or writing to different audiences. The approach I advocate here conflicts with a traditional view of the canonical texts that sees them as a faithful represention of the words of the Buddha. Although the Pāli texts may indeed accurately represent much of what the Buddha taught, given that these traditions were transmitted orally for some 300 years by followers of the Buddha, and that we possess no pre-modern manuscripts, we cannot responsibly assume that these texts reliably report the Buddha's teachings.[19] Another way of reading the

Theravādin texts as unified in meaning seeks to recover the meaning of a text for the tradition as a whole, that is, for the commentators and for other hearers and readers of the texts. Steven Collins refers to the object of this hermeneutic as the "Pali imaginaire," "a mental universe created by and within Pali texts."[20] This kind of canonical reading is of interest not only for Buddhists, but for all who want to understand Theravāda Buddhism as a living religious and intellectual tradition.[21] Nonetheless, if we wish to discover the meanings that this literature had in its original contexts, we must recognize the sometimes competing voices within our texts.

Understanding the conversations and debates that inform a textual tradition requires that we form hypotheses about the development of that tradition. Historical-critical methods offer ways of developing and testing such hypotheses; however, we face particular problems in applying such approaches to the study of ancient South Asian literature, including the Pāli canon.[22] As Gregory Schopen has observed, since archeological and epigraphic evidence is scarce, any reconstruction of the history of early Buddhist textual traditions rests almost entirely on textual evidence. The first redaction of the Pāli canon (or of any Buddhist canon) was that of Aluvihāra in the first century BCE, and we have no definite knowledge of the contents of the canon prior to the composition of the commentaries in the fifth and sixth centuries CE.[23] During the centuries between the time of the Buddha and these redactions, oral traditions were no doubt expanded and extensively revised. Schopen shows that we cannot reconstruct the original oral tradition by comparing versions of texts from different Buddhist traditions, as he disproves what he calls the cardinal tenet of higher criticism, "that if all known 'sectarian' versions of a text or passage agree, that text or passage must be very old, i.e. it must come from a pre-sectarian stage of the tradition." He argues instead that such agreement more likely represents "the conflation and gradual leveling and harmonization of earlier existing traditions."[24]

If comparison between traditions is unreliable, reconstructing the development of the textual tradition on the basis of internal evidence is also problematic. Wilhelm Geiger notes that the language of the canonical *gāthās*, or verses, is very heterogenous and contains many archaic forms, while the language of the prose is more homogenous, contains fewer archaic forms, and is governed by more rigid rules.[25] While this observation suggests that the verses predate the prose, a number of scholars have argued that the authors of some verses may have deliberately used archaic forms in order to give the appearance of antiquity.[26] A. K. Warder argues that the comparative study of meter provides a way of establishing a chronological classification of verses; however, his conclusions have not been widely adopted by scholars.[27] More typical is the conclusion of K. R. Norman, that chronological stratification of the Pāli texts is "in the absence of better methods than we have at present, a very subjective matter."[28]

Despite these significant problems, we cannot abandon historical approaches in favor of a purely literary, philosophical, or devotional reading of the canonical texts. In asking what meaning a text had for its original author and audience, or what meaning the traditions incorporated into a text may have had in their original social contexts, we necessarily make explicit or implicit assumptions about the context in which that text was composed. My argument here is not that we should attempt to establish a chronological stratification of the texts as an end in itself, but that we make explicit the historical assumptions that guide our reading. I am less interested in historical-critical approaches to Pāli literature as means to reconstructing early Buddhist history than as tools of literary analysis.[29] An example from biblical criticism may clarify my argument. The hypothesis that the Pentateuch incorporates traditions dating from different historical periods has been of great value for reconstructing the development of ancient Israelite religion. This theory has, however, been equally valuable for the insights it gives into the literary and religious character of the Pentateuch. For example, a careful reader who does not recognize that Genesis 1–2 contains two creation stories is likely to wonder why the narrative is repetitious, disordered, and self-contradictory. An interpreter who sees that this passage combines two narratives can ask different questions, such as, "Why did the redactors include both of these stories? What does each story add to the redactors' representation of God and the world? What does the existence of contradictions between the two accounts imply about the redactors' understanding of these narratives – did the redactors intend for them to be taken as history or as fiction?" Text-critical hypotheses allow us to see the redactors of a text not simply as reciters and scribes, guardians of a tradition, but as authors with their own views concerning the materials they reshaped. Without some idea of how a text came into being, we can recognize neither the diversity of views expressed by that text nor the intention of its authors in combining its sources.

We know that the texts that are now part of the Pāli canon developed from oral traditions. I assume that during the period of oral transmission the prose *suttas* did not exist in the same form as they do today, but that Buddhist monastics would have memorized verses, lists, and prose formulas, on the basis of which they would have composed sermons. John Brough and Noritoshi Aramaki have argued that aphoristic verses and even parts of verses were very likely transmitted independently before being incorporated into larger texts.[30] L. S. Cousins and Rupert Gethin similarly show that Buddhists used lists in order to aid memorization of doctrinal discussions.[31] The Pāli texts as we have them are probably similar in form to these early Buddhist sermons, in which these mnemonic elements were explained through discourses and narratives. For example, Gethin shows that lists were expanded in different ways to form a number of *suttas* and *Abhidhamma* texts. Verses provided the basis for mixed verse and prose compositions, as occasional remarks in the commentaries that prose passages were composed after the verses attest.[32] Prose passages often comment on verses, or, in texts such as *Sagāthavagga* (S I), simply provide a narrative frame for the verses. As I argue in chapter 2, prose passages frequently present significantly different points of view from those of the verses on which they comment.

If this account of the formation of the canonical texts is correct, we may hypothesize regarding the parts of the canon generally considered most likely to be oldest – *Vinaya*, the first four *Nikāyas* of *Suttapiṭaka*, and *Dhammapada*, *Udāna*, *Itivuttaka*, *Suttanipāta*, *Theragāthā*, *Therīgāthā*, and *Jātaka* – that the verses often represent an older tradition than does the prose.[33] Of course the prose may also be very old; however, even if the prose and the verses dated from the same period, the prose would likely have undergone greater changes than the verse during the centuries of oral and written transmission, because the metrical structure of the verses helps to insure accurate transmission. As N. A. Jayawickrama writes of the mixed verse and prose narratives of *Suttanipāta*:

> The language of the prose is quite similar to that of the prose Nikāyas in idiom, syntax, and style. The stereotyped expression of the prose of Sutta Nipāta does not permit one to infer that it preserves the exact words of the narrators or reciters of these ballads. Generally, ballad-reciters state *in their own words*, such facts as are necessary for the listeners to follow the narrative in

> the ballads. Here the prose states the same facts though clothed in the standard Canonical garb; and probably this standardisation has taken place long after the composition of the ballads themselves.[34]

Norman notes that the grammar of the canonical texts underwent revision at least as late as the twelfth century,[35] but the presence of archaic forms in the *gāthās* indicate that they were not standardized in this manner in form or content, or at least to a much lesser extent than was the prose. Of the verses, external evidence shows that *Aṭṭhakavagga* and *Pārāyaṇavagga* of *Suttanipāta* likely belong to the oldest Buddhist literature: these *vaggas* are both mentioned by name and quoted in other Pāli canonical texts, and the canon includes a commentary on these passages and on *Khaggavisāṇasutta* (Sn I.3), but on no other text.[36]

This account suggests that purificatory and sacrificial discourses predate and were largely replaced by karmic discourse. As Lambert Schmithausen observes, the oldest verse literature represented by *Aṭṭhakavagga* and *Pārāyaṇavagga* identifies the cause of existence in *saṃsāra* not as karma but as harmful mental states.[37] In other words, they present the path to nirvāṇa in purificatory discourse, not karmic discourse. Other verse literature contains sacrificial and purificatory discourse as well as karmic language; sacrificial discourse appears most often in non-narrative, didactic verses, while karmic expressions are usually found in verse narratives. Prose discussions of action and rebirth, however, consist almost entirely of karmic discourse, and rarely incorporate sacrificial discourse apart from fixed formulas. These data indicate that the earliest form of Buddhism of which we have knowledge was not articulated in karmic discourse, but that karmic discourse eventually became the standard idiom for the expression of Buddhist teachings.

Other explanations are of course possible: as N. A. Jayawickrama argues, because *gāthās* may have been deliberately composed in archaic language, an assertion that verses are old must be supported by additional arguments:

> The Pali of the gāthās represents the standard vehicle of poetic expression, the archaic colouring being the outcome of a close adherence to what may be termed as the gāthā-style. Yet, the Vedic elements in Sn., as a rule, are generally confined to those sections to which an early date can be assigned on *collective data*.[38]

As I show in chapter 2, the hypothesis that karmic discourse replaced sacrificial discourse as a mode for explaining the effects of gifts also provides the simplest explanation of the difference in content between the sacrificial verses and the canonical prose.

The major contribution of my argument, however, lies not in its reconstruction of early Buddhist doctrinal history, but in offering a new way of reading the canonical texts. According to most accounts of early Buddhism, karmic theory pre-existed Buddhism: the Buddha or his followers adopted the idea of karma from late Vedic religion and modified it by taking the moral quality of actions, rather than their ritual character, to be the determinant of rebirth.[39] One who accepts this hypothesis will tend to find the same meaning in all canonical statements about action and rebirth. The hypothesis that sacrificial-purificatory discourse is older than karmic discourse (or at least, older than the karmic discourse as elaborated in the canonical prose) opens up ways of reading the Pāli *sutta*s that recognize the varied intentions of their authors. We can see that the authors of the sacrificial verses actively appropriate Vedic sacrificial ideology by representing almsgiving as an act of sacrifice in which the Buddha or a Buddhist monastic replaces sacred fire and Vedic deity as recipient of the offering. We can also discern that the authors of the karmic prose do not simply adopt and modify a pre-existing karma theory, but engage in an innovative and largely successful attempt to reduce sacrifice and mental purification to a unified soteriological system. When we read our texts in this manner, words, images, and arguments that had formerly seemed opaque become meaningful and expressive products of authorial decisions.

The plan of this book

In the first half of this book I characterize the sacrificial and karmic discourses, drawing primarily on the non-narrative sections of *Vinaya*, the first four *Nikāyas* of *Suttapiṭaka*, and *Dhammapada*, *Udāna*, *Itivuttaka*, *Suttanipāta*, *Theragāthā*, and *Therīgāthā*. In chapter 1, I argue that the didactic verse of these texts present two complementary soteriological paths: a purificatory soteriology oriented toward attainment of nirvāṇa, and a sacrificial soteriology oriented toward the attainment of heaven. Most of this chapter consists of a description of the expressions and concepts that characterize this sacrificial discourse. In the last section of this chapter, I show that some *Jātaka* stories present an understanding of giving not as sacrifice but as heroic generosity. In chapter 2, I describe the karmic discourse as presented in the discursive prose passages of the books named above, and demonstrate that while it accounts for acts of giving and of mental purification, it differs significantly from the sacrificial and purificatory discourses in the language it employs and in its understanding of how good actions produce their effects. I also argue that in systematic and philosophical writing, the karmic discourse largely replaced the sacrificial discourse, and I place this development in the larger context of the history of South Asian religions.

In the second half of the book I turn to the use of sacrificial and karmic themes in narrative. I demonstrate, through a study of four important and representative narrative texts, that both sacrificial and karmic discourses inform later Theravāda in significant ways. In chapter 3, I examine how the verse narratives of *Vimānavatthu* and *Petavatthu* combine elements of sacrificial and karmic discourse to dramatize the effects of good and bad actions. I argue in chapter 4 that the commentary to these texts attempts to give them a consistently karmic interpretation, but aspects of sacrificial discourse resist explanation in karmic terms. Finally, in chapter 5, I show that the medieval story collection *Sīhaḷavatthuppakaraṇa* draws freely on both sacrificial and karmic idioms, showing that despite the dominance of karmic discourse in systematic thought, the sacrificial tradition continues to be a vital part of Theravāda Buddhism. *Sīhaḷavatthuppakaraṇa* also demonstrates the importance of *Jātaka* in the tradition by liberally incorporating heroic asceticism and other themes drawn from that text.

The phrase 'invention of karma' in the title of this book therefore has a double reference. In the first part of the book I argue that Buddhists did not inherit the classical doctrine of karma from late Vedic religion, but that they, like their Jain and Brahmanical contemporaries, invented the idea of karma as a way of unifying the sacrificial and purificatory soteriologies within a single doctrinal system. However, in reading the stories of *Vimānavatthu*, *Petavatthu*, *Paramatthadīpanī*, and *Sīhaḷavatthuppakaraṇa*, we see their authors continuing to try to render coherent and meaningful the notion of karma, and in particular to reconcile it with other understandings of action and rebirth. The Buddhist invention of karma is an ongoing process.

Part One

Sacrifice and Karma in Didactic Verse and Discursive Prose

CHAPTER ONE

The Discourse of Sacrifice

Many verses of *Vinaya*, the first four *Nikāyas* of *Suttapiṭaka*, *Dhammapada*, *Udāna*, *Itivuttaka*, *Suttanipāta*, *Theragāthā*, and *Therīgāthā* present *dāna*, or giving to monastics, as a kind of sacrifice (*yañña*). These verses do not present this equivalence of almsgiving and sacrifice as a claim to be argued for or to be qualified; rather, they appropriate ideas and expressions from Vedic ritual discourse and apply them to Buddhist almsgiving, thereby articulating a distinctively Buddhist sacrificial discourse. In this chapter, I outline the Vedic antecedents of Buddhist sacrificial practice, and then trace the continuities and discontinuities between Brahmanical and Buddhist practice in relation to three themes: almsgiving as sacrificial action, observance of *sīla* as sacrificial action, and almsgiving as transfer of sacrificial substance. I then consider why Buddhists adopted Vedic beliefs and practices, and finally, I discuss some canonical verses that present giving not as sacrifice but as heroic generosity.

The structure of Brahmanical sacrifice

In a Vedic sacrifice, the patron, often with the assistance of priests, makes an offering to a deity or group of deities, usually by burning the offering in a consecrated fire. The Brahmanical texts provide a number of explanations of how performance of the sacrifice benefits the patron; these center on the object offered or on the act of offering it. These two ideas of reward constitute complementary ways of thinking about the effects of sacrifice. As I will show, Buddhists applied both understandings of the workings of sacrifice to the act of giving to monastics, and thereby ascribed meaning and efficacy to the act of almsgiving.

Vedic literature presents various understandings of how the material offering benefits the patron. According to the older literature, the burnt offering reaches the gods, who enjoy it and reward the patron. These rewards usually consist of long life and material goods, such as rain, cattle, and wealth. A typical prayer expressing this understanding states, "Let Dhātar, Rāti, Savitar enjoy this, Prajāpati, Agni, our treasure-lord; let Tvaṣṭar, Viṣṇu, bestowing liberally assign wealth with offspring to the sacrificer."[1] The few references to the afterlife in this older literature present it as a Hades-like underworld.[2] In later texts, explanations of the mechanism of reward in terms other than divine counter-gift become more prominent, as do descriptions of benefits to be enjoyed in a heaven after death.[3] For example, sacrifices and *dakṣiṇā*, the gift to the priest who officiates at a sacrifice, sometimes referred to collectively as *iṣṭāpūrta*,[4] are said to accumulate for the future enjoyment of the donor. A late hymn of the *Ṛg Veda* addresses a dead man at his funeral with these words:

> Meet with the fathers, with Yama [the god of the dead], and with your sacrifices and gifts in the highest heaven. Having abandoned imperfections, reach your home again; Meet a (new) body, O radiant ones.[5]

Elsewhere we find the idea that the sacrificial oblation becomes the body (*ātman*) of the patron in the next life, as in *Śatapatha Brāhmaṇa* 11.2.2.5–6:

> . . . having become the sacrifice, he is freed from that death, and all his sacrificial rites are freed from that death. What oblation he offers becomes his body in that world; when he goes away from this world it is at his back, calling: "Come, here I am, your body."[6]

These passages thus in different ways represent the material offering as reaching heaven and producing (or becoming) a reward for the patron.

Other passages of the *Brāhmaṇas* and ritual *sūtras* emphasize less the offerings and gifts themselves as productive of reward, than the correct performance of the rite. The efficacy of the rite in this view depends primarily not on the substance of the material offering but on the conformity of the ritual performance to a cosmic prototype. A good example of this understanding is provided by the *Śatapatha*

Brāhmaṇa's prescriptions for the *agnicayana* sacrifice.[7] The text elaborates a system of correspondences between the parts of the ritual, the parts of the sacrificial patron's body, and the parts of the year and of the cosmos, which are identified with the gods Prajāpati and Agni. For example, five layers of bricks in the altar are said to correspond to the five parts of the patron's body, and also to the five seasons and the five directions. Alternatively, twelve layers of brick and mortar correspond to the twelve parts of the patron and to the twelve months of the year.[8] By performing this rite, the patron repeats Agni's act of restoring the body of Prajāpati after the creation of the world (6.1.2.13, 21–27), and thereby creates an immortal body for himself.[9]

Some important expressions in this act-centered discourse are *sukṛt-*, one who does well, and *sukṛta*, well-done or well-made, which may refer to a ritual action, a world won by ritual action, or merit, the potential to attain such a world in the future.[10] *Puṇyakṛt-* and *puṇya* (cognate to Pali *puñña*), meaning 'good' or 'auspicious,' are frequently used with the same range of referents.[11] Merit is said to accumulate for the ritual actor in a heaven, or to accompany him there.[12] The continuing effect of past action is only rarely referred to as *karman*.[13]

These material-centered and act-centered ideas of reward accruing from sacrificial substance and action are represented not as two competing discourses as much as two complementary ways of thinking about the effects of ritual action. This point is made clear by those passages that combine these conceptions, such as *Muṇḍaka Upaniṣad* 1.2.6:

> Saying "Come! Come!," the radiant oblations carry the sacrificer on rays of the sun,
> Saying pleasing words and praising him, "This is your auspicious (*puṇya*) and well-made (*sukṛta*) Brahmaloka."[14]

Here oblation and merit cooperate to bring the sacrificer to heaven. In *Aitareya Brāhmaṇa* 8.15.3, a king is instructed to offer in guarantee of an oath his sacrificial offerings and gifts (*iṣṭāpūrta*), his world (*loka*), his merit (*sukṛta*), his life, and his offspring. *Iṣṭāpūrta* and *sukṛta* are here regarded as different things. Of these two basic mechanisms of reward for the sacrifice, based either on the material offering or on the ritual act, the latter understanding was heavily appropriated by the Buddhist tradition. But as I will show, conceptions of the material offering reaching a divine recipient also inform Buddhist conceptions of religious giving in significant ways.

To understand how Buddhists could view almsgiving as sacrifice, we must see that the Brahmanical texts themselves equate sacrifice with dakṣiṇā, the gift given to the officiating priests. These texts view dakṣiṇā as essential to the sacrifice, and refer to Dakṣiṇā as the wife of the sacrifice.[15] *Śatapatha Brāhmaṇa* 2.2.2.1–2 and 4.3.4.1–2 explain the origin of the word *dakṣiṇā* by telling that after the gods killed the *soma* offering, they enabled (*dakṣayan*) it by giving dakṣiṇā to the priests. *Śatapatha Brāhmaṇa* 1.9.3.1 and 4.3.4.6 tell that when the sacrifice goes to the world of the gods, the dakṣiṇā follows with the patron holding on to it. Other texts present dakṣiṇā as a sacrifice in itself. *Ṛg Veda* 10.107, a hymn to dakṣiṇā, states, "Dakṣiṇā is a gift to the gods, a sacrifice to the gods."[16] A number of texts assert that Brāhmaṇs are gods on earth,[17] or the human counterparts of the gods;[18] to give dakṣiṇā is therefore to sacrifice. *Śatapatha Brāhmaṇa* 2.2.2.6 states that there are two kinds of gods: gods (themselves) and Brāhmaṇs; accordingly, sacrifice is divided into oblations for the gods and dakṣiṇā for the "human gods."[19] We also read that the recipient of dakṣiṇā should turn away from it and dedicate it to various deities.[20] Here the priest consumes or keeps the material gift, while the gods receive its essence or heavenly counterpart; in this way the priest serves as intermediary between the patron and the gods. Similarly, descriptions of sacrifices in which priests eat part of the offering represent them either as recipients of the sacrifice, or as the sacrificial fire, "the mouth of Agni," mediating between the patron and the deities.[21] In the funerary *śrāddha* feast, food eaten by priests is said to be consumed by the dead. Āpastamba explains, "In this rite the ancestors are the deity to whom the offering is made, while the Brāhmaṇs stand in the place of the offertorial fire."[22]

A discussion of the *agnihotra* sacrifice in *Yajur Veda* illustrates well the interpretation of dakṣiṇā as sacrifice. Among the solemn, or *śrauta*, rites,[23] the *agnihotra*, the twice-daily oblation of milk into the three domestic fires, held a central position as the paradigmatic sacrifice.[24] Its performance was compulsory for everyone who had established the sacred fires in his home. Although only Brāhmaṇs could perform the *agnihotra*, the *Yajur Veda* allows that Kṣatriyas may nonetheless participate in Vedic ritual on a daily basis by giving dakṣiṇā:

> The Kṣatriya has no *agnihotra*, because he is not fit for it; he kills (or, he kills a vow). One (i.e., a Brāhmaṇ) should not interrupt one's vow. One

> should offer oblations (on behalf of the Kṣatriyas) on the night of the full moon and of the new moon, for those two protect the vow (i.e. they cause the Kṣatriyas to keep their vow). During those days when one does not offer oblations (on behalf of the Kṣatriyas), they should first (i.e. before their own meal) present (food) to a Brāhmaṇ at their homes. The Brāhmaṇ is identical with Agni. Thereby they offer in Agni. What has been tasted by him, thereby has been sacrificed.[25]

This text offers two remedies for the Kṣatriya's lack of religious observance. The Kṣatriya may sacrifice during the two days of the month when he observes his vow, which consists in partial or full fasting, and in retiring in the hall in which the sacrificial fire is kept.[26] The other solution is that just as the Brāhmaṇ makes offerings into Agni, the fire, and so offers hospitality to the gods, so the Kṣatriya may sacrifice by feeding Brāhmaṇs in his home.[27] Here dakṣiṇā stands alone as an independent sacrifice.

Both of the rites described in this passage are mirrored in major forms of Theravādin practice. Buddhists adopted the custom of undertaking ascetic restrictions at the time of the full moon and new moon; many lay Buddhists keep these Uposatha days by staying at a monastery and observing rules similar to those obeyed by monastic novices.[28] Buddhists also give to monastics gifts, usually of food, and Buddhist texts identify this activity as sacrifice.[29] In addition to these ways of making merit, Buddhists also adopted the Vedic practice of giving dakṣiṇā as a means of giving to deities and to the dead. In these ways, Buddhists made the Vedic sacrificial cult their own.

Almsgiving as meritorious sacrifice

The most important aspect of Vedic sacrificial theory and practice to be appropriated by Buddhists was the interpretation of giving to clergy as meritorious sacrifice. Theravādin sacrificial discourse employs vocabulary and concepts borrowed from the Vedic tradition to attribute meaning to the act of giving and to show how it produces its meritorious effects. Giving is frequently identified as sacrifice in verses such as, "I sacrifice to the fire worthy of dakṣiṇā; I venerate the Tathāgata."[30] One arhat is described as "worthy of oblations, having knowledge, developed, worthy of the dakṣiṇā of deities and humans."[31] The Saṅgha is similarly named as "the best for those who sacrifice, desiring merit."[32] A worthy recipient is often called a field for merit (*puññakkhetta*). In this extended metaphor, the field is the recipient of a gift, the sower is the donor, and the seed is the gift. If the seed is planted in a good field, viz. the Buddha, an upright monastic, or the Saṅgha as a whole, it will yield great merit:

> A gift given with discernment is praised by the Sugata: gifts given to those worthy of dakṣiṇā here in this world produce great fruit, as seeds planted in a field.[33]

In another verse the Buddha claims to be, "the unsurpassed field for merit, / The sacrificial recipient for all the world; what is given to the Blessed One yields great fruit."[34] The recipient need not be an arhat to be a fruitful field:

> In this world, disciple and adept are worthy of the oblations of those who sacrifice,
> Those who are upright in body, speech and mind
> Are a field for those who sacrifice; what is given here is of great fruit.[35]

A lay donor is praised by the members of her family with these words:

> You indeed recognize this unsurpassed field of merit;
> These ascetics (will) also receive our dakṣiṇā.
> An abundant sacrifice will surely be established for us here.[36]

Other verses designate the Saṅgha as the recipient:

> For those persons sacrificing, for those people seeking merit,
> For those making merit from material [offerings], what is given to the Saṅgha is of great fruit.[37]

As this metaphor of the field for merit illustrates, a worthy recipient is an essential component of a meritorious gift.

A donor should regard the recipient of a gift with an attitude of confidence and trust, or *saddhā*.[38] Vedic tradition similarly regards *śraddhā*, understood as trust in the gods and in the efficacy of the sacrifice that manifests itself in generosity, as necessary for success in sacrifice.[39] Another set of Pāli verses stresses the importance of maintaining a happy state of mind before, during, and after the act of giving:

> Before giving one is glad, while giving one makes one's mind devoted,
> Having given one is elated: this is successful attainment of sacrifice.
> Without lust, hatred, delusion, or *āsavas*,
> Restrained *brahmacārins* are a perfect field for sacrifice.

After cleansing oneself and giving with one's own hands,
The sacrifice is of great fruit for oneself and for others.
Having sacrificed in this way, the wise, faithful, mentally liberated,
Intelligent one arises in an undisturbed, happy world.[40]

Other verses stress the need to give with a devoted, clear, friendly, and liberated mind, and further specify that the donor should be self-controlled, modest, wise, approachable, generous, dispassionate, faultless, resolute, and unconfused.[41]

The immediate result of an act of giving, which produces its final effect, is usually called *puñña*. In canonical non-narrative verse literature, use of this term correlates closely with other features of sacrificial discourse.[42] In these verses, *puñña* usually means 'auspiciousness' or 'merit,' the potential to produce a good effect that is created by a sacrificial act. The sacrificial verses typically say that one makes (*karoti*) or produces (*pasavati*) *puñña*. While *puññaṃ karoti* could also be construed to mean, "one does a good deed," or, "one does well," the verb *pasavati* implies an understanding of *puñña* as the effect of action, and other usages confirm this interpretation.[43] Merit is said be something that people seek (*pekkha*), for which they have need (*attho*) or desire (*kāma, ākaṅkhā*).[44] People obtain (*labhati*) and have (*puññavant-*) merit which is amassed (*cīyate, upacita*) to form a heap (*uccaya, nicaya, sañcaya*), a store (*nidhi*), a provision (*patheyya*) or an island (*dīpa*).[45] The merit of one who does good is said to be difficult to measure; a good person is said to be full of merit.[46] It is said that one's merits follow one to heaven like a shadow; alternatively, it is said that one's merits receive one in heaven as do relatives.[47] Merits are said to be helpers (*upakāra*), friends (*mitta*), or supporters (*patiṭṭha*) in the next world.[48] Merits bring happiness (*sukhāvaha*);[49] they come (or return, *āgacchati, āgama*)[50] to their makers, and persons and actions are said to share in merit (*puññabhāgin-*).[51] Some passages describe merit as *opadhika*, "resulting from the donation of material objects (*upadhi*)."[52]

In addition to the root metaphor of the field for merit, merit is represented as fruit or as bearing fruit (S I 20, 97). We read that merit grows, as in a set of verses about those devoted to the Buddha, "the best, the one most worthy of dakṣiṇā," the Dharma, "the best, cleansing and calming, pleasant" and the Saṅgha, "the best, the unsurpassed field for merit":

For those giving a gift to the best, the best merit grows,

The best life, beauty, glory, fame, happiness, and strength.[53]

That is, giving produces not only merit for the next life, but rewards for this life as well. It is also written that the merit of those who supply the physical needs of monastics grows always, day and night (A II 65).

The Theravādin sacrificial discourse predicts that those who make merit will go to the heavens, while those who fail to make merit will experience a bad fate. Thus we read that at the breaking up of the body, the fool who has not made merit arises in a bad destiny, while the wise man who has made merit arises in heaven.[54] Other verses state that one who does not give goes to a bad destiny, while givers go to an auspicious place,[55] and that those who behave badly toward monks and parents go to a bad destiny, while those who behave well rejoice in heaven.[56] In their descriptions of the heavens, the Pāli verses follow Vedic patterns. *Dhammapada* 44 and 45, which state that the virtuous disciple is able to conquer "the world of Yama with its gods," expresses the Vedic idiom of conquering a 'world' (*loka*) and the ancient belief that the god Yama rules over the happy dead.[57] The sacrificial-purificatory verses also resemble the Vedic texts in saying little about the unhappy destiny of those lacking in merit. No didactic verses that speak of merit indicate that *niraya* should be understood as a place of torment.[58] One verse suggests that the bad fate may have been understood as being caught in the cycle of rebirth as a lower form of life: *Suttanipāta* 278 describes the downfall (*vinipāta*) as "from womb to womb, from darkness to darkness."[59] This phrase perhaps echoes a passage in *Chāndogya Upaniṣad* which states that those who lack in knowledge and merit are reborn as "tiny creatures revolving here ceaselessly."[60]

Although some Pāli sacrificial-purificatory verses speak of gifts bringing benefits for this life as well as merit for the next,[61] none speaks of merit producing or conditioning rebirth as a human or as an animal after one leaves heaven.[62] In this regard, the Pāli verses follow the pattern set out in the earliest *Upaniṣads*.[63] *Bṛhadāraṇyaka Upaniṣad* tells that people win worlds "by offering sacrifices, by giving gifts, and by performing austerities," and *Chāndogya Upaniṣad* says that villagers who worship with the thought, "Gift-giving is offerings to gods and to priests," reach the world of the fathers.[64] When their time in the heavens is over, these people return to earth and are reborn through entering plants, being eaten, becoming semen, and being deposited in a womb. *Chāndogya* does includes a verse

(5.10.7) that asserts that one's past behavior conditions one's rebirth, because good souls come to be eaten by twice-born men, and bad souls by low-caste men and animals; however, as Wilhelm Halbfass observes, this verse appears to be a later addition, as it does not explain this phenomenon in relation to the text's naturalistic paradigm.[65]

Also like the Pāli verses, these *Upaniṣads* contrast the performance of meritorious actions leading to a limited sojourn in heaven with another path leading to a permanent state of bliss. BĀU 6.2.15 states that those with special knowledge, and those in the wilderness who venerate truth as faith, go after death to the Brahmalokas, from which they do not return. ChU 5.10.1–10 similarly tells that those with special knowledge, and those in the wilderness who venerate by thinking that austerity is faith, go after death to Brahman.[66] The purificatory discourse as represented in the didactic verses of *Suttanipāta* and *Dhammapada* similarly presents meritorious action and mental purification as distinct soteriological paths. While merit leads one to heaven after death, purification strikes at the fundamental causes of death and rebirth: passion, attachment, clinging, thirst, and other mental states.[67] Through attaining nirvāṇa, the extinguishing of these states, one may put an end to rebirth.[68] These verses never present merit and demerit as fundamental causes of renewed existence, nor do they describe merit as a means to the attainment of nirvāṇa.[69] In the *Suttanipāta*'s account of the temptation of Gotama by Māra, the Bodhisattva regards the possession or non-possession of merits as immaterial to his attaining awakening (427–431). Some verses do, however, present *attachment* to merit and to evil action as causes of rebirth. The problem with merit is not that it produces rebirth, but that it is a potential object of clinging to be abandoned and rejected.[70] The Buddha states,

> But whoever has passed beyond merit and evil, both attachments,
> Without grief, without pollution, purified, him I call a Brāhmaṇ.[71]

The ascetic Sabhiya praises the Buddha with these words:

> As a beautiful lotus flower does not cling to water,
> So you do not cling to merit and evil, both.[72]

Similarly, we read,

> Not clinging to merit or evil, [the Brāhmaṇ] abandons what has been taken up, and does not fashion (anything more) here.[73]

Again, the *Upaniṣads* present a precedent: KṣU 1.4 states that a person on his way to the Brahmaloka shakes off his merit and demerit (*sukṛtaṃ, duṣkṛtaṃ*).

The hypothesis that Buddhists recognized sacrifice and mental purification as two distinct soteriologies gives a way of making sense of an obscure verse from *Suttanipāta*: *uccāvacā hi paṭipadā samaṇena pakāsitā: / na pāraṃ diguṇaṃ yanti, nayidaṃ ekaguṇaṃ mutaṃ.*[74] We can interpret the first line, "For high and low are the paths revealed by the ascetic [i.e. the Buddha]," by noting that the preceding verse instructs monks not to despise a small gift or to disparage a giver. This context is particularly relevant if the particle *hi* is understood as *for* or *because*. If we interpret this verse in connection with the Buddha's approval of giving, we may take it to mean that the Buddha has revealed the low path of sacrifice as well as the high path of purification. We may then translate the second line as, "They do not go to the far shore two ways; this [far shore] is in no way felt." In other words, only one of the two paths reaches nirvāṇa, which is not experienced with the senses.[75]

A set of verses from *Aṅguttara* II 43–44 brings together many aspects of the Theravādin sacrificial discourse:

> Restrained practioners of *brahmacariya* approach a sacrifice
> That is ritually prepared, without killing, and done at the proper time.
> Those for whom the veil has been removed in this life, who have overcome death,
> Awakened ones, knowers of merit, praise this sacrifice.
> Properly making an offering in a sacrifice or in a śrāddha rite,
> A person of devoted mind sacrifices in a good field, among *brahmacārins*.
> What is done among those worthy of offerings is well-offered, well-sacrificed, and well-obtained;
> The sacrifice is abundant and the gods are pleased.
> Having sacrificed in this way, the wise, faithful, mentally liberated,
> Intelligent one arises in an undisturbed, happy world.[76]

This passage invokes a number of Brahmanical terms and concepts. It affirms, in continuity with Vedic thought, the importance of the physical act of giving and of faith (*saddhā*). The result of this sacrifice is merit leading to a happy world. This author of this passage constructs *dāna* as a ritual action by specifying how it is to be performed. The text uses a term with sacrificial connotations, *abhisaṅkhata* (Sanskrit *abhisaṃskṛta*), to describe how the gift must be prepared. The requirement that the gift be timely, which also appears in other verses,[77] in part reflects a practical concern that monks and nuns be given food at the time they make their morning almsrounds. But in these passages which are heavy with allusions to Vedic sacrifice, attention to the time for giving serves to ritualize the time for sacrifice, to mark it off from profane activities. Most importantly, the gift must be made to a recipient who is a restrained *brahmacārin*, whose worthiness as a field for merit is a product of mental and behavioral purity. At the same time, this passage also distances itself from the Vedic tradition by describing a sacrifice that is without killing (*nirārambha*). In affirming both continuities and discontinuities with the older tradition, this text co-opts the powerful symbolism of sacrifice.

Three *suttas* at *Saṃyutta* I 165–170 similarly revalue Brahmanical categories in order to assert the superiority of Buddha and Saṅgha as recipients of offerings.[78] In the second of these *suttas*, the Buddha proclaims that one becomes worthy to receive offerings not through birth as a Brāhmaṇ and knowledge of the three Vedas (literally 'knowledges'), but through attainment of a different three knowledges (*tevijjo*): knowing that one has lived before, seeing the heavens and the bad destinies (*saggāpāyañca*), and having attained the destruction of rebirth (S I 166–167). This redefined threefold knowledge appears elsewhere as the standard marks of awakening.[79] In the third *sutta*, the Buddha contrasts the external purity of Brahmanical ritual with the inner purity of the arhat:

> Brāhmaṇ, do not think that purity comes from gathering wood; that is external.
> The good say that he who desires external purification does not attain purity.
> Brāhmaṇ, I, having abandoned wood gathering, make burn an inner fire.
> Having a permanent fire, always composed, I, an arhat, live the *brahmacariya* life.[80]

In this passage, unusual for Theravāda in its use of the inner flame as a symbol of internalized sacrifice, the Buddha makes his mental purity the basis for his worthiness to receive offerings.

Finally, a pair of *suttas* from *Suttanipāta* develop the theme of the worthy recipient in extended dialogs. In *Sundarikabhāradvāja Sutta* (III.4), the Buddha proclaims that "a Brāhmaṇ who seeks merit should sacrifice" and "at the right time should offer an oblation" to sages who are without passion.[81] The Buddha convinces a Brāhmaṇ that the Tathāgata "deserves the sacrificial cake" and that he is "an unsurpassed field for merit, a sacrificial recipient for the entire world."[82] *Māgha Sutta* (III.5) begins with the following exchange:

> 'I ask, sir, the munificent Gotama,' said the young Brāhmaṇ Māgha, 'who wears a yellow robe, (and) wanders houseless: If any open-handed householder, a lordly giver, seeking for merit, looking for merit, sacrifices, giving food and drink to others here, wherein would the oblation be purified for the one sacrificing?'
>
> 'Any open-handed householder, a lordly giver, Māgha,' said the Blessed One, 'seeking for merit, looking for merit, sacrifices, giving food and drink to others here, would succeed because of those worthy to receive dakṣiṇā.'[83]

The Brāhmaṇ's question is pertinent in the context of the Vedic rite: because only pure oblations were believed to be acceptable to the gods and therefore efficacious, priests would undertake preparatory rituals to insure the purity of offerings.[84] The Buddha indicates that an offering is purified not by external ritual but by a worthy recipient, and proceeds to describe at length the ideal sacrificial recipient.[85] In response to further questions, the Buddha states that the donor should clear his mind, eliminate his faults, and cultivate unbounded lovingkindness; one who thus "sacrifices the threefold successful performance of the sacrifice" arises in the Brahmaloka.[86] The authors of these *suttas* not only appropriate Vedic categories, but argue that Buddhist *dāna* represents a superior form of sacrifice.

Uposatha observance as meritorious votive asceticism

As the *Yajur Veda* passage cited in the first section of this chapter indicates, lay practice of Vedic ritual included, in addition to sacrifice and giving, fortnightly austerities at the time of the full moon and new moon sacrifices. This observance was called *vrata*, after the vows undertaken, or *upavasatha*, 'dwelling near,' because during this observance the sacrificers stayed near the sacred fires and the gods were believed to draw near (ŚB 1.1.1.7). The Pāli texts indicate that Buddhists similarly observed the Uposatha as a periodic exercise of asceticism in the presence of the Saṅgha, and these texts present Uposatha observance as a means of making merit.

For Theravādins, observance of the Uposatha typically consists in going to a monastery, giving *dāna*, hearing sermons, and most importantly, observing the *aṭṭha sīla*, or eight precepts:

> He should not kill any being, he should not take what is not given,
> He should not tell a lie, and he should not be a drinker of intoxicants;
> He should abstain from sexual activity, from intercourse;
> He should not eat an untimely meal at night;
> He should not wear garlands or use perfume;
> He should lie on a bed or a mat on the ground:
> This, they say, is the eightfold Uposatha
> Made known by the Buddha, who has gone to the end of suffering.[87]

Keeping the Uposatha is said to produce merit:

> Therefore the woman and the man who possess *sīla*,
> Having observed the eight-limbed Uposatha,
> Having made merits yielding happiness,
> Go blameless to a heavenly place.[88]

These eight precepts are similar to the ten *sikkhāpada*s, or training rules, observed by novices, which consist in abstention from:

1 killing (*pāṇātipāta*)
2 stealing (*adinnādāna*)
3 sexual activity (*abrahmacariya*)
4 lying (*musāvāda*)
5 intoxication (*surāmerayamajjapamādaṭṭhāna*)
6 untimely eating (*vikāla bhojana*)
7 seeing shows of dance, song, and music (*naccagītavāditavisūkadassana*)
8 wearing garlands, perfumes, and ointments (*mālāgandhavilepanadhāraṇamaṇḍanavibhūsanaṭṭhāna*)
9 high beds and large beds (*uccāsayanamahāsayana*)
10 receiving gold and silver (*jātarūparajatapaṭiggahaṇa*)[89]

The only differences between these two codes is that the seventh Uposatha precept corresponds to the seventh and eighth *sikkhāpada*s, and the Uposatha precepts do not include a rule against handling money. Novices and lay practitioners therefore observe very similar sets of rules, but for different purposes. While novices are to observe the rules as a means of cultivating self-discipline with the ultimate goal of attaining nirvāṇa, the Uposatha is recommended to laity as a means of making merit.

The contents of these two lists, especially of their second halves, suggest that common translations of *sīla* as morality, moral conduct, or virtue are not appropriate here. In this context, *sīla* indicates observing a set of ascetic restrictions ritualized by the taking of vows. Each of the precepts is of the form, "I undertake the training rule of abstaining from . . ." (. . . *veramaṇīsikkhāpadaṃ samādiyāmi*). These precepts are similar in form and content to vows undertaken by Jains and Brāhmaṇs.[90] This interpretation of *sīla* as votive asceticism is supported by uses of the compound *sīlavata* (or *sīlabbata*), which appears in numerous places in the *Tipiṭaka*. Although this compound is often taken to mean, 'good conduct and vows,' this interpretation does not fit the many passages in the canon in which this expression has a negative connotation, as it is difficult to see why a Buddhist text would criticize good conduct.[91] However, such passages are easily understood if we construe this compound as "vows of ascetic behavior," as excessive asceticism could easily attract censure.

These *aṭṭha sīla* and *sikkhāpada* lists are marked by the particularity of the actions they forbid. Vows to abstain from such practices as sleeping on high and large beds do not follow necessarily from a governing ethical principle. Nor do these vows imply a definite goal: one could undertake them in order to progress toward nirvāṇa, to make merit, or to attain some other end. These sets of precepts constitute only two of many possible ascetic regimens for beginners in monastic life. This particularity indicates that the purpose of these lists is not to establish an absolute and universal morality but to bind the practitioner to the life of the Buddha's community. Just as gifts given to mentally pure Buddhist monastics are the most meritorious, so the most meritorious ascetic practice is that performed by observing in the presence of Buddhist monastics the rules that they themselves follow.

Sacrifice and Uposatha observance thus share a structure that reveals why Buddhist and Vedic traditions class them together as meritorious acts. In Durkheim's succinct formulation, sacrifice consists of renunciation of an offering and the communion with the deity that this offering produces.[92] In the case of Buddhist *dāna*, the role of the deity is filled by individual monastics or by "the Saṅgha with the Buddha at its head," as a common formula has it. Although keeping the *aṭṭha sīla* is renunciation of a rather different kind, it also produces communion with the Saṅgha. It is this contact with the Saṅgha that, in the logic of sacrifice, makes the act fruitful.

Almsgiving as transfer of sacrificial substance

Although most canonical Pāli texts attribute the efficacy of sacrifice to the act of giving, some verses appropriate Vedic beliefs in the efficacy of the material offering itself.[93] According to Vedic tradition, dakṣiṇā received by a Brāhmaṇ priest may pass to another recipient. Offerings dedicated to deities may earn the deities' favor, while food given to deceased ancestors in a śrāddha feast nourishes the dead and helps them move from their liminal post mortem condition into a state of being happy and benevolent ancestors. In all of *Vinaya*, the first four *Nikāyas* of *Suttapiṭaka*, *Dhammapada*, *Udāna*, *Itivuttaka*, *Suttanipāta*, *Theragāthā*, and *Therīgāthā*, only three sets of *gāthās* present this material-centered understanding of *dāna*.[94] In addition, three *suttas* from *Petavatthu* also exemplify this sacrificial pattern. I discuss these three *suttas* in this section because they are similar in form and style to other sacrificial didactic verse. In addition, circumstantial evidence supports the supposition that they are relatively old: *Aṅguttara* V 269–273 appears to be dependent on *Tirokuḍḍa Sutta* (Pv I.5), and *Tirokuḍḍa* appears in *Khuddakapāṭha* as well as in *Petavatthu*.

These six sets of verses exhibit marked continuities with Vedic accounts of the dedication of dakṣiṇā.[95] A verse that appears at *Aṅguttara* III 43 and *Dīgha* III 189 includes among the five duties of a son giving dakṣiṇā for the dead. The set of verses at *Aṅguttara* II 43–44, discussed in the second section of this chapter, refers to both act-centered and material-centered understandings of sacrifice. The first it calls sacrifice, or *yañña*, which the commentary glosses as *pakatidāna*, or ordinary *dāna*. The second form of offering is *saddha* (śrāddha), which the commentary glosses as *matakadāna*, *dāna* for the dead (Mp III 84). This form of offering corresponds to the Brahmanical practice of feeding Brāhmaṇs as surrogates for deceased ancestors. In *Vinaya* I 229, *Dīgha* II 88, and *Udāna* 89, the Buddha expresses his appreciation for a meal with a set of verses about the dedication of gifts to deities:

> Wherever a wise man takes up his abode,
> If after having fed there those possessing morality, restrained
> practioners of *brahmacariya*,
> He then assigns that dakṣiṇā to the deities that are there,
> They, being worshiped, worship him; being thought highly of, they
> think highly of him.

Consequently, they have compassion for him, like a mother for a son at her breast;
The man for whom the deities have compassion always sees auspicious things.[96]

The movement of the dakṣiṇā from donor to worthy recipient, and from recipient to deity, and its reciprocation by the deity to the donor, form a complete cycle. The expression used here for assigning the dakṣiṇā is *ādise*; this usage is also found in Vedic texts.[97] The use of the verb √*dis*, usually with the prefix *ā-* or *ud-*, becomes in Pāli texts the standard way to refer to the dedication of a gift for the benefit of designated deities and ancestors.[98]

Petavatthu I.1 integrates dakṣiṇā dedication into a concise statement of the merit field metaphor:

Arhats are like fields, givers are like plowmen,
The thing to be given is like seed: from these comes the fruit.
Seed, plowing, and field are for the departed (*peta*) and for the giver:
The departed enjoy this and the giver increases in merit.
Doing good here and honoring the departed,
One goes to a heavenly place having done an auspicious act.[99]

These verses articulate two benefits of giving to worthy recipients: the dead enjoy the offering while the donor increases in merit leading to heaven. *Petavatthu* I.4 similarly encourages giving to the Saṅgha for the benefit of the formerly deceased (*pubbapete*), local deities (*vatthudevatā*), and the world-protecting deities, the Four Great Kings.

The passage that develops the material-centered understanding of the rite most fully is *Tirokuḍḍa Sutta*, which appears at *Petavatthu* I.5 and *Khuddakapāṭha* VII, and which is regularly chanted at dedications of dakṣiṇā for the dead. The text describes the state of the dead as follows:

1 They stand outside the walls and at crossroads and forks;
They go to their own homes and stand at the doorposts.
2 When drink and hard and soft food are set out,
No one, recalling their past deeds, remembers them.
3 Those who are compassionate give for relatives
Pure, excellent food and drink in a timely and appropriate manner:
"Let this be for you, [our] relatives, let [our] relatives be happy."
4 And those departed relatives assembled there
Respectfully express appreciation for the excellent food and drink:

5 "Long live our relatives, on account of whom we have gained;
Honor has been done to us, and the givers are not without fruit."
6 For there is no plowing there, nor is cowherding found there.
There are not the likes of trading, or buying and selling with gold.
The departed dead subsist there on what is given from here.
7 As water that falls on high ground flows downward,
Even so, what is given from here benefits the departed.
8 As swollen rivers fill up the sea,
Even so, what is given from here benefits the departed.
9 "She gave to me," "He worked for me," "They were my relatives, friends, and companions,"
[Thus] remembering what they did in the past, give dakṣiṇā for the departed.
10 For neither weeping, nor sorrow, nor other kinds of mourning
Serves the welfare of the departed; those relatives remain the same.
11 But dakṣiṇā given and well-established in the Saṅgha,
"May it be for [their] good a long time," benefits [them] immediately.
12 This duty of relatives has been shown,
Great honor has been done to the departed,
Strength has been given to monks,
And you have produced considerable merit.[100]

Unlike the Vedic rites, which were performed to benefit only ancestors in the paternal line, the dedication of dakṣiṇā is here said to benefit all deceased relatives as well as friends and companions. However, in other regards the rite described here is much like the Vedic śrāddha. The words of dedication spoken in verse 3, *idaṃ vo ñātīnaṃ hotu*, resemble the Brahmanical *tyāga*, the words spoken by the patron of a sacrifice when relinquishing an oblation.[101] *Tirokuḍḍa* also represents the beneficiaries of the rite much as the Brahmanical texts do. The deceased are said to inhabit liminal spaces at the edge of human habitation: outside of walls and at crossroads and doorposts. Although they haunt their old homes, they are not portrayed as horrific or miserable. The living who remember their former relationships with those now dead are said to give dakṣiṇā to benefit the departed and thereby to pay them honor. The departed, in turn, respectfully bless the donors with wishes for long life. This *sutta* does not suggest that the departed exist as tormented ghosts.[102] It instead offers the happy prospect of living in a continuing relationship of mutual aid with one's deceased relations. This view is much like Brahmanical representations of the deceased as unhappy beings who depend on regular offerings of food from their former families to transform them into ancestors (*pitṛs*) and to maintain them in that state.

These six sets of verses present a straightforward adoption of the Vedic understanding of the sacrifice as the transfer of the offering to another recipient, either a deity or an ancestor. Although references to the dedication of gifts in the didactic verse literature of the Pāli canon are few, the dedication of dakṣiṇā seems to be better represented in other Buddhist traditions. Gregory Schopen writes that expressions such as *dakṣiṇādeśana* are much better represented in Sanskrit texts, especially those of the Mūlasarvāstivāda school.[103] That the earlier Pāli texts include few references to the dedication of gifts, and no explanation of this practice, may indicate not that this practice was absent in early Buddhism, but that those who formed the Theravādin canonical texts (other than *Petavatthu*) had, for the most part, an ambivalent attitude toward this rite. In the following two chapters, I will show that this ambivalence can be seen in discussions of the dedication of gifts in canonical prose and in the *Petavatthu* narratives.

Why sacrifice?

We therefore find in the verse literature of the Pāli canon a remarkably homogenous discourse about the causes and effects of merit, and about the relationship of merit to the path of purification. This discourse served important purposes for early Buddhist communities. As Buddhist monks and nuns competed with Brāhmaṇs and with other ascetics for material support from laity, the sacrificial discourse provided reasons why people should give to Buddhist renouncers. Buddhist preachers no doubt used sacrificial *gāthās* to encourage giving. Many verses praise donors, saying, for example, that they outshine other men as the moon outshines the stars, or that they attract arhats as a great fruit tree attracts birds.[104] Through the dedication of dakṣiṇā, the sacrificial discourse also provided a way for those who had abandoned Vedic religion to care for their deceased ancestors and to interact with deities.

Buddhists adopted Vedic sacrificial beliefs rather than some other ideology of giving in part because Vedism was the most prestigious religious tradition in ancient north India; consequently, the first generations of Buddhists and their supporters would have found sacrificial discourse both intelligible and persuasive.[105] A sense of the power and prestige of Vedic sacrifice for early Buddhists can be gained from canonical references to the *agnihotra* that are remarkably positive, given that other passages condemn its performance.[106] A list of things best in their class calls the *agnihotra* the best of sacrifices.[107] In *Suttanipāta* 428, Māra tempts the Bodhisattva on the eve of his awakening by suggesting that he live the *brahmacariya* life, sacrifice the *agnihotra*, and thereby accumulate merit.[108] The Bodhisattva responds not by criticizing the *agnihotra*, but by denying that he needs to acquire any merit. The prestige of the Vedic tradition for Buddhists is also attested to by their appropriation of non-sacrificial Vedic expressions like *brāhmaṇa* and *tevijja* (*trividya*).[109]

Additional evidence that the Buddhists appropriated Vedic ritual in a straightforward way is given by the *Arthaśāstra* of Kauṭilya, which recommends imposing a fine of one hundred *kahāpaṇas* on anyone who invites "base ascetics such as Buddhists and Ājīvakas" to a meal for gods or ancestors.[110] If this rule was formulated in response to actual practice, we may conclude that some laypeople and Buddhist monastics did regard the śrāddha rites observed by Brāhmaṇs and Buddhists to be the same rite, and did not see such rites as inherently Brahmanical and therefore not Buddhist. The existence of this rule also indicates, however, that some Brāhmaṇs rejected the aspirations of Buddhist monks to perform this ritual function.

Vedic sacrificial ideology had appeal not only for laity, but for monastics as well. The scant data available to us suggest that large numbers of Buddhist monastics were from high status backgrounds. B. G. Gokhale shows that of the elders identified in the *Theragāthā* and *Therīgāthā*, about 41% were from Brāhmaṇ families and 94% twice-born; his analysis of a list of 41 monastic leaders in *Aṅguttara* yields similar findings.[111] Furthermore, Gregory Schopen's studies of early Buddhist inscriptions have shown that Buddhist monastics were occupied not only with their own progress toward nirvāṇa, but were very much concerned with the welfare of their families.[112] As Schopen observes, for persons from Brāhmaṇ and other twice-born families, joining the Saṅgha would have involved the loss of a prestigious social identity and often would have evoked strongly negative reactions from family members. If monastics could continue to perform traditional religious roles to aid their families, doing so would no doubt have eased these difficulties. Monastics could believe that by pursuing nirvāṇa, they were transforming themselves into fertile fields for their families' donations. By dedicating dakṣiṇā, monastics could have continued to make their traditional offerings to protective deities and to their ancestors; dedicating offerings to ancestors would have been especially important because as celibates, monastics would have been unable to produce sons to make offerings in the future.[113]

The appeal of the Buddhist sacrificial discourse is, however, explained not only by its continuities with Brahmanical practice, but also by its discontinuities. Buddhists rejected animal sacrifice, the hereditary authority of Brāhmaṇs, and complex and esoteric ceremonial codes. For example, *Saṃyutta* I 75–76 and *Aṅguttara* II 42–43 consider violent sacrifices including the horse sacrifice and human sacrifice to be of little fruit, but praise those who always offer victimless sacrifices according to their family custom.[114] Most importantly, while participation in the Brahmanical rites was restricted to married males of the first three social classes (*varṇas*), Buddhist *dāna* and Uposatha were open to all. Numerous canonical verses present women as independent donors,[115] and even the poor could make merit by offering a small gift of food, or by approving or assisting in another's act of giving:

> Those who then rejoice or perform service
> Do not lack dakṣiṇā; they share in the merit.[116]

Furthermore, while Brahmanical texts name only father, paternal grandfather, and paternal great-grandfather as the beneficiaries of śrāddha,[117] *Tirokuḍḍa Sutta* includes other ancestors as well as friends and companions among those who receive offerings. The Buddhists made the prestige and efficacy of the Vedic sacrifice available to many who formerly had no direct access to it.

On the other hand, the sacrificial *gāthā*s do not indicate that nuns were ever regarded as sacrificial recipients. As we will see, although they extend to women the opportunity to act as patrons of sacrifice, Theravādin texts have generally reserved the role of priest for men.[118]

Another ideology of the gift

Although the sacrificial discourse presents the most widespread understanding of religious giving in the canonical didactic *gāthā*s, many of the oldest and most popular Theravādin stories of giving are informed by a different ideology of the gift. In a number of *Jātaka* stories, donors such as Dhanañjaya, Sivi, and Vessantara give to all who ask without regard for their personal qualities.[119] These givers are celebrated not for the worthiness of their recipients, but solely for the greatness of their generosity.

Biḷārikosiya Jātaka and *Saṃyutta* I 18–19 present a number of didactic *gāthās* that express this understanding of religious giving.[120] Like the sacrificial verses, these verses claim that by giving gifts the good gain merit to be enjoyed in heaven, while evil persons experience a bad destiny. On the other hand, by stressing the need to overcome avarice, negligence, and fear of hunger and thirst, these verses present giving as more akin to mental purification than to worship.[121] These verses never mention the qualities of the recipients of gifts, but instead praise acts of giving for their difficulty:

> Evil persons imitate neither those who give what is difficult to give, nor those who do what is difficult to do. The dharma (or duty) of good persons is hard to follow.[122]

Other verses claim that one gift given by a person who has little is equal to a thousand.[123] The worth of a gift lies not in its monetary value, nor in the qualities of the donee, but in its cost to the donor.[124]

Vessantara Jātaka (hereafter VJ), the story of a prince who gives away all he has, even his wife and children, exemplifies well these stories' understanding of giving not as sacrifice, but as heroic performance of dharma. Even after relinquishing his children to the Brāhmaṇ Jūjaka, Vessantara asks, "Who, knowing the dharma of good persons, regrets giving a gift?"[125] Sakka likewise regards Vessantara's gift of his wife, Maddī, as the fulfillment of dharma, and praises Vessantara "because he does what is difficult."[126] Earlier in the story, after Vessantara has been banished from his kingdom because of his excessive giving, Maddī expresses a similar sentiment, saying that the gods praise a wife who is content whether richer or poorer, because she does what is difficult.[127]

While praising ascetic feats of generosity, the poet places no importance on the qualities of the donee. Despite once instructing Maddī to give to those who possess *sīla*, throughout the story Vessantara gives indiscriminately to all, even supplying liquor to those who want it.[128] The poet describes at length the wickedness of the Brāhmaṇ recipients of Vessantara's largesse, especially Jūjaka, whose greed, cruelty, and ignobility are matched by his grotesque appearance. Jūjaka's prominent role in the poem precludes any interpretation of Vessantara's giving as sacrifice to a worthy recipient.[129] Although Vessantara is in his capacity as donor called a sacrificer (*yajamāno*),[130] an incident in the story shows that the poet does not understand this word to denote worship. When a hunter overhears Jūjaka inquiring after Vessantara, the hunter threatens to make of Jūjaka's flesh a sacrifice to the birds along the road. The hunter does not use a neutral word like *bali*, but the markedly Vedic terms *yajati* and *āhuti*.[131] The hunter thus likens the Brahmanical recipients of Vessantara's largesse to vultures and crows. The poet also mocks sacrificial rhetoric by having Jūjaka tell Vessantara, "King, after giving wealth to someone like me, one will go to heaven."[132] Ironically, this claim turns out to be true, but not because Jūjaka is in any way a worthy field for merit.

VJ thus reverses the understanding of giving presented by sacrificial-purificatory discourse. In the latter, the donor desires merit, while the ideal recipient is free from desire. In VJ, the mendicants are greedy, while Vessantara is *cāgādhimānaso*, intent on relinquishing.[133] The poet identifies the true ascetic not with the mendicant, but with the donor. This identification is embedded in the plot of the story, as Vessantara's pursuit of giving leads to his living as a "royal seer" in the woods.[134] Vessantara and the other forest-dwelling ascetics forage for their food and worship at their own sacrificial fires; their self-sufficiency contrasts with the dependency of the Brāhmaṇ beggars. Despite their poverty, the ascetics are quick to extend hospitality to guests, as Accuta and Vessantara do for Jūjaka.[135] After restoring Maddī to Vessantara, Sakka says to these two:

> "Kṣatriyas of good families, well-born on mothers' and fathers' sides,
> You both were banished here in the forest; live in peace in a hermitage
> So that you may make merits, giving again and again."[136]

With these words Sakka concisely links noble birth, forest-dwelling asceticism, and meritorious giving.

VJ shows that giving leads to the highest religious goals. Vessantara aspires that by the gift of his children he would make the world cross the sea of existence (Ja VI 546); this gift thus becomes the basis for his attainment of buddhahood. After Vessantara gives away his wife, Sakka grants him eight wishes; with the last of these he wishes that when he dies he would attain an excellent state in heaven, and not be reborn from there.[137] It is difficult to reconcile this wish not only with Vessantara's aspiration to become a buddha, but also with the Buddhist axiom that everything is impermanent. Ludwig Alsdorf has pointed out, however, that Vessantara's aspiration to buddhahood, which is the only explicitly Buddhist element of the story, is inconsistent with many other parts of the poem; for this reason Alsdorf concludes that this aspiration was added to a pre-existing work.[138] If we read this *jātaka* without this aspiration to buddhahood, we see that Vessantara's imagining liberation from rebirth as permanent residency in a heaven does cohere with the rest of the poem. Vessantara's wish also has non-Buddhist parallels, notably with *Bṛhadāraṇyaka Upaniṣad*'s statement regarding those who through knowledge attain the Brahmalokas that, "For them there is no return."[139]

An understanding of giving similar to that presented by VJ and related *jātakas* informs the edicts of Aśoka. Inscribed a century or two after the Buddha's death, these edicts are the oldest Buddhist writings that can be reliably dated.[140] Lambert Schmithausen's characterization of their ethics and eschatology makes apparent their affinity to the *jātakas*:

> Now, in the Aśokan inscriptions, there is no mention of rebirth as an animal or *preta* nor even of a return to the world of men, nor is there any instance of rebirth or transmigration terminology (like *upa-pad*, *cyu*, *praty-ā-jan*). The only thing we find is that . . . Aśoka contrasts, with this world, the yonder world (*palaloka*, etc.), and that he seems to equate the yonder world more or less with heaven (*svaga*, *suaga*) which will be attained (*āladhi*) by those who zealously practise his *dhaṃma*, i.e. moral behaviour. There is no mention of an underworld or hell as an alternative for people not practising the *dhaṃma* or doing evil. Only once does Aśoka say that not acting in accordance with his admonition will entail great loss or misfortune (*apāya*), but the subsequent sentence shows that this does not refer to an underworld, let alone hell, but simply means that such a person will not attain heaven (nor the favour of the king).[141]

Like Vessantara, Aśoka defines his ethics in terms of dharma, or duty, which he explains as obedience to parents, elders, and "those who receive high pay," courtesy and liberality to friends, acquaintances, relatives, Brāhmaṇs, and ascetics, proper courtesy to slaves and servants, and non-injury to animals.[142] As in VJ, dharma includes giving to Brāhmaṇs, ascetics, and even acquaintances.

In two edicts Aśoka articulates this message in a ritual idiom. In the Ninth Rock Edict, Aśoka decrees that while rites (*maṃgala*) ought to be performed, most are of little fruit (*apa-phala*); one should therefore perform the rite of dharma (or a dharmic rite, *dhaṃmamaṃgala*). In Rock Edict XI, Aśoka recommends dharmic giving, dharmic acquaintance, dharmic distribution, and dharmic kinship. In both edicts, Aśoka presents the explication of dharma I cite in the preceding paragraph. Both edicts end with what are the only uses of the term *puṇya / puñña* in the Aśokan corpus.[143] Rock Edict IX twice states that through the rite of dharma endless merit is produced in the other world (*atha paratra anaṃtaṃ puñaṃ prasavati; aṭho paratra cha anaṃtaṃ puñaṃ prasavati tena dhramaṃgalena*), while Rock Edict XI promises the same result from dharmic giving (*paratra cha anataṃ puña prasavati [te]na dhrama-danena*). Although this rhetoric is like that of the sacrificial *gāthās*, in meaning these edicts more closely resemble VJ. Even Aśoka's reference to endless merit, an oxymoron within the sacrificial-purificatory system, corresponds to Vessantara's wish to remain in heaven forever. Apart from Vessantara's aspiration to buddhahood, neither Aśoka nor Vessantara mentions a religious goal higher than the eternal existence in a heaven they hope to gain through their fulfillment of dharma.

Comparison of VJ and the Aśokan edicts with the sacrificial verses reveals, therefore, that even though they all assume a similar cosmology and eschatology, they present very different ethics of giving.[144] While sacrificial passages treat giving as worship, Vessantara and Aśoka understand giving as the exercise of generosity. These (legendary and historical) princes adhere to an ideal of Kṣatriya conduct that Thomas Trautmann has shown to be well represented in the Epics; among other things, this warrior ethic prescribes that a king is to give freely to all, but to accept no gifts.[145] By denying reciprocity, this ideology asserts the moral and material superiority of the donor over the recipient.[146] An episode of *Mahābhārata* encapsulates this understanding of the gift and of the relationship between kings and Brāhmaṇs in the taunting words delivered by the princess Śarmiṣṭhā to the Brāhmaṇ girl Devayānī:

> "Your father humbly stands below my father, whether he is sitting or lying, flattering and praising constantly! You are the daughter of one who begs, who praises, who accepts gifts; I am the daughter of one who is praised, who gives, who does not accept gifts."[147]

VJ's depictions of Jūjaka reveal a similar attitude. The Cetan hunter, Accuta, and Vessantara all show hospitality to Jūjaka, but the one time he tries to reciprocate, the hunter refuses Jūjaka's offer and instead urges him to take more food.[148] The meaning of this episode is clear: even the hunter considers Jūjaka his inferior.

The difference between ideologies of sacrificial and heroic giving in Buddhism therefore exemplifies a fundamental paradox in ancient Indian society, in which "religious gifts flow upward to superior beings, but royal gifts flow down a hierarchy of dependency."[149] While Vessantara's gifts threaten to undo the relationships of dependency they create, Aśoka's aspirations to religious authority over his beneficiaries can be seen in his edicts establishing disciplinary rules for Buddhist monastics, and instructing them on what texts contain the true Dharma.[150] As the linkage between kings and forest sages in VJ suggests, the ideal of heroic giving is more akin to mental purification than to sacrifice, in that heroic giving and purification both involve renunciation rather than devotion. However, there are also important differences between heroic and purificatory discourses: the purificatory verses focus on thoughts, while VJ stresses the performance of particular difficult acts; the purificatory verses promote detachment, while Vessantara's relinquishing his children and wife is seen as great precisely because he is deeply attached to them. Sacrifice, purification, and heroic generosity therefore constitute three distinct soteriologies in early Buddhism. Karmic discourse, I argue, provides a way to understand all three in terms of a single ethics and soteriology.

CHAPTER TWO

The Discourse of Karma

A number of canonical verses, especially narratives, describe actions and their effects not in terms of sacrifice and merit, but with a discourse that centers on the category of karma, or action. This karmic discourse is developed and systematized in the canonical prose, in which karma is the standard idiom for talking about acts and their effects. In this chapter, I describe this karmic discourse as developed in the prose *suttas*, including the ethics, eschatology, and cosmology that it entails. I argue that karmic discourse attempts to account for the sacrificial and purificatory soteriologies within a single theoretical framework, and I suggest that the development of this discourse was motivated by social and religious needs as well as by a desire for philosophical coherence. I also locate the development of this karmic discourse within the larger history of ancient South Asian religions.

Karma in early Buddhist prose literature

The prose sections of *Vinaya*, the first four *Nikāyas* of *Suttapiṭaka*, *Udāna*, *Itivuttaka*, and *Suttanipāta* contain some expressions of sacrificial themes, most notably an oft-repeated formulaic description of worthy recipients of *dāna* as "worthy of oblations, offerings, dakṣiṇā, and salutations, an unsurpassed field for merit for the whole world."[1] For the most part, however, the sacrificial discourse is in the canonical prose displaced by ways of speaking of action and rebirth that center on the categories of *kamma* (karma, action) and *saṅkhāra* (mental construct or formation). This karmic discourse encompasses all forms of action – physical, verbal, and mental – that may produce the attainment of nirvāṇa or of rebirth, as well as a number of effects in the here and now. Unlike sacrificial discourse, which is concerned only with whether one goes to heaven or to a bad destiny after death, karmic discourse describes effects to be experienced in the lifetime in which the act was performed, and others to be experienced many rebirths in the future. These afterlife effects include not only the attainment of heaven or hell, but also the conditions of one's rebirths as human, animal, or ghost (*peta* or *petī*).[2] Good karma may also lead to awakening, often as the conclusion of a process that extends over the course of multiple lifetimes. In this understanding of action and rebirth, the sole criterion for whether an act produces a good or bad effect is whether that act conduces to mental purification. Karmic discourse thus presents a unitary soteriological ethic that encompasses both giving and renunciation.

Kamma and its Sanskrit cognate *karma* derive from the verbal root √*kṛ*, to do or to make, and convey a wide range of meanings centered around the idea of doing or making. In Vedic literature, *kárman* refers especially to praiseworthy acts such as the great deeds of the gods, poetic composition, and sacrifice.[3] The double meaning of 'action and especially sacrificial action' made *karma* and its cognate *kriyā* useful terms for Brahmanical, Jain, and Buddhist thinkers. These terms allowed teachers to allude to notions of the effectiveness of ritual action while extending the range of actions considered to be productive of good or ill; the *Bhagavadgītā*, for example, exploits this slippage in meaning (e.g. 3:8–9). The Pāli term *kamma* is likewise not limited by its sacrificial connotations, but refers to a wide range of actions.[4]

Karmic discourse uses certain characteristic expressions to describe how actions produce future rebirth effects. The prose texts say that one does (*karoti*) or wills (*ceteti*)[5] acts (*kamma*), and that those acts that are accumulated (*upacita*) will ripen (*vipaccati*) to produce their fruit (*phala*) or result (*vipāka*). The original actor feels (*paṭisaṃvedati*, *vediyati*) or experiences (*anubhavati*) this outcome of the act, which thereby comes to an end (*vyantibhāva*) or is exhausted (*khīṇa*). Although this karmic discourse employs some of the agricultural imagery of the *puññakkhetta* metaphor, it significantly lacks the elements of the physical gift as seed and the recipient as field. Because the karmic discourse defines the efficacy of action in terms of the purity of the actor's intention, an act need not be directed toward a field for merit in order to be effective. Even solitary actions such as holding right or wrong views may produce karmic effects to be experienced by the actor. Interestingly, however, the image of the field was adopted and reinterpreted by later Sautrāntika and Yogācārin karma theorists, who identified the field not with the object of worship but with the actor's own mental continuum, in which are deposited good and bad karmic seeds.[6] This transformation of the field metaphor illustrates nicely the fundamental difference between sacrificial and karmic discourses.

The difference between sacrificial and karmic models can also be seen clearly in how two *suttas* from *Aṅguttara* use karmic language to analyze *dāna* and its effects. In A IV 59–63, the Buddha describes eight motivations that will produce *dāna* that is not of great fruit or profit:[7] these lead to rebirth among the Four Great Kings, i.e. as a terrestrial deity, and then to rebirth as a human being. The first of these eight employs typical sacrificial terms like *pekha* and *nidhi* to caricature the sacrificial understanding of *dāna*:

> Here, Sāriputta, someone seeking for himself, enslaved in mind, and seeking treasure, gives a gift thinking, "After I die, I will enjoy this." He then gives to an ascetic or a Brāhmaṇ a gift: food, drink, clothing, a vehicle, garlands and scented ointments, bed, dwelling, and a lamp with accessories.[8]

The ninth intention, by contrast, leads to birth among the Brahmā deities, and eventually to becoming a non-returner bound for awakening:

> On the other hand, Sāriputta, here someone [gives not for any of these eight reasons] . . . however, he gives a gift with the purpose of adorning and equipping his mind (*cittālaṅkāraṃ cittaparikkhāratthaṃ*). He then gives to an ascetic or a Brāhmaṇ . . . (A IV 62–63).

This *sutta* thus defines the proper purpose of giving as improving the mind of the donor, and explicitly rejects desire for external rewards. In other words, mental purification replaces sacrifice as the rationale for giving. A IV 239–241 tells that a gift can lead to births ranging from wealthy human being to Brahmā deity; a virtuous donor attains the birth to which he or she aspires because of his or her purity and dispassion.[9] Here again, an ethic of mental purity displaces that of sacrifice.

In neither of these texts does the worthiness of the recipient affect the merit produced by the gift. Both *suttas* simply state that the gift is given to an ascetic or Brāhmaṇ. This pair of recipients appears often in canonical prose; sometimes lists of donees also include wayfarers, beggars, and the needy.[10] These texts are not concerned with the worthiness of the recipient; he need not possess any particular qualities and need not even be a Buddhist. These *sutta*s clearly reject an understanding of giving as an act of sacrifice or worship, and instead view giving as an act of relinquishment or detachment, much as VJ and related *jātaka*s do. What is lacking in the *jātaka*s that these prose *sutta*s supply is an explanation of the karmic mechanism by which these acts produce their effects.

A similar change can be seen in comparing the Uposatha ascetic code and the ten *sikkhāpada*s with another set of ten precepts that appears in canonical prose. Known as the ways of action, or *kammapatha*, these consist of the following behaviors to be avoided:

1 killing (*pāṇātipāta*)
2 stealing (*adinnādāna*)
3 sexual misconduct (*kāmesu micchācāra*)
4 lying (*musāvāda*)
5 slander (*pisuṇāvācā*)
6 harsh speech (*pharusāvācā*)
7 frivolous talk (*samphappalāpa*)
8 covetousness (*abhijjā*)
9 malevolence (*byāpāda*)
10 wrong view (*micchādiṭṭhi*)

Although it begins as the *sikkhāpada*s do, this explication of *sīla* is not an ascetic code; rather, it is a summary of all forms of morally significant action – physical, verbal, and mental. The last three items correspond to lust (*rāga*), hatred (*dosa*), and delusion (*moha*), the three roots of bad action; anyone who abstains from these three will necessarily abstain from the first seven actions as well. Abstention from these ten acts constitutes the karmic process of mental purification. Descriptions of these *kammapatha*s link them to a unified eschatology that encompasses all good karmic effects. Thus in *Aṅguttara* V 263–268, the Buddha teaches that following the ten wrong ways of action produces rebirth in a hell, as an animal or ghost, or in some other bad birth, while following the ten right ways of action produces rebirth as a deity, as a human, or some other good birth. In *Aṅguttara* V 57 the Buddha says that one who follows the ten right ways of action will put an end to suffering, i.e. attain nirvāṇa.[11]

These passages also exemplify another view characteristic of the karmic discourse, that volition (*cetanā*) determines the identity and effect of an action. In *Aṅguttara* III 415, the Buddha states, "Monks, I say that willing is acting; [by] willing, one performs an action with body, speech, or mind."[12] Although this statement does not (as is often claimed) equate volition and action, as the second half of the statement assumes that verbal and physical action are also action, it does present volition as determinative of all action. In *Mahākamma-vibhaṅga Sutta* (M III 207–215), the Buddha explains the workings of action as follows:

> 'Friend Potaliputta, having done an intentional action by way of body, speech, or mind to be experienced as pleasant, one feels pleasure. Having done an intentional action by way of body, speech, or mind to be experienced as painful, one feels pain. Having done an intentional action by way of body, speech, or mind to be experienced as neither-pain-nor-pleasure, one feels neither-pain-nor-pleasure.'[13]

The Buddha then develops this theme in terms of the ten *kammapathas*. This discussion makes intention a necessary component of karmic action, and presents purely mental acts as productive of good and bad karmic effects. It dispenses completely with the sacrificial model, instead using the idiom of sensation to show that action is its own reward or punishment. *Aṅguttara* V 292–297 and 300–301 similarly state that all volitional actions done and accumulated (*sañcetanikānaṃ kammānaṃ katānaṃ upacitānaṃ*) will be experienced.

The most sophisticated explanations of how volitions produce their effects employ the category of the *saṅkhāras*.[14] One of the five aggregates (*khandha*) of which all things are made, the *saṅkhāras* are the mental formations, the most important of which are the volitions. As the second link in the process of dependent origination (*paṭiccasamuppāda*), a person's *saṅkhāras* give rise to a new consciousness at the time of death. For example, a discussion of three different types of action begins with the following:

> Here, monks, someone generates a harmful mental formation pertaining to body, speech, or mind. Having generated a harmful mental formation pertaining to body, speech, or mind, one arises in a harmful world.[15]

The passage goes on to characterize analogously the effects of formations that are harmless and of those that are partly harmless and partly harmful. Mental formations thus form the link between action and rebirth effect. The category of mental formation is also used to describe the elimination of mental defilements and progress toward nirvāṇa. *Saṅkhārupapatti Sutta* (M III 99–103) uses the term *saṅkhāra* to refer to aspirations leading to rebirth or to final liberation. *Sāleyyaka Sutta* (M I 285–290) describes in very similar terms how a person of righteous conduct (*dhammacārī samacārī*) may through a wish (*ākaṅkheyya*) attain good rebirth or liberation. The karmic discourse thus presents meritorious acts leading to a good rebirth as the same in kind as good acts conducive to nirvāṇa.

As indicated above, the karmic discourse also encompasses a much wider range of eschatological effects than does the sacrificial discourse. Karmic texts assume an eschatology in which one may be reborn into one of five or six destinies (*gatis*): birth in a hell, or as a ghost, animal, human being, deity, or, according to some passages, an *asura*.[16] The particular circumstances of these existences are explained with reference to past actions, so that, for example, bitterness leads to ugliness, stinginess to poverty, and so forth.[17] Actions may produce effects not only in the next life, but in this life and in future lives as well. According to *Majjhima* III 214–215, "a bad action to be experienced as unpleasant" or "a good action to be experienced as pleasant" may be experienced "either here and now, or in his next rebirth, or in some subsequent existence."[18] This karmic eschatology is linked to a cosmology in which the entire world is vertically ordered by the force of past actions. The earth is inhabited by ghosts, animals, humans, and terrestrial (*bhumma*) deities; below the earth are the hells. Above are 26 heavens whose elevations correspond to the karma of the deities that inhabit them. Those heavens closest to the earth are the worlds of the Four Great Kings, the Tāvatiṃsa deities, the Yāma deities, the Tusita deities, the Nimmānarati deities, and the Paranimmitavasavatti deities. Above these are the 20 Brahmalokas, each of which corresponds to a different level of meditational attainment.[19] The entire world is ordered such that as one ascends, materiality and desire decrease yet pleasure increases. In the karmic cosmology, the world both symbolizes and embodies the path to nirvāṇa.

The Theravādin karmic discourse thus represents an attempt to account for all ethically significant actions, and to order them on a single scale. The texts that employ this discourse rationalize religious acts like giving *dāna* and observing *sīla* as means to mental purification, and describe a hierarchy of effects corresponding to these acts. In place of the dual soteriology of ritual action and mental purification presented by the didactic *gāthās*, the canonical prose presents a unified soteriology that reduces all causes of rebirth to mental action. The sacrificial-purificatory and karmic discourses thus present two systems of ethical value, one based on the two complementary goods of merit and mental purity, and the other based on the single value of karma.

Representations of Vedic sacrifice in karmic prose

The marked differences between the sacrificial-purificatory discourse of the canonical verse and the karmic discourse of the canonical prose are most easily explained by the hypothesis that the sacrificial-purificatory verses predate the karmic prose. As we have seen, old verse anthologies such as *Aṭṭhakavagga* and *Pārāyaṇavagga* do not employ karmic discourse, but speak of purifying the mind of craving, ignorance, and other harmful mental states. As noted in chapter 1, VJ and related *jātakas* and the Aśokan inscriptions likewise contain no elements of karmic discourse. (Although they certainly differ from sacrificial and purificatory discourses in their soteriology and ethics, these *jātakas* and inscriptions resemble sacrificial verses in their vocabulary and rhetoric.) Furthermore, sacrificial discourse is virtually absent from canonical prose and from later Theravādin doctrinal and philosophical texts, while karmic discourse became the standard way of explaining rebirth in Theravāda (as well as in other Indic religions). By applying the principle well established in biblical criticism that discontinuity with later tradition is a strong indication that a particular tradition is old,[20] we may conclude that sacrificial discourse predates the extant prose. The simplest explanation of all of these data is that karmic discourse was not part of the earliest Buddhist tradition, but that by the time that the prose achieved its present form, systematic karmic discourse had largely replaced sacrificial discourse in doctrinal discussions of rebirth. If this hypothesis is correct, then karma was not the soteriological problem for which the Buddhist path was originally intended to provide a solution.[21] Rather, as Schmithausen points out, the oldest Buddhist formulations of the fundamental human problem center on suffering caused by craving, ignorance, and other mental states. Systematic karmic discourse, in the Buddhist context, can be understood as a second-order theory developed to account for two different determinants of rebirth: sacrificial merit and mental purity. The discourse of karma provided a way to rationalize discourse about giving and mental purification in terms of a unified ethics and soteriology.

Of course, other explanations of the relationship of sacrificial verse to karmic prose are possible; the most plausible of these is that the authors of the verses adopted the Vedic idiom of sacrifice as a metaphorical expression of their karma theory. They may have done so for some of the reasons I give above, notably, to supply a rationale for lay donations to Buddhist monastics and to borrow the prestige of Vedic religion. However, this hypothesis fails to explain why, apart from citing some sacrificial formulas, the prose does not incorporate sacrificial ideas as the verses do. If the verses expressed provisional formulations of the Dharma, and the prose more adequate statements, then we would expect that verses and prose would be intended for different audiences or contexts. In the *suttas*, however, the Buddha preaches in verse and prose to both lay and monastic audiences. Furthermore, verse and prose do not differ only in their wording, but they differ significantly in their understandings of how giving produces its effects. Such differences can best be explained by supposing that the prose is of later authorship than the verses.

Comparison of how sacrificial verse and karmic prose treat the Vedic tradition lends further support to this hypothesis. As I argue in chapter 1, the sacrificial discourse deliberately appropriates the symbolism and practice of Vedic sacrifice, dakṣiṇā, and *upavasatha* (Uposatha). Theravādin sacrificial discourse criticizes not these practices in themselves but perceived Brahmanical abuses, and claims that the Buddha and his Saṅgha constitute the best recipients of worship. The canonical prose does not use this sacrificial discourse, and the few prose passages that do use sacrificial imagery do not embrace it as a living symbol, but employ it merely as a rhetorical device. This difference in how the didactic verse and discursive prose of the Pāli canon treat the Vedic tradition reveals that the sacrificial verses are much closer to the Vedic milieu from which Buddhism emerged than is the karmic prose.

An example of the rhetorical use of sacrifice in canonical prose is given by *Aṅguttara* IV 41–46, in which the Buddha uses the image of the three sacred fires of Vedic religion in two very different ways.[22] The Buddha begins a discourse on the subject of sacrifice by criticizing the slaughter of animals. He then speaks of three fires to be abandoned, the standard triad of ignorance (*avijjā*), lust (*rāga*), and hatred (*dosa*). However, he also revalues the three fires as a positive religious image, saying that the three fires worthy of worship are parents, dependents, and Brāhmaṇs and ascetics. Finally, he mentions natural fire as another fire in need of tending. Unlike the sacrificial verses, this passage does not appropriate sacrifice as a powerful religious symbol. It instead deconstructs the *agnihotra*, treating fire as an empty signifier capable of representing evil, good, or simply itself.

In the *Sigālaka Sutta* (D III 180–193), the Buddha similarly teaches a householder that the proper way to pay homage (*namassati*) to the six directions is not to salute them, but to protect the following six groups of people: parents; teachers; wife and children; friends and companions; servants, workers, and helpers; and Brāhmaṇs and ascetics.[23] This story does not appropriate a ritual of worshiping the six directions but rather uses it as a rhetorical figure to criticize Brahmanical ritualism, and to assert Buddhist notions of social duty.

In *Kūṭadanta Sutta* (D I 127–149) the Buddha adopts the category of sacrifice but in a way that renders it almost meaningless. In this text, a Brāhmaṇ asks the Buddha how to perform "the threefold successful performance of the sacrifice with its sixteen requisites."[24] This phrase perhaps alludes to the *soḍaśin* soma sacrifice, which included three animal victims and sixteen hymns (ŚB 4.5.3). The Buddha responds by telling a *jātaka* story in which the Bodhisattva was a priest who taught his king how to perform a non-violent sacrifice of dairy and vegetable substances. The Buddha does not identify the recipient of this sacrifice, but he does define the three modes and the sixteen requisites as the participants in the rite and their good personal qualities. After thus unfavorably contrasting animal sacrifice with this non-violent rite, the Buddha does not then advocate performance of this ritual. Instead, he describes a number of superior forms of sacrifice (*yañña*) which he ranks on a scale of increasing fruitfulness (*mahāphalataro ca mahānisaṃsataro ca*). These sacrifices are large donative festivals; regular family offerings to virtuous ascetics; providing shelter for the Saṅgha; taking the five precepts (*sikkhāpadāni*); going forth, becoming perfected in *sīla*, and attaining the four *jhānas*; and attaining knowledge of the destruction of the *āsavas*. This text thus appropriates the sacrifice only to discard it. In the *jātaka* story the Buddha describes a form of sacrifice superior to animal sacrifice, but after winning the acclamation of his audience, he rejects this rite in favor of other religious practices. Although the Buddha labels these as sacrifices, by assigning to the term *yañña* such a wide range of referents, the Buddha gives to this word a sense that is only vaguely connected with its primary meaning.

If the authors of these *suttas* deliberately deconstruct Vedic concepts of sacrifice and ritual, the authors of another set of prose narratives seem simply not to have understood the meaning of a Vedic motif present in these accounts. A rule that appears at a number of places in *Vinaya* and *Majjhima* allows a monk to dispose of leftover alms by throwing them where there is little grass or dropping them in water devoid of living beings.[25] Three related narratives at *Saṃyutta* I 167–170, *Suttanipāta* I.4, and *Vinaya* I 224–226 provide some context for this rule. In the first two passages, the Buddha rejects a Brāhmaṇ's offer of the remains of a sacrifice, saying that a buddha cannot accept food over which verses have been chanted.[26] The Brāhmaṇ asks what should be done with the food. The Buddha replies that no one except a Tathāgata or his disciple could eat it,[27] and he directs that it be thrown where there is little grass, or immersed in water devoid of living beings. The Brāhmaṇ drops the food in water, where it hisses and seethes, steams and smokes, just as a plowshare that had been heated all day would.[28] The Brāhmaṇ, trembling and with hair standing on end, then approaches the Buddha to take refuge. In the *Vinaya* story, a donor tries to give to the Buddha and his monks 500 cartloads of sugar, and the monks take all they can, as do those who live off the remains of the monks' meals.[29] The story then proceeds almost identically to the other two accounts. The Buddha states that only a Tathāgata or his disciple could digest the remainder of the sugar, and so it should be disposed of in a grassless spot or in lifeless water. The donor dumps the sugar in water where it hisses and seethes, etc. The donor, trembling and with hair on end, then approaches the Buddha, hears a sermon, and takes refuge.

Because the miraculous heat in these accounts would surely harm any creature in the water, the rationale for the injunction to avoid living beings is apparently to keep from harming them. But what does heat signify in these passages? As it inspires the donors to convert, they apparently take it to be a sign of the Buddha's power. According to Buddhaghosa, the heat results from the power of the Buddha, and not from the water, the food, the Brāhmaṇ, or any other source.[30] André Bareau suggests further that the offering takes on the *tapas*, the ascetic heat, of the Buddha.[31] Bareau argues that the transformation of the gift is meant to show that the gift has been filled with the Buddha's power, and that the donor will experience karmic rewards even though the Buddha does not consume the gift. Bareau contends that this pericope is meant to calm the doubts of those offering gifts to images of the Buddha after his death. It seems unlikely, however, that this was the meaning intended in these passages, as the Buddha neither accepts the gifts, nor assures the donors of the success of their offerings. In addition, neither the texts, nor Buddhaghosa, nor Bareau explains why the Buddha's heat should destroy life, or why only rejected gifts should become heated.

In order to understand the element of heat in this cycle of stories we can profitably look to Vedic antecedents. Jan Gonda, J. C. Heesterman and Stephanie Jamison all discuss Brahmanical stories of dakṣiṇā becoming destructive when rejected. Often the dakṣiṇā becomes a dangerous beast: a lioness, a tigress, or a female hyena.[32] The reason for these animals being female (in addition to the fact that dakṣiṇā is grammatically feminine) is that they implicitly stand in opposition to the cow, a standard dakṣiṇā; when a dakṣiṇā is thwarted she is transformed from beneficent to vicious. In two passages the dakṣiṇā burns (*nirdahati, atapat*) the donor (KS 28.4/KapS 44.4) or the recipient (AB 6.35). Jamison shows that the destructive power of the rejected dakṣiṇā is one of the many forms of *mení*, the harmful force believed to be released through the disruption of prescribed exchange relations.[33] This Vedic belief that rejected dakṣiṇā becomes hot and destructive provides a compelling rationale for the *Vinaya* rule, and it is likely that this rule and story motif originated in a context in which Vedic beliefs regarding the potentially destructive power of dakṣiṇā held sway. In their present form, the stories give no indication that they understand the destructive heat to be a property of the dakṣiṇā, but instead present the heat as a demonstration of the power of the Buddha.

By intentionally or unknowingly distancing themselves from Vedic traditions, the authors of these karmic passages about sacrifice and dakṣiṇā show that they are much further removed from Vedic attitudes and practices than are the authors of the sacrificial verses. Greg Bailey has argued that the conflicting attitudes toward Brahmanical tradition that we find in the mixed verse and prose conversion stories of *Suttanipāta* should be attributed to the Buddhists' "uncertainty about their identity in a social situation where in order to survive without undertaking practical work they had to project themselves as religious elites."[34] I would nuance this interpretation by noting that the difference in views between the sacrificial verses and the karmic prose reflects the changing social status of Buddhism. Although Buddhism emerged in a cultural milieu dominated by Vedic religion, Buddhism enjoyed a period of cultural ascendancy in India under the Mauryas, and was the dominant religious force in Sri Lanka for perhaps two centuries before the Aluvihāra recension was made. During this period, the Brāhmaṇs had little if any presence in South India and Sri Lanka. Consequently, for over two centuries Buddhists transmitted and shaped their religious traditions free from Brahmanical hegemony. The hypothesis that the prose literature reflects these post-Aśokan conditions accounts for the shift from the appropriation of Brahmanical ritualism in the didactic verse to the disdain and misunderstanding toward Brahmanism shown by the prose.[35]

The reduction of sacrifice to karma

With the creation of karmic discourse came the need to explain sacrificial and purificatory terminology and verses in terms of the new paradigm. The process of mental purification could be explained as a series of momentary mental actions; similarly, *Jātaka*'s accounts of heroic generosity easily lent themselves to karmic interpretation. Sacrificial discourse, invested in the objective aspects of giving, presented more problems. In this section I will show how the karmic passages, with varying degrees of success, reduce sacrificial discourse to karmic discourse in their treatments of the act of giving, the observance of Uposatha, merit, and dakṣiṇā dedication.

While the recipient is essential to sacrificial understandings of giving, in karmic ideology only the donor's intention determines the karmic fruit. Most prose passages that incorporate a sacrificial verse or formula either do not comment on its sacrificial themes or use it only to describe and to praise worthy recipients of offerings, but do not develop or explain the sacrificial idiom in any other way.[36] However, a few karmic prose texts, most notably *Dakkhiṇāvibhaṅga Sutta* (M III 253–257), discuss the idea that the qualities of the recipient affect the degree of merit produced.[37] This *sutta* describes with mathematical precision how the status of the recipient of a gift affects its karmic result:

> "Ānanda, when a gift is given to an animal, a hundredfold return (*sataguṇā dakkhiṇā*) may be expected. When a gift is given to an immoral ordinary person, a thousandfold return may be expected. When a gift is given to a virtuous ordinary person, a hundred-thousandfold return may be expected. When a gift is given to one outside [the Buddha's dispensation], who is free from lust for sensual pleasures, a trillionfold return may be expected.[38]

The passage goes on to state that a gift to a *sotāpanna* yields an incalculable reward, and to ask rhetorically how much greater would be the effect of gifts given to those who had made still greater progress toward nirvāṇa.[39] By ranking gifts to worthy and unworthy recipients on a single scale of efficacy, this *sutta* retains the idea that the worthiness of the recipient affects the merit produced by a gift, but it also relativizes this claim. As giving *dāna* to an animal can hardly be construed as an act of worship, such giving must be understood in terms of some other value, such as detachment or compassion. This passage does not construe *dāna* as a sacrifice, and it includes no sacrificial terminology other than *dakkhiṇā*. Furthermore, the author idiosyncratically uses this term to refer not to material offerings but to their effects, suggesting that he is unfamiliar with its older usage.

Against the sacrificial emphasis on giving to worthy individuals, this *sutta* asserts that gifts designated for the whole Saṅgha, even when given to immoral monks, are more efficacious than gifts made to individual monastics (M III 255–256). This passage establishes the Saṅgha and not individual monks as the true recipient of offerings and the guarantor of their efficacy. By assigning to the act an ideal object, this interpretation moves toward a thoroughly psychological analysis of giving. The text also thereby removes the lay donor from the position of judging the worthiness of the monks to receive *dāna*.[40]

This *sutta* treats the theme of the purification of *dakkhiṇā* (*dakkhiṇāvissudhiyo*) by tersely explaining that *dakkhiṇā* may be purified by its donor, its recipient, both, or neither (M III 256–257). The text does not explain what purification of *dakkhiṇā* might mean, but if *dakkhiṇā* refers here, as it does earlier in the *sutta*, not to the offering itself but to its result, then *to purify dakkhiṇā* would mean *to make an offering fruitful*. The commentary gives this interpretation, and this interpretation is perhaps implied by the accompanying verses.[41] The idea of the purification of *dakkhiṇā* apparently derives from a sacrificial context like that represented by *Suttanipāta* 487–488; however, as earlier in the *sutta*, a belief in the importance of the recipient in determining the result of an act of giving is here divorced from the sacrificial context that gives it meaning.

Karmic interpretations of undertaking *sīla* vows during the Uposatha are provided by the prose passages that frame the Uposatha verses discussed in chapter 1. *Aṅguttara* I 207 defines the Uposatha as "purification of a defiled head (i.e. mind) through action,"[42] and *Aṅguttara* IV 248–251 and 251–255 present Uposatha observance as imitation of the life of an arhat. Although these passages do not replace the *aṭṭha sīla* precepts with the *kammapathas*, they do define the purpose of Uposatha observance as the karmic goal of mental purification.

The prose literature also reinterprets the central category of merit (*puñña*) to indicate good karma. *Mahācattārīsaka Sutta* (M III 71–78) appears to represent a transition between sacrificial and karmic discourses. In this text, the Buddha considers view, intention, speech, action, and livelihood, distinguishing with regard to each between 1. wrong; 2. right but "affected by the taints, partaking of merit, ripening on the side of attachment;" and 3. right and "noble, taintless, supramundane, a factor of the path."[43] As in the sacrificial discourse, this text applies the term *puñña* only to the attainment of good rebirth, and not to the attainment of nirvāṇa. But as in karmic discourse, this *sutta* does not differentiate between the kinds of actions and states that lead to each of these ends; rather, the two types of good practice represent two levels of attainment on the same scale. In addition, this text includes a standard summary of right view that incorporates both sacrificial and karmic idioms; it begins, "There is what is given and what is offered and what is sacrificed; there is fruit and result of good and bad actions."[44]

In other prose (and some verse) literature, *puñña* denotes all beneficial actions and their proximate effects, whether leading to a good rebirth or to nirvāṇa. This expansion of the semantic range of *puñña* can be traced in discussions of giving, right conduct, and meditation as constituting the three bases for making merit (*puññakiriyavatthūni*). This theme seems to have developed out of exegesis of a set of verses that appears at *Itivuttaka* 15–16 and at 51–52:

> If one would train oneself for merit which lasts long and yields happiness,
> He should cultivate giving, right conduct, and lovingkindness.
> Having cultivated these things which are three sources of happiness,
> The wise man arises in a happy world that is free from harm.[45]

These typically sacrificial *gāthās* incorporate themes of giving, merit, and heavenly world (*loka*); right conduct (*samacariya*) is perhaps a synonym for *sīla*. The mention of lovingkindness (*mettā*) is unusual, but is certainly consonant with sacrificial discourse. The two frame texts give a karmic reading to these verses. The prose at It 15 glosses the three actions with distinctly karmic language, referring to the fruit and result of three actions (*tiṇṇaṃ kammānaṃ phalaṃ . . . vipāko*).

The other prose frame, at It 51, describes the three as bases for making merit (*puññakiriyavatthūni*): *dānamayaṃ*, *sīlamayaṃ*, and *bhāvanāmayaṃ*.[46] While in the verses all three elements are objects of the verb *bhāvaye,* in this gloss *bhāvanā* (meditation) becomes the name of one of them. In this way, meditation, an activity generally presented as a means to mental purification leading toward awakening, is classified as a merit-making activity. This same definition of *puññakiriyavatthūni* appears in a *mātika* list at *Dīgha* III 218 and is the basis of a *sutta* at *Aṅguttara* IV 241–243. This *sutta* states that one who makes the bases of giving and *sīla* to a small degree is reborn among poor men, and if he makes them to a medium degree he is reborn among men of average wealth. If he makes them to a high degree, he is reborn among wealthy men, or the Four Great Kings, or the Tāvatiṃsa deities, or the Yāma, Tusita, Nimmānarati, or Paranimmitavasavatti deities. This correlation of actions with wealth in a future life and this elaborate list of heavens contrast starkly with the *Itivuttaka* verses' simple promise of a happy world free from harm. Strangely, this *sutta* does not tell what becomes of those who develop the basis of meditation.[47] Nonetheless, these interpretations in prose of the theme of the three meritorious actions all present an understanding of merit as encompassing all good karma.

Merit and demerit are also identified with the *saṅkhāras*, understood as causes of rebirth or of the attainment of nirvāṇa:

> Monks, if an ignorant person forms a meritorious mental formation, there is consciousness following merit; if he forms a demeritorious mental formation, then there is consciousness following demerit; if he forms a neutral mental formation, then there is consciousness following what is neutral.[48]

Because the word *puñña* is ordinarily a noun in canonical Pāli, the phrases *puññaṃ ce saṅkhāraṃ* and *apuññaṃ ce saṅkhāraṃ* could be rendered more literally as "mental formation that is merit" and "mental formation that is demerit." This passage defines merit and demerit, the proximate effects of good and bad action, as mental formations.

A few passages explicitly identify *puñña* as the cause or effect of attaining nirvāṇa. *Nidhikaṇḍa Sutta* (Khp VIII) tells that a treasure of merit gives every pleasure, including the attainment of nirvāṇa, liberation (*vimutti, vimokkha*), insight (*paṭisambhidā*), pratyekabuddhahood (*paccekabodhi*), and buddhahood (*buddhabhūmi*).[49] *Saṃyutta* V 392 and 401–402 call the attainment of arhatship a flood of merit and good (*puññābhisando kusalābhisando*).[50] The second of these *suttas* adds that this attainment produces an incalculable, immeasurable heap of merit,[51] and includes these verses:

> He who, desiring merit and established in what is wholesome,
> Cultivates the path to the attainment of deathlessness,
> Understanding the heart of the Dharma, delighting in the destruction [of the taints],
> Does not tremble when the king of death comes.[52]

"Desiring merit," a standard epithet for donors in sacrificial verse, is here applied to individuals seeking nirvāṇa. *Aṅguttara* V 248–249 lists ten things whose possessor will produce much merit; these ten are the eight elements of the Noble Eightfold Path plus right knowledge and right release. This passage thus presents merit as an effect of liberation.

Finally, two prose passages from *Aṅguttara* address the dedication of dakṣiṇā. While both *suttas* reproduce the sacrificial pattern for this rite, in their current forms they also include elements of karmic discourse.[53] A V 269–272 begins with a young Brāhmaṇ telling the Buddha about Brahmanical śrāddha rites:

> "O Gotama, we Brāhmaṇs of course give gifts, we make śrāddhas, saying, 'Let this gift benefit our departed kinsmen; let our departed kinsmen enjoy this gift.'[54]

The Brāhmaṇ asks the Buddha whether the dead enjoy such gifts. This question seems to presume an eschatology similar to that of *Tirokuḍḍa* and of the early Brahmanical texts, wherein the dead live a liminal existence, dependent on descendants for food but happy and beneficent when fed.

The Buddha's reply expresses ambivalence toward dakṣiṇā dedication. He says that śrāddha offerings cannot reach a person who has arisen in a hell or as an animal, a human, or a deity, but that only those wrongdoers who arise in the *pettivisaya* are able to receive dedicated gifts. *Pettivisaya* is a harsh pun that identifies the Brāhmaṇs' world of the fathers (*pitṛloka*) with the realm of the *petas* (ghosts, literally, 'departed'), a miserable destiny. This *sutta* does not understand the śrāddha rite in terms of the old eschatology in which the dead exist in a transitional state. Instead, this text presents an eschatology in which one is reborn in one of five *gatis*, or destinies, soon after dying. Because only those reborn as ghosts may benefit from the dedication of dakṣiṇā, the Buddha views this rite as a rather ineffective means for aiding deceased ancestors. The Buddha instead encourages the Brāhmaṇ to perform meritorious actions in order to ensure his own happiness after death. This *sutta* thereby brings the practice of dakṣiṇā dedication in line with both the karmic eschatology and the Theravādin ethos of soteriological self-sufficiency.

The authors of this *sutta* underscore their attack on the dedication of dakṣiṇā by making its proponent a Brāhmaṇ, thereby suggesting that this ritual is not truly Buddhist. They do so even though the Brāhmaṇ's question contains a number of verbal parallels with *Tirokuḍḍa Sutta*, including *ñāti-*, *dāyakā ca anipphalā*, and *upakappati*.[55] These parallels show that the authors are using the character of the Brāhmaṇ as a device to criticize a Buddhist practice. The authors' admission that dakṣiṇā dedication is effective in some cases indicates that this rite was too popular at the time of this *sutta*'s composition for its authors to dismiss it outright. However, if the *sutta*'s polemic is representative of a hostile attitude toward the dedication of dakṣiṇā among the authors and redactors of the texts, this fact would explain why the Pāli canon contains relatively few references to this practice.

The other prose account of dakṣiṇā dedication, A IV 63–67, follows the sacrificial pattern, but with one important deviation. In this episode, the lay follower Nandamātā attracts the god Vessavaṇa with her singing, which she offers to him as a guest-offering.[56] He tells her that a group of monks led by Sāriputta and Moggallāna will be coming to that place the next day, and asks that she feed the monks and dedicate the dakṣiṇā to him as a guest-offering.[57] On the next day Nandamātā feeds the monks and dedicates the offering to Vessavaṇa, but she does so by saying to Sāriputta, "Sir, let what merit there is in this gift be for the happiness of the great king Vessavaṇa."[58] That this injunction refers to merit, but not to food or dakṣiṇā, suggests that the author of this phrase understands the effectiveness of this act to depend on the merit of the act, rather than on the transfer of the item given. In interpreting dakṣiṇā dedication as a dedication of merit, this story is unique among canonical accounts of the dedication of dakṣiṇā.

We have good reason to believe, however, that this dedicatory formula has been interpolated into the text. First, Nandamātā's statement awkwardly interrupts the narrative. After he has finished eating, Sāriputta asks Nandamātā who told her that the monks were coming. She relates that it was Vessavaṇa, and that he asked her to prepare a meal and dedicate the dakṣiṇā to him. She then abruptly utters the dedication formula. Sāriputta does not acknowledge this dedication with an *anumodana* (thanksgiving or benediction) verse, as one would expect, but continues to speak with Nandamātā about her meeting with Vessavaṇa. Second, in *Cūḷasaccaka Sutta* (M I 227–237) the Buddha rejects the use of dedication formulas like the one Nandamātā uses. After being defeated by the Buddha in a debate, a man named Saccaka has his supporters prepare a meal which he presents to the Buddha. When the Buddha has eaten, Saccaka initiates the following exchange:

> "Gotama, let what merit and greatness [?] of merit there is in this gift be for the happiness of the givers."
> "Aggivessana, what [merit] there is in relation to a sacrificial recipient such as yourself, who is not without lust, hatred, and delusion, that will be for the givers. What [merit] there is in relation to a sacrificial recipient such as myself, who is without lust, hatred, and delusion, that will be for you."[59]

The Buddha rejects Saccaka's attempt to dedicate the merit resulting from his gift, and asserts that merit accrues automatically to the donor and cannot be transferred to another.

To explain Nandamātā's use of this dedicatory formula will require a brief digression, for although this episode is unique in the Pāli canon, it represents an important development in Buddhism, the reinterpretation of dakṣiṇā dedication as a function of merit. Similar '*yad puññaṃ*' formulas are used for the dedication of dakṣiṇā in other Buddhist literature. For example, in the *Avadānaśataka* (second century CE), the Buddha dedicates dakṣiṇā to ghosts (*pretas*, Sanskrit cognate of *peta*) with the following words:

> Let the merit that is from this gift reach this ghost.
> Let this one immediately arise from the very terrible ghost realm.[60]

Inscriptional evidence, however, suggests that such usages did not originate with dakṣiṇā dedication, but with other practices for dedicating the effects of action. Many donative inscriptions dating from the Common Era are also of the form, "What merit is here, let it be for. . . . "[61] A number of earlier donative inscriptions simply designate that a gift is for someone, for the worship (*pūjā*) of someone, or for someone's welfare, health, or happiness.[62] Some of the oldest inscriptions of this type are from Sri Lanka, and include a group of inscriptions from the third or second century BCE that dedicate a gift "for the welfare and happiness of beings in the boundless universe."[63] Such dedications differ from the dedication of dakṣiṇā as described in the Pāli canon in that the recipients of dakṣiṇā are always deities or *petas*, while the beneficiaries named in the inscriptions are often living people. More fundamentally, in dakṣiṇā dedication a material offering gives rise to a material effect similar in kind to the offering, while in the inscriptions a person aspires that a good action, usually of giving, would produce an immaterial benefit, such as welfare, health, or the attainment of nirvāṇa. The inscriptions therefore show that from at least as early as the third or second century BCE Buddhists engaged in practices of merit dedication that differed fundamentally from dakṣiṇā dedication.[64]

These practices of dedicating the effects of action likely had their origin not in the dedication of dakṣiṇā, but in the practice of forming aspirations (*paṇidhi / praṇidhāna, patthaṇā / prārthanā*) to direct the effects of good actions to benefit oneself or others. In the first section of this chapter I give some examples of aspirations made for one's own benefit; canonical verse narratives also provide examples of aspirations made for the benefit of others. In the conclusion of VJ, Maddī recounts the vows she performed for the sake of her children, and then aspires that her children would attain deathlessness by virtue of their parents' actions:

> Whatever meritorious deeds have been done by me and by your father,
> By this truth and goodness, become free from aging and death.[65]

Buddhavaṃsa tells that the future Gotama Buddha lay in the mud so that the buddha Dīpaṅkara could cross over his body; the Bodhisattva then resolved,

> By this service, done for the greatest of persons,
> When I attain omniscience, let me deliver many people.[66]

In *Apadāna*, the Bodhisattva creates a vision of buddhas, pratyekabuddhas and disciples, summons beings to worship it, and then makes two aspirations for the benefit of others.[67] He first wishes that all beings be sharers in the fruit of his meritorious action:

> 'Whatever beings are conscious [of this act], and whatever beings are not conscious,
> Let them all share in the fruit of the meritorious act done by me.'
> To those who knew the deed well I gave the fruit of the meritorious act,
> And to those who did not then know, when the gods went they revealed it.[68]

Beings here share in the fruit of the Bodhisattva's act by worshiping the vision he creates; that the Bodhisattva considers it necessary that beings have knowledge of his act shows that these beings make merit through their own efforts.[69] This reading is also suggested by the expression "sharing in merit," which echoes the claim made in *Aṅguttara* III 41 that those who rejoice over another's gift share in merit. The Bodhisattva's second aspiration, on the other hand, requires no effort on the part of the beneficiaries:

> 'Let all beings in the world that subsist on food
> By my thought obtain all delightful food.'[70]

Like the dedicatory inscriptions, these aspirations from *Jātaka*, *Buddhavaṃsa*, and *Apadāna* direct the effect of an action toward some particular named end. The verbal parallels between literary aspirations and inscribed dedications become more marked in the Common Era.[71]

The insertion of the "*yad idaṃ*" formula into A IV 63–67 therefore most likely represents an attempt to identify dakṣiṇā dedication with practices of merit dedication. As I argue in later chapters, the interpretation of dakṣiṇā in terms of karma becomes common in post-canonical Theravādin texts.

We should also note that verbal aspirations themselves represent another pre-Buddhist practice that has been incorporated into karmic discourse. The verbal aspirations cited in the previous paragraphs closely resemble verbal acts such as oaths or truth acts (**satyakriyā / saccakiriyā*). The standard form of the Vedic and Buddhist truth act is for the basis of the act to be in instrumental case and in sentence-initial position, with the object usually stated in imperative mood.[72] The three clear examples of merit dedication cited above are of this form. The practice of forming aspirations to direct the effects of action, if not derived from the truth act itself, is certainly grounded in similar ideas about the power of solemn speech acts. However, in the canonical prose passages cited in the first section of this chapter (A IV 239–241, M III 99–103, M I 285–290), purely mental aspirations (*cetopaṇidhi, saṅkhāra, ākaṅkheyya*) shape the effects of actions. These passages represent a karmic understanding of these acts as essentially mental rather than verbal.

Why karma?

The development of systematic karmic discourse constituted a crucial development in Buddhist thought. Buddhists used karmic discourse to articulate new understandings of ethics, psychology and eschatology and thus to move beyond Vedic views of the world. The idea of karma allowed Buddhists to rationalize received practices, including giving and dedicating *dāna*, in the context of a unified philosophical system. But karma theory appealed to the wishes and fears of Buddhists as well as to their intellects. The sacrificial discourse depicts those who give to monastics and observe Uposathas as trapped in *saṃsāra*: one may make merit and gain heaven, but when she falls from heaven she returns to a human birth. VJ and the Aśokan edicts both witness to the aspirations of laity that their religious practices would provide a way to an eternal salvation. Similarly, the purificatory *gāthās* do not indicate that those who devote themselves to renunciation and meditation but fail to reach nirvāṇa have anything lasting to show for their efforts. The karmic discourse addresses both problems by positing that the path to nirvāṇa extends over numerous lifetimes, and allows both householders and monastics to progress toward their ultimate salvation while enjoying countless pleasant births along the way.[73]

This unification of the path can be seen in a number of prose narratives that recommend that monks and nuns make merit.[74] In *Sāmaññaphala Sutta*, two men go forth thinking, "I should make merit."[75] *Dīgha* II 28–29 similarly names merit-making (*puññakiriya*) as one of the defining characteristics of one who has gone forth (*pabbajito*). A number of passages in *Aṅguttara* state that monks produce merit or demerit depending on whether they rightly carry out such typically monastic actions as interpreting and teaching the Dharma.[76] The *Cakkavattisīhanāda Sutta* begins and ends with the Buddha instructing monks on how they may make merit grow through the cultivation of wholesome mental states.[77]

Some passages clearly express an understanding of monks' merit as leading to a good rebirth. *Aṅguttara* V 76 says that one who heals a schism in the Saṅgha produces *brahmaṃ puññaṃ*, meaning that he will rejoice in heaven for an eon (*kappa*). At *Aṅguttara* IV 88–89 and *Itivuttaka* 14–15, the Buddha addresses his monks with these words:

> Monks, do not fear merits, for this is a name for happiness, [for what is desirable, lovely, dear, and pleasant]. For I know the desirable, lovely, dear and pleasant result experienced for a long time of merits made over a long time.[78]

The Buddha goes on to describe various blissful lives he lived in the heavens and on earth as a *cakkavatti* king because he cultivated thoughts of lovingkindness for seven years. The *Itivuttaka* version of this account ends with the *puññakiriyavatthūni* verses, while the *Aṅguttara* account ends with a verse version of the prose. In both passages, the Buddha clearly enjoins his monks to make merit.

That these passages admonish monks not to fear merits suggests, however, that some monks did believe that merit was not a proper goal for them.[79] While some religious impulses motivated the adoption of karmic discourse, others resisted it. The belief that the worthiness of the recipient affects the merit of a gift survived the rise of karma theory because the economy of gift-giving and merit generation that is at the heart of the lay-monastic relationship is predicated on this doctrine. If laypeople believed that the benefits of giving lay only in the renunciation of wealth, they might, like Vessantara, give to any beggar who asked. That a desire to encourage giving to Buddhist monastics motivated the survival of sacrificial discourse is shown by the majority of prose passages that comment on sacrificial verses or incorporate a sacrificial formula in praise of the Saṅgha or of individual monks: these passages use sacrificial verses or formulas to describe and to praise worthy recipients of offerings, but do not otherwise develop or explain the sacrificial idiom.[80] The dedication of dakṣiṇā likewise continued despite attempts to rationalize it in terms of karma theory because this rite provides a means of caring for one's special dead and propitiating guardian deities. As I will show, these aspects of sacrificial discourse continue to play a prominent role throughout later Theravādin tradition.

The invention of karma in ancient South Asia

In this chapter I have described the karmic discourse of the Pāli *suttas* and, on the basis of these *suttas*, I have attempted to reconstruct the Buddhist invention of karma during the half millennium BCE, a time when other South Asian intellectual traditions were also developing ideas of karma as a mechanism linking a great variety of ethically significant actions with a complex array of effects. If it is useful for us to think of karma as an idea constructed by Buddhists rather than simply inherited from Vedic religion, then we should also think of other traditions' notions of karma as similarly invented during this period. The various karmic discourses created during this time are remarkable for their similarities as well as for their differences. A thorough study of the development of ideas of karma in ancient South

Asia would map out a complex web of influences, appropriations, and arguments. In the following paragraphs I would like to give a sense of what this project would involve by briefly comparing the picture suggested by the Theravādin texts with that which emerges from two other groups of texts, the earliest literature of the Brahmanical legal (Dharma) and Śvetāmbara Jain traditions.

The earliest literature of the Brahmanical legal and Śvetāmbara Jain traditions dates from roughly the same period as the Pāli canonical texts. Patrick Olivelle argues largely on the basis of internal evidence that the *Dharmasūtras* of Āpastambha, Gautama, and Baudhāyana date from the third or second centuries BCE and that that of Vasiṣṭha dates from between the second century BCE and the first century CE.[81] Olivelle dates *Manusmṛti*, the first of the *Dharmaśāstras*, to the first couple centuries of the Common Era.[82] This difference in time allows us to observe developments between the three earlier texts and Manu. According to Śvetāmbara tradition, the oldest Jain texts were lost, and the extant scriptures, although they present authentic teachings of Mahāvīra, were not redacted until the fifth or sixth century CE.[83] Walther Schubring identifies *Āyāraṃga* (*Ācāraṅga*), *Sūyagaḍaṃga* (*Sūtrakṛtāṅga*), *Uttarajjhāyā* (*Uttarād-hyayana*), and *Dasaveyāliya* (*Daśavaikālika*) as the texts containing the oldest traditions, although like other scholars he recognizes that these texts contain materials from different periods and that any attempt to date these texts would be highly speculative.[84] With these caveats in mind, I will in the following paragraphs discuss these four texts as those most likely to represent early Jainism.[85]

The mutual influence exerted by Indic traditions as they developed concepts of karma is exemplified by the eschatologies presented in Theravādin, Śvetāmbara, and Brahmanical legal texts. Many of the features that characterize Theravādin karmic eschatology can also be found in the other two traditions. The Śvetāmbara texts, for example, demonstrate that karma produces repeated rebirth in four *gatis* (denizen of hell, animal, human, or god) or as a simpler form of life, and they dramatize at length the miseries of *saṃsāra*, especially the torments of hell.[86] The Dharma literature presents similar ideas; moreover, in comparing the three earlier *Dharmasūtra* texts with *Manusmṛti* we can trace the development of a karmic eschatology. The *Dharmasūtras* contain very few descriptions of the afterlife effects of action. The most detailed of these, ĀpDhS 2.2.2–3 and GDhS 11.29, both state that one who follows his dharma enjoys pleasures in heaven and then, upon his return to earth, a remainder of the fruits of his actions produces a good human rebirth.[87] The accounts of the fates of evildoers differ: ĀpDhS 2.2.6–7 asserts that when a sinner returns from boundless (or endless) *niraya* he is reborn in a low birth corresponding to his former *varṇa* (a Brāhmaṇ is reborn as a Cāṇḍāla, etc.), while GDhS 11.30 simply states that wrongdoers scatter and perish. In these verses we can see elements of classical karmic eschatology, notably that past actions condition human births; however, these descriptions for the most part assume a late Vedic worldview, according to which one performs good actions on earth and enjoys their fruits in heaven, and when those fruits are exhausted one returns to a human birth on earth. The differing descriptions of the fate of wrongdoers shows that a consensus had not emerged regarding their destiny. ĀpDhS 2.2.3 likens the process of repeated death and rebirth to a wheel, but it presents this situation as a happy one and not one from which a person would wish to escape. Baudhāyana is even farther from the classical outlook; he makes no reference to the impermanence of heaven or to actions as determinants of human rebirth, and instead presents Vedic worship as the means to becoming Brahman and attaining the Brahmaloka.[88]

In the twelfth chapter of *Manusmṛti*, on the other hand, we find an elaborate if not entirely consistent karmic eschatology.[89] Manu describes at length how the three qualities of existence (the *guṇas* of Sāṅkhya philosophy) produce actions that lead after death directly to rebirth as a particular variety of god, human, or animal (12.39–59). Those who commit great misdeeds are first tormented for a long time in terrible hells, and are then reborn as a low status human, an animal, or a *preta* (12.53–81). Manu links specific deeds to their effects; e.g. for stealing grain one becomes a rat; for brass, a goose; for water, an aquatic bird; for honey, a stinging insect, and so forth.[90] Manu also expresses the revulsion with *saṃsāra* characteristic of karmic discourse: "Through their repetition of evil actions, men of little intelligence experience miseries in womb after womb in this world."[91] These descriptions plainly resemble developed expositions of rebirth processes in Theravādin and Jain karmic texts. Furthermore, a comparison of the Vedic texts to the *Dharmasūtras* and to *Manusmṛti* reveals a clear line of development that parallels the change from sacrificial to karmic discourses that I argue occurred in the Buddhist tradition.

In the ethical and soteriological value that they assign to meritorious actions, these three traditions begin from very different assumptions; nonetheless, the Brahmanical legal and Śvetāmbara traditions, like the Theravādin, develop ways of integrating the performance of meritorious actions and the pursuit of liberation within a unified soteriology. As BDhS 2.7.22, cited above, exemplifies, the *Dharmasūtras* present a single soteriological path in which meritorious action is the way to the highest religious ends. Against the claims of renouncers, Āpastambha asserts that Vedic rites must be performed and that those who perform them will obtain the eternal fruit called heaven.[92] The text goes on to say that one may by action or asceticism win a finite world, but that this is no grounds for claiming that one way of life is superior to another.[93] Gautama and Baudhāyana go further, claiming that the renouncer's way of life is inferior to that of the householder, because the householder's way of life is the only one authorized by the Vedas, and only he produces offspring.[94] These three texts present a soteriology similar to that of VJ and the Aśokan inscriptions, in that meritorious action – in the Brahmanical texts defined as Vedic ritual, performance of one's dharma, and perhaps also asceticism – is believed to lead to the ultimate goal of eternal existence in a heaven.

Manu similarly upholds Vedic ritual and the life of the householder as the best way of being religious, but he also incorporates into his soteriology the renouncer's ideal of liberation from rebirth. Manu does so in part by presenting renunciation not as the rejection of Vedic sacrifice, but as its culmination: after a life of ritual performance, the renouncer internalizes the sacrificial fires and thereafter constantly chants the Vedas (6.25, 83). The renouncer is thus able to perform his dharma even as through knowledge and detachment he avoids the karmic effects that would keep him in *saṃsāra* (6.66, 73–81). In Manu's synthesis, Vedic ritual provides the way to the highest goal of *mokṣa*, but as one nears that goal one performs that ritual in a way that does not produce karmic effects.

The early Śvetāmbara *sūtras* suggest that although Jains viewed karma very differently than did Buddhists and Brāhmaṇs, Jains also found ways to synthesize the paths of merit and *mokṣa*. K. K. Dixit argues on the basis of his study of the *Bhagavatī Sūtra* (*Viyāhapannatti*) that the early Jain tradition had no notion of good karma, but viewed karmic acts (*kamma* and *kiriyā*) as essentially violent and karmic effects as the primary obstacle to gaining *mokṣa*.[95] *Āyāraṃga* and *Sūyagaḍaṃga* lend support to this interpretation. Both texts frequently refer to karma as *daṇḍa*, meaning 'rod' or 'punishment,'[96] and Āyār 1.3.1.4 declares killing to be the root of karma.[97] Both texts repeatedly identify ceasing to produce karma and annihilating karma already made as the way to attain nirvāṇa.[98] The reason that karma has such a negative value in the Jain tradition lies in the meaning of *kamma* and *kiriyā* as 'action but especially ritual action.' The paradigmatic ritual act of Vedic sacrifice of course involves violence against the offering which is consumed, but the Jain texts even represent feeding clergy as morally problematic, and they therefore deemphasize the ritual and donative character of this action. *Sūyagaḍaṃga* asserts that one should not praise a gift of alms because food preparation always involves killing, and by praising an act one becomes accessory to that act. On the other hand, neither should one criticize a gift because by doing so one may deprive monastics of their livelihood. One should therefore say nothing (1.11.16–21). *Uttarajjhāyā* 6.7 and 12 state that because accepting gifts leads one to hell, one should eat the food placed in one's bowl only to preserve one's life, and one should preserve one's life only in order to eliminate karma. Monastics should not accept food prepared especially for them, but should gather small amounts of food from many donors.[99] The Jain *sūtras* accordingly condemn the large, premeditated gifts accepted by Buddhists and Brāhmaṇs. *Sūyagaḍaṃga* represents Buddhists and Brāhmaṇs as advocating feeding 2000 mendicants at a time in order to make merit and attain rebirth as a deity. The author condemns such feasts because their preparation involves violence against animals.[100] Such qualms notwithstanding, it must have been necessary to give laypeople some rationale for feeding ascetics, and a few passages do present a more positive evaluation of almsgiving. Sūyag 2.2.76 includes almsgiving in a list of actions that will lead to a good rebirth.[101] Utt 12 remarkably includes an exposition of the merit field doctrine; however, the text reveals its reservations on this point by putting these words in the mouth of a yakṣa (a terrestrial deity) who, by an act of ventriloquism, speaks for a silent monk (vv. 8, 12–15).[102]

These Jain texts thus present a unitary ethic in which the elimination of karma is the soteriological goal; however, *Dasaveyāliya* and *Uttarajjhāyā* find different ways to accommodate good or meritorious action within this system.[103] *Dasaveyāliya* encourages the performance of good actions, which it describes with words that elsewhere often indicate merit or auspiciousness, including *cheya* (*śreya*, 4.10), *kallāna* (*kalyāṇa*, 4.11), and *puṇṇa* (*puṇya*, 4.15–16, 10.18), and which it contrasts with *pāva* (or *pāvaga*; *pāpa*). However, when describing the *effects* of actions, Dasav 4.1–9 does not contrast the binding of evil karma with the accumulation of good karma;

rather, this passage contrasts the binding of evil karma with not binding evil karma. The implication seems to be that good acts do not produce the binding of karma. *Uttarajjhāyā*, on the other hand, asserts that both merit and demerit (*puṇṇapāvaṃ*) must be destroyed (21.24), indicating that good action does produce karma. However, *Uttarajjhāyā* also attributes to meritorious karma the capacity to produce birth in a good family, the attainment of permanent bliss, and even birth as a Tīrthaṅkara (29.10, 23, and 43). While maintaining that final salvation consists in the destruction of all karma, *Uttarajjhāyā* thus paradoxically allows that acquiring merit may help one reach that goal. The ambivalent understanding of good action represented by these two texts, wherein an act is thought either to create or to destroy karmic bonds (or simultaneously to liberate or to entrap), even today forms the characteristic Jain synthesis of the paths of action and non-action.[104]

From this very brief discussion of the shared history of Indic religions, some general patterns emerge. In all three traditions, we can trace the development of a karmic discourse as a way of synthesizing divergent soteriological goals within a single religious system. While the *Dharmasūtras* exclude renunciation and *mokṣa*, Manu accommodates them within his system of duty and merit-making. *Āyāraṃga* and *Sūyagaḍaṃga* present karma as the chief obstacle to be overcome by one seeking nirvāṇa, but *Uttarajjhāyā* finds a place for merit-making in this very quest to eliminate karma.[105] And as we have seen, in the Buddhist texts a dual soteriology of merit-making and mental purification is replaced by a unified karmic soteriology. This cursory comparative exploration suggests that it is not the case that during the half millennium before the Common Era a single idea of karma was adapted in different ways by various traditions, but rather that these traditions created similar ways of thinking and speaking about karma. This convergence of ideas must have occurred through a complex process of mutual appropriation and response that we do not yet understand. Yet in none of these traditions did the invention of karma eliminate all ambiguities; there remains in each of these traditions a conflict between the classical karmic eschatology and soteriology and elements of the older worldview and ethos which remain embedded in the scriptures and rituals of that tradition. In the second half of this book, I trace some of the ways in which this conflict has played out in the Theravādin tradition.

Part Two

Sacrifice and Karma in Narrative

CHAPTER THREE

The Centrality of Sacrifice in *Vimānavatthu* and *Petavatthu*

The narrative verse sections of *Suttapiṭaka* include most of *Jātaka*, *Vimānavatthu*, *Petavatthu*, *Cariyāpiṭaka*, *Buddhavaṃsa*, and *Apadāna*, as well as portions of other texts. *Jātaka*'s tales are believed to differ widely in their dates of composition, and many are thought to be non-Buddhist in origin.[1] The rest of these books belong to what Wilhelm Geiger called "the later and least happy parts of the canon."[2] If they are sometimes difficult to appreciate, these narrative verse texts nonetheless add significantly to Buddhist literature about giving and rebirth by articulating ideas of sacrifice, ascesis, and karma in the forms of myth, legend, and drama. *Cariyāpiṭaka*, *Buddhavaṃsa*, and *Apadāna* tell stories of progress toward nirvāṇa, while *Vimānavatthu* and *Petavatthu* relate tales about acts leading to rebirth as a denizen of hell, a ghost, or a deity. In so doing, these stories give specificity and realism to processes of action and rebirth.

Jonathan Walters argues, however, that *Cariyāpiṭaka*, *Buddhavaṃsa*, and *Apadāna* do more than simply express older ideas in narrative form; he claims that these texts are of central importance to the development of Buddhism because they construct a universal soteriology in which meritorious acts performed by laypeople as well as by monastics may lead to pleasant rebirths and eventually to the attainment of nirvāṇa.[3] In the previous chapter I showed that the karmic prose also creates a unified soteriology through systematic discourse; Walters therefore may seem to overstate the significance of these verse texts in the development of the tradition. On the other hand, the judgment of Geiger and other past scholarship on the dates of the canonical texts should be called into question. Although *Vimānavatthu*, *Petavatthu*, *Cariyāpiṭaka*, *Buddhavaṃsa*, and *Apadāna* may be among the later canonical verse literature, there is no compelling reason to believe that, prior to the composition of these verse texts, the canonical prose traditions closely resembled the forms in which they exist today. As I state in the Introduction, the canonical prose was probably not fixed prior to the Aluvihāra recension, and it underwent at least minor revisions after that time as well. If these allegedly late verse narratives took shape during the same period as the prose traditions, then these verse texts present less translations of classical karmic theory into narrative than efforts to invent a discourse of karma. This interpretation is supported by a number of the stories contained in these texts which do not assume a sophisticated concept of karma like what we find in discursive canonical prose, but rather present various understandings of action and rebirth.

Cariyāpiṭaka, for example, appears not to be informed by the classical karma theory of the prose, but draws more frequently on ideas of sacrifice and heroic asceticism than on karmic discourse. Like *Buddhavaṃsa* and the *Buddhāpadāna* section of *Apadāna*, *Cariyāpiṭaka* tells stories of the Bodhisattva's progress toward awakening over the course of numerous rebirths.[4] Each of *Cariyāpiṭaka*'s 35 stories retells a tale from *Jātaka*, emphasizing how the Bodhisattva cultivated perfection of some virtue – giving, *sīla*, renunciation, determination, truth, lovingkindness, or equanimity – in order to attain awakening and omniscience. The author uses very little markedly karmic language or ideas: the first verse tells that over thousands of eons the Bodhisattva's conduct ripened for awakening, two verses speak of aspirations, and another tells that a character was attached to his past karma.[5] Within this loosely karmic frame, *Cariyāpiṭaka*'s ten stories about the perfection of giving include tales of sacrifice as well as stories of ascetic generosity. Cp I.1, 2, 7, and 10 exemplify the sacrificial discourse: in I.2 the Buddha speaks of desiring and needing merit and of giving to a fruitful field, and in I.1, 7, and 10 he speaks of the importance of giving to a recipient worthy of dakṣiṇā. In I.3–6 and 8–9, on the other hand, the Bodhisattva gives to all who ask without regard for their moral qualities; in I.6 he gives even to birds and animals. These stories, which include a version of the Vessantara legend, present giving not as worship, but as heroic generosity.[6] *Cariyāpiṭaka* thus accommodates both sacrificial and ascetic soteriologies within a karmic model, but gives no explanation of how the differences between these soteriologies are to be understood.[7]

In contrast to *Cariyāpiṭaka*, whose author retells a number of older tales to form a larger story, *Vimānavatthu* and *Petavatthu* consist primarily of a series of unconnected variations on two basic conversations. In these dialogs, deities, ghosts, and inhabitants of the hells describe to human interlocutors their present happiness or unhappiness, and the deeds that they did in their previous lives to bring about their present condition.[8] In one scenario, a person remarks on the condition of a deity (usually commenting on the *vimāna*, or celestial palace or domain, that the deity inhabits) and asks what deed the deity did to attain that state, and the deity tells the story of an act performed in its previous life. In the other plot, the interlocutor comments on the appearance of a ghost (or deceased person, *peta* or *petī*) and asks the ghost who he or she is, and the ghost responds. The interlocutor then asks about the deed performed to cause rebirth in that state, and the ghost tells its story.[9] All 85 *Vimānavatthu* poems and 37 of the 51 *Petavatthu* poems consist of dialogs of these types.[10] The other 14 *Petavatthu* poems are also about death and the afterlife: three are dialogs in which one person convinces another of the futility of mourning for the dead, five are didactic discourses attributed to the Buddha, four consist of verses attributed to another speaker or speakers, and two consist entirely of third person narration.[11] Many of these poems are informed primarily by sacrificial terminology and emphases, while others are typical of karmic discourse. They appear to have been written by different authors and at different times.[12] Taken as a whole, these accounts present a varied picture of existence in *saṃsāra*.

Meritorious and demeritorious acts

Although they include elements of karmic discourse, the primary emphases and assumptions of *Vimānavatthu* and of many *Petavatthu* narratives are those of the sacrificial discourse. In particular, *Vimānavatthu* presents sacrifice and devotion as the primary means of making merit. Acts of worshiping or giving to worthy recipients are named as the meritorious acts in 62 of the 87 *Vimānavatthu* stories.[13] In most of these tales, a deity credits his or her blissful existence to a single act, which is frequently described with sacrificial language. One goddess states:

> Tathāgatas indeed arise for the benefit of many:
> Worthy to receive the dakṣiṇā of humans, mines of merit fields,
> The giver who pays homage to them rejoices in heaven.[14]

A god exhorts his audience to make merit:

> Merits should be made by the wise and discerning;
> What is given to perfected buddhas is of great fruit.[15]

Another god states that his act of giving, which he calls an "unconfined, three-moded, pure sacrifice," was effective because buddhas are the best recipients of oblations for those in need of merit, who seek abundant fruit.[16] One goddess tells that a dakṣiṇā given to the Buddha Kassapa is well-established; other deities say that gifts should be given at the proper time and to the upright, to released, calm *brahmacārins*.[17]

Some stories dramatize the importance of the recipient of the gift. Pv II.9.46–57 tells that a man named Aṅkura sought to attain merit by giving a great donative festival (*mahādāna*) which lasted for years, and for which 95,000 people prepared the food.[18] When he is reborn as a deity (*devatā*) he is greatly outshone by one who in his previous life gave a spoonful of food to the elder Anuruddha. In this story, the extreme incommensurability of the gifts highlights how the worthiness of the recipient is much more important than the object given in determining the result of a gift.[19] This theme is restated at the conclusion of the dialog through a treatment of the merit field simile in six verses. Similarly, in Vv III.6, two sisters have been reborn as deities named Bhaddā and Subhaddā. Bhaddā complains that although she fed many more restrained *brahmacārin* monks than did her sister, Subhaddā enjoys greater splendor as a deity. Subhaddā explains that once when she was giving a meal to a group of monks, one of them out of compassion instructed her to give to (or in respect of) the Saṅgha (*saṅghe dehī*), and she did so. She remarks:

> The dakṣiṇā gone to the Saṅgha is established in the immeasurable;
> What was given by you to individuals is not of great fruit for you.[20]

In both of these stories, the givers who receive lesser rewards do so not because of any bad thoughts or actions, but for reasons beyond their control. Aṅkura's gifts did not reach any worthy recipients because he lived at a time when there was no Buddhist community in the world, while Bhaddā failed to give to the entire Saṅgha because she had not been instructed to do so.

Other stories emphasize that while proper intention is essential to a meritorious donation, the physical action is also important. In Vv IV.9.6, a deity tells she enjoys her present state because once while on her way to present an offering to a stūpa she was killed by a cow. If she had reached the stūpa and accumulated that merit, she reasons, the result would have been greater.[21] Vv IV.6 tells that a woman who gave a dwelling (*vihāra*) to the Saṅgha was reborn as the chief queen of the god Sunimmita among the Nimmānarati deities, while her friend who rejoiced (*ānumodiṃ*) in the gift received a lesser reward of rebirth as a deity with her own *vimāna*. Here, and also in Pv II.9.19, a person made merit simply by rejoicing over another's gift, although the donor made more merit.

The following verses spoken in Vv III.6 and Vv IV.6 add to the theme of sacrifice that of recollection:

> For this Saṅgha is abundant and great; it is immeasurable like the ocean,
> For these disciples of the hero of men are the best; these radiant ones proclaim the Dharma.
> Well-given, well-offered, and well-sacrificed is the gift of those who give designating it for the Saṅgha.
> The dakṣiṇā established in the Saṅgha is of great fruit and is praised by the world-knowers.
> Those who wander through the world recollecting such a sacrifice, thrilled,
> Having removed the stain of avarice with its root, go blameless to a heavenly place.[22]

This last verse indicates that recollecting (*anussarantā*) a sacrifice done in the past and being thrilled (*vedajātā*) over it leads to a heavenly birth. Pv II.9.49 quotes a verse also found at *Aṅguttara* III 337 that stresses the importance of maintaining a joyful mental state before, during, and after giving.[23] Similarly, in Vv VII.5.11 a deity counts as part of his past meritorious deed his recollection of the act, by which he filled his entire body with joy (*so pītiya kāyaṃ sabbaṃ pharati attano*). These stories extend the sacrificial discourse's concern with proper intention to the preparation for giving and to the recollection of the act. A single interaction with a worthy recipient provides the basis for a lifetime of meditation. By remembering a past act of giving, one is able to continue to make merit even in the absence of a field for merit.

The term *anussarantā* suggests a connection between this act of recollection and lists of six or ten *anussati* or subjects for recollection found in *Dīgha* and *Aṅguttara*.[24] The more common list of six consists of *buddha, dhamma, saṅgha, sīla, cāga* [relinquishing], and *devatā* [deity]. *Aṅguttara* III 287 and V 331 define *cāgānussati* as reflection on one's own generosity and happiness in giving. Vv III.6 and Vv IV.6 give specific content to this practice by encouraging their audience to recall particular acts of giving. Paul Harrison has drawn attention to the difference between formulaic definitions in *Aṅguttara* of *buddhānussati* as an abstract exercise, and the use of visualization in *buddhānussati* in later texts.[25] In a similar manner, in these *Vimānavatthu* stories, persons give specific content to the recollection of giving by thinking of particular actions.

A number of *Petavatthu* stories show the other side of the sacrificial eschatology by telling what happens to those who abuse mendicants, obstruct potential givers, or simply fail to give. One ghost blames her misery on her having never been told to give to ascetics and Brāhmaṇs.[26] Other ghosts afflicted by terrible thirst and heat when asked the cause of their suffering explain that although they formerly had things to give, they failed to make an island for themselves.[27] Another ghost attributes aspects of her current suffering to various past deeds: she is naked because she stole clothes, she is covered with dust because she poured dust on another, and so forth. However, when asked the cause of her bad destiny (*duggatā*), she replies that although there were things to give, she failed to make an island for herself.[28] This line appears in at least four other places in *Petavatthu*.[29] Failure to give is a sufficient cause of a miserable rebirth.

In the 25 *Vimānavatthu* stories that are not about a single act of giving or worship, deities attribute their happiness to another meritorious act or to a lifetime of good actions, including giving *dāna*. Besides giving, the acts most often named are possessing *sīla*, observing the Uposatha, keeping the five precepts, taking the Refuges, becoming a lay follower, and being devoted to the Buddha. Such acts are considered meritorious in both sacrificial and karmic discourses. Obeying one's husband and serving one's family are occasionally mentioned in *Vimānavatthu*; these acts are specifically said to be meritorious in such didactic verses as A III 38. In four *Vimānavatthu* stories, the deity indicates that he or she attained divine birth by having progressed toward nirvāṇa; I will return to these stories later in this chapter.[30]

Although these 25 *Vimānavatthu* stories are not about single acts of giving, many of them share the sacrificial emphasis on devotion to a worthy recipient. In Vv V.1, a frog hears the Buddha preach and attains a moment of devotion (*muhuttaṃ cittappasādassa*) just before being killed, and he is reborn as a deity. Taking the Refuges is similarly an act of devotion to the Three Jewels. One deity construes her keeping the five precepts as an act done toward the Dharma. She remarks:

> Even a small thing done in accordance with (or, with respect to) the Tathāgata's Dharma is abundant and of great result.[31]

The language used here parallels that of verses which discuss actions done with respect to worthy recipients, such as:

> In the same way, even a small act of homage performed with respect to those who possess *sīla* and virtue is a meritorious act of great fruit.[32]

Just as verses like this one present the Buddha or his Saṅgha as the intentional object of an act of giving or worship, the goddess who kept the precepts presents the Buddha's Dharma as the intentional object of an act of conforming to that Dharma. Obedience to the Dharma is thereby construed as an act of worshiping the Dharma, just as giving food or garlands is viewed as an act of worshiping Buddha or Saṅgha.

Although sacrifice plays a prominent part in representations of good actions in *Vimānavatthu* and *Petavatthu*, these texts also draw on karmic models and language to describe how actions produce their effects. They speak of action as something that one experiences (*anubhavati*) and feels (*vedeti*).[33] In sixteen *Petavatthu* stories, the interlocutor asks a ghost a question of the form, "What bad deed did you do in body, speech, or mind? By the ripening of what deed . . .?"[34] In Pv IV.1 a yakṣa (Pāli *yakkha*, a terrestrial deity) presents karma as the cause of all existence:

> "See and hear, and believe. This is the result of good and evil.
> If there were not both good and evil, how would there be beings in good or bad destinies?
> And if mortals did not commit good and evil actions in this world of human beings,
> There would be no beings in good or bad destinies, and no low and exalted in the world of human beings."[35]

Later in this story, it is said that every deed must be felt, but that through good action one may help to determine where one will experience these effects.[36]

Eschatology and cosmology

Just as *Vimānavatthu* and *Petavatthu* include sacrificial and karmic descriptions of actions, their eschatology and cosmology draw on both sacrificial and karmic discourses. Although some stories compare the effects of two acts, these texts do not present systematic expositions of mechanisms of cause and effect, rebirth destinies, or of the structure of the cosmos, nor do they share clearly defined beliefs regarding these matters. This is the case in part because different poems are informed by different understandings of action and rebirth, and in part because these poems are not treatises about the nature of reality, but series of dramatic improvisations on the theme of the effects of good and bad actions.

Most of these stories present a marked similarity between the act and its effect. Persons who make merit are reborn as deities, who are usually said to be of glorious appearance and to possess a world, or *vimāna*, over which they rule; in some stories they are instead said to possess a vehicle or mount.[37] Often a gift resembles the possession or world to which it gives rise; for example, a gift of a chair produces a heavenly chair (Vv I.1–4), and a gift of water produces a *vimāna* with a boat and rivers (Vv I.6–8). Conversely, those who fail to give are reborn as ghosts and experience hunger, thirst, and want. Other stories link specific wrongs to specific effects. For example, two women who caused their co-wives to miscarry are reborn as ghosts who give birth daily and then eat their own children (Pv I.6–7). A man who rudely gave a piece of sugar cane by handing it behind his back in his next life owns a field of sugar cane from which he can eat only by reaching behind his back (Pv IV.5). Mixed actions may produce mixed fates, such as that of two men who hunted by day but refrained from killing at night: in their next lives they are devoured by hounds during the day but enjoy pleasures at night (Pv III.7–8). A man who was restrained in body but not in speech is reborn as a ghost with a golden body and the head of a boar; another who practiced asceticism but slandered others has a divine appearance except for a worm-eaten and foul-smelling mouth.[38] In a few stories, evildoers are reborn not as ghosts but in a hell (*niraya*), where they are tormented for their evil deeds.

People also direct the effects of their actions by forming aspirations. A goddess tells a man to reach her *vimāna* by doing a deed to be experienced there, and then fixing (or bending or leading)[39] his mind on that place (Pv III.3.7). Another deity after telling of her good deeds goes on to explain,

> Hearing constantly of Nandana, desire arose in me;
> Fixing my mind there, I am arisen in Nandana.
> I did not do the word of the Teacher, the Buddha, the kinsman of the sun;
> Having fixed my mind on the inferior, I am remorseful.[40]

In another story Sakka remarks:

> When the mind, whether remaining or extinguished, is calm [or even], the fruit is calm [or, is likewise];
> Because of fixing the mind, beings go to a good destiny.[41]

According to this verse, even those who have attained nirvāṇa may direct their thoughts to shape the effects of their actions. Speech acts can also have harmful karmic effects. In some stories, a person pronounces a curse only to have it fall on him or her (e.g. Pv I.9, II.10). In other stories people falsely assert their innocence, wishing that if they be lying some terrible consequence should befall them. After death, they suffer that result (e.g. Pv I.6–7, II.12, III.4).

While they vividly describe the pains and felicities experienced in the next life, these stories generally do not distinguish sharply between classes of beings. A few *Vimānavatthu* stories assign a deity to one of the heavens or classes of deities catalogued in the classical karmic cosmology. One goddess is said to be a daughter of King Vessavaṇa, four stories state that a deity belongs to the Tāvatiṃsa deities, and three deities are said belong to the Nimmānarati deities.[42] The majority of *Vimānavatthu* stories, however, simply describe the splendor of deities and their *vimāna*s without classifying them or locating them in a named heaven.[43] Other stories seem to confuse birth as a ghost, a yakṣa, or a deity. In Pv II.9 a being refers to himself as a *yakkha* of the greatest powers and as a *peta* (vv. 10–11), while another being is called both a *Tāvatiṃsa deva* and a *yakkha* (vv. 58, 68). In Pv IV.1 a being is called both a *peta* and a *yakkha* (vv. 1, 6, 13, 18). In Pv IV.3 a being with the appearance of a *deva* says that he is a *peta* and neither a *deva* nor a *gandhabba* (Sanskrit *gandharva*), but he is later called a *yakkha* and a *devatā* (vv. 14, 18, 51). In Vv VII.9 a *Tāvatiṃsa deva* is addressed as *yakkha* and *devatā* (vv. 12, 19). Beings that experience the results of both good and bad actions in the same existence experience aspects of divine and ghostly life. Among these are beings who possess a *vimāna* but who are otherwise miserable.[44] In Pv I.9 and 11, members of families are reborn together on earth where some enjoy bliss while others suffer torment. In I.9 neither person is labeled as belonging to a particular class of being, while in I.11 the unfortunates are called *petas*. In a number of stories, a being formerly called a *petī* or *peta* is after receiving dedicated dakṣiṇā called a *devī*, *devatā*, or *yakkha*.[45]

The texts also do not always clearly distinguish birth as a ghost from birth in hell. Both births are designated as Yama's realm.[46] In Pv IV.6, two inhabitants of the world beyond (*paralokaṃ*) complain that having fallen to the *pettivisaya* is the greatest evil that could have befallen them; they (or the authors) are apparently unaware of the hells. In Pv I.11, *petas* state that Yama's inmates (*ṭhayino*) (such as themselves), being burned for a long time, are consumed in fire; this sounds like a description of the fires of the hells. In Pv IV.16 a person who slung a stone at the Buddha Sunetta, splitting his head, has been reborn as a *peta* who experiences 60,000 hammers constantly falling on and splitting his head. As murdering a buddha ranks among the most grievous of sins, we would expect that this person would be reborn in the most horrible hell.[47] Moreover, because this constant hammering more resembles the infliction of a punishment than a personal condition, this state is more typical of descriptions of hell than of the *petaloka*. The author of this story does not seem to differentiate existence in a hell from existence as a ghost.

Pv III.10 presents the existence that perhaps most defies classification. The interlocutor addresses a being as one who stands in the air giving off a foul odor and with a worm-eaten mouth, a typical description of a ghost. The questioner further notes that the being is repeatedly carved up and sprinkled with lye, a characteristically infernal punishment, and the being himself states that he and 86,000 others are being cooked intensely in a hell (*paccāma niraye bhusaṃ*). The being also uses the term *ito*, from here, to refer to his current state or location (i.e. hell), while normally in *Petavatthu*, *ito* refers to the human world in which the encounters occur. The tormented being says that he is being cooked in a hell; however, the commentator identifies him as a ghost living in this world, and takes the reference to hell as hyperbole. Perhaps the author views this being as appearing in this world while simultaneously suffering in hell, and understands the existential metaphor of having departed (*peta*) and the spatial metaphor of being in a hell as two ways of describing the same reality. In any case, the line between *petaloka* and *niraya* is here very difficult to locate.

The looseness with which the authors of most of these stories apply terms like *yakkha*, *peta*, and *niraya* shows that their purpose was not to name clearly bounded classes, but to characterize the speaker's quality of life. In order to make sense of the "shadowy borderline cases" in which beings experience both happiness and suffering, Peter Masefield suggests that such *petas* be viewed as *devatās* "whose enjoyment is to some extent incomplete."[48] Wilhelm Stede offers the opposite interpretation, seeing *yakkhas* as *"Preta Mahārddhika," petas* of great wondrous powers.[49] These are reasonable solutions, but they solve a problem that exists only when we try to fit the beings described in the texts into a paradigm of five or six discrete *gatis*. Most of *Vimānavatthu* and *Petavatthu* is not informed by an understanding of the *gatis* as distinct forms of existence; in fact, these texts contain only one reference to a scheme of distinct *gatis* (Pv IV.11). The goal of the authors is not precision of taxonomy, but richness of description.

The attainment of nirvāṇa

Six *Vimānavatthu* narratives describe progress toward nirvāṇa. In three stories a goddess tells of attaining the Eightfold Path after hearing the Buddha preach; a fourth goddess attained the path after being devoted to the Buddha and keeping the *sikkhāpadas*.[50] For at least three of these deities, attainment of the path is the deed that leads to their heavenly rebirths; these tales thus illustrate the unity of karmic soteriology. Conversely, one of these goddesses describes her reaching "deathlessness, peace, nirvāṇa, the immovable place" with strongly devotional language:

> I am firmly established because of love, unwavering in vision,
> Through faith born from its root, I am a true daughter of the
> Buddha.[51]

With these references to love and vision the author asserts that the devotion characteristic of sacrificial soteriology informs progress toward nirvāṇa as well.

Although the other two stories about the attainment of nirvāṇa use karmic language, they also reproduce the dual soteriology of sacrifice and purification. In Vv III.9, a goddess states that she gained her present state by placing a garland on a stūpa. She continues:

> That I possessed *sīla* has not ripened for me,
> But my hope, lord of gods, is that I would be a once-returner.[52]

This deity describes becoming a once-returner not in terms of an ongoing mental purification, but with the karmic idiom of ripening; however, as in the sacrificial-purificatory model, giving leads to heavenly rebirth, and asceticism to nirvāṇa. In Vv VII.7, a god tells that he attained his *vimāna* because in his past life he was Kanthaka, the horse which Gotama rode during his great renunciation. The god continues:

> Laughter was mine when I heard word of the awakening:
> Because of that good root, I will touch the destruction of the taints.[53]

Like the goddess in Vv III.9, this god imagines his progress toward nirvāṇa not in relation to his current thoughts, but in terms of a past action that will ripen to produce a future effect. At the same time, this story embodies the duality of sacrifice and purification: devotion produces rebirth as a deity, while the thought of awakening leads to nirvāṇa.[54]

The dedication of dakṣiṇā

Petavatthu contains twelve dialogs that describe dedications of dakṣiṇā.[55] These dialogs differ from didactic *gāthā*s that appropriate the Vedic understanding of dakṣiṇā dedication, including Pv I.1, 4, and 5, as well as from *Aṅguttara* V 269–272, which accepts this practice only grudgingly. Instead, these twelve stories promote dakṣiṇā dedication even as they modify it to conform to their own eschatology and ethos.

As in the sacrificial texts, the dedication of dakṣiṇā in the *Petavatthu* stories consists in the transfer of a transformed sacrificial offering to a divine, deceased, or ghostly recipient by means of a worthy recipient.[56] The items dedicated are more varied than in the sacrificial verses, and the authors dramatize the transformations of these gifts: in ten of these twelve stories, the ghost is explicitly said to receive items similar to those offered to the monastics, but of much greater quality and quantity.[57] For example, in Pv III.2 the author describes five separate offerings and five corresponding results: a gift of rags produces an abundance of clothes and coverings, a gift of a hut produces heavenly houses, and so forth. Of the other two stories, Pv II.8 does not name the material result of gifts of food, drink, and robes, but the text does state that the ghost is satisfied with plenty. Only Pv III.6 does not specify the nature of the gift or name a material result, saying only that as a result of the dedication the ghost became happy with a beautiful body.

As in the didactic verses, the acquisition of these heavenly items transforms these beings. In five stories, beings that were formerly called *peta* or *petī* are after receiving the dakṣiṇā called *devī* (goddess), *devatā* or *yakkha*.[58] Beings initially said to be hideous are later said to become pure, or surpassing in appearance or in wondrous powers. A ghost begs the elder Sāriputta to dedicate dakṣiṇā to her, saying, "release me from this bad destiny (*mocehi maṃ duggatiyā*," Pv II.1.6). In two stories the donor expresses devotion to the deity that he had just saved from misery.[59]

These metamorphoses have been variously interpreted. As noted above, Stede and Masefield collapse the distinction between *peta* and *devatā* or *yakkha*, and therefore maintain that the transformation of these beings does not involve a change of *gati*.[60] Jean-Michel Agasse, on the other hand, asserts that receipt of a dedicated gift produces an immediate passage to another state, an instant rebirth.[61] Common to these readings is a reification of the names given to different beings into distinct forms of existence. But as already noted, even narratives that do not involve dedication of dakṣiṇā imprecisely distinguish *peta*s from *yakkha*s, and *yakkha*s from Tāvatiṃsa deities. *Vimānavatthu* and *Petavatthu* generally use terms like *peta*, *yakkha*, and *devatā* not to mark distinct and mutually exclusive modes of existence, but to name beings that exhibit certain qualities. If a departed spirit experiences misery and want, she is called a *petī*, but if all her desires are fulfilled and she becomes happy, she is called a *devī*. A partial exception to this generalization is Pv IV.3, whose author tries to be precise about terminology.[62] A being who has received a dedicated gift is said to have the appearance of a *deva*, and he tells a traveler that he is neither a *deva* nor a *gandhabba* but a *peta* (vv. 14, 18). However, the traveler later addresses the *peta* as *yakkha* and *devatā*, blurring the distinctions established earlier in the story (51).

Traditional commentators and modern scholars have both described these ghosts' transformations as a function of merit.[63] The strongest support for the claim that these stories involve merit transfer is provided by the following verse, which appears in half of the *Petavatthu* dedication stories:

> Immediately, when [the offering] was dedicated, the result arose;
> Food, clothing and water: this was the fruit of that dakṣiṇā.[64]

As Schmithausen observes, the terms *phala* (fruit) and especially *vipāka* (result) suggest a karmic interpretation. But this verse describes an occurrence very much unlike the way that karma is ordinarily said to operate. As the words *phala* and *vipāka* (literally, ripened or cooked) suggest, actions are usually said to develop before producing their results. This verse, by contrast, emphasizes the synchronicity of act and effect, creating a tension between the immediacy of this result and the usually slow ripening of actions.[65] Rather than describing a sort of "instant karma,"[66] this verse is better understood as employing typically karmic language in order to dramatize that dakṣiṇā dedication produces results like those of merit, but by different means. The transformations of *peta*s and *petī*s into *deva*s and *devī*s have also been cited as evidence that these dedications are about merit transfer. But as I argue above, this conclusion only follows if one assumes a classical eschatology involving five or six distinct *gati*s that is alien to these stories. It should further be noted that although dedicated offerings improve the quality of life for departed beings, three stories show that such gifts cannot save beings from hell.[67] If the dedication of dakṣiṇā were a matter of transferring merit, then a large enough quantity of merit presumably could save a being from that fate. Furthermore, donors never give out of their store of accumulated merit, even though an arhat like Sāriputta should have merit to spare. Instead, even Sāriputta presents dakṣiṇā to other monks and dedicates these offerings to ghosts.[68]

These stories from *Petavatthu* also differ from the didactic *gāthā*s in how they represent the relationship between the donor and the recipient. In these *Petavatthu* stories, the beneficiaries of dakṣiṇā dedication are usually not the donor's ancestors or other loved ones; in only one of the twelve stories does a donor initiate an act of giving in the hope of benefiting a deceased parent.[69] In the other eleven stories, donations are occasioned not by memories of the departed, but by an encounter with a ghost or yakṣa. In four of these stories, these beings appear to former relations, but in six stories they appear to strangers.[70] In either case, the donor gives not out of filial piety, but from disinterested compassion.[71] For example, in Pv II.1 a ghost appears to Sāriputta, and he, being compassionate, dedicates dakṣiṇā on her behalf. In the following story, Sāriputta encounters another miserable ghost, who reveals that she was his mother in her previous life. Sāriputta, however, makes no expression of affection or familial obligation, but again, being compassionate, performs the same act that he performed for the stranger.

Unlike *Aṅguttara* V 269–272, these *Petavatthu* stories affirm that the dedication of dakṣiṇā for the dead is efficacious, and they encourage its performance; however, they de-emphasize the concern for one's ancestors that no doubt provided the main motivation for the performance of this ritual. These stories suggest that one perform the rites not in order to care for deceased relatives and to maintain relationships with them, but with the same attitude of compassion that the mentally pure individual feels toward all creatures. Even in those stories in which someone performs a rite for a deceased parent, the donor does not do so as a routine expression of filial duty or affection, but in response to a chance encounter with a ghost. These narratives therefore suggest a meaning and motivation for the śrāddha rite that is very different from that of most ancestral rites, including the Brahmanical śrāddha. These stories do not negate the element of caring for deceased ancestors, but they extend it by making an entire class of beings the potential beneficiaries of the rite. By attributing to this rite the Buddhist values of detachment and universal compassion, these *Petavatthu* stories legitimate it as one in which even arhats may engage.

This emphasis on detachment in the dakṣiṇā dedication stories is complemented by a set of stories about mourning for the dead. Pv I.4.3 and I.5.10 both contrast the efficaciousness of dedicating dakṣiṇā for the dead with the futility of grieving. Pv I.12 develops this theme in ten verses, saying among other things that lamenting the dead is as effective as trying to repair a broken pot. In four stories, one person cleverly convinces another of the foolishness of mourning the dead. In Pv I.8, a man pretends to try to rouse a dead ox in order to demonstrate the futility of hoping that the dead will return. In Pv II.6, a man cries out for the moon, and later points out that grieving over the dead is an even greater folly. Vv VII.9 is a similar story about a god who wishes for the sun and moon as wheels for his chariot. In Pv II.13, a seer facetiously asks a widow which Brahmadatta she is mourning, as 86,000 persons of that name have been cremated in that same place. In all four of these stories, the converted recite the same three verses in which they liken their sorrow to a dart that has been removed, and to a ghee-sprinkled fire (*pāvakaṃ*, literally 'purifier') that has been extinguished (*nibbāpaye*). The latter metaphor contrasts the Brahmanical sacrificial fire with the image of nirvāṇa, or extinguishing. In Vv VII.9, the convert takes the Three Refuges, while in Pv II.13 she goes forth and eventually attains the Brahmaloka. Those who persuade others of the foolishness of grieving for the dead are said to have wisdom (*paññā*) and compassion (*anukampā*) (Pv I.8.8, II.6.19). These stories form with stories of dakṣiṇā dedication a pair of distinctively Buddhist responses to death:

by not mourning one cultivates detachment, while by aiding the dead through giving to the Saṅgha one both exercises compassion and makes merit for oneself.

Representations of givers

Another remarkable aspect of accounts of giving in *Vimānavatthu* and *Petavatthu* is the way in which they portray donors. As one would expect, the great majority of donors are laity, and the majority of recipients are monks. In *Vimānavatthu*, the donors are all laypeople; the sole deity said to have formerly been a monastic says that as a monk he had nothing to give (Vv VII.8). However, in three of *Petavatthu*'s twelve dakṣiṇā dedication stories the donor is a monk,[72] suggesting that the authors thought it more appropriate for monastics to give *dāna* in order to benefit others than to make merit for themselves.[73] In *Vimānavatthu* and in the dakṣiṇā dedication stories, the recipients of gifts are monks, a buddha, a stūpa, or, in only a few cases, a layman. This pattern of laypeople giving to monks suggests a reading of *Vimānavatthu* and *Petavatthu* that sees these stories as only so many carrots and sticks intended to lure and frighten credulous laity into giving *dāna*. However, the stories are more complex than they may at first seem. While some stories tell of large gifts like a *vihāra* or numerous offerings of food, clothing, and shelter, most tell of only a single, small gift, such as a meal or a garland of flowers. Sometimes the act is as small as offering an *añjali* salute, or rearranging a garland on a stūpa (Vv IV.11 and VII.9, VII.11). These small donations produce heavenly rewards as great as those resulting from large gifts. *Vimānavatthu* emphasizes this appeal to the economically and socially subaltern by naming among its donors servants (II.1, IV.1, IV.12), a poor, wretched, dependent woman (II.3), a Caṇḍālī (II.4), poor, wretched, homeless workers (VII.1, VII.2), a hireling gardener (VII.5), and a hireling cowherd (VII.6).[74] *Vimānavatthu* presents a virtually free path to heaven, requiring only that the donor give to a worthy recipient with an attitude of devotion.

Even more striking than *Vimānavatthu*'s appeal to the poor, however, is the prominent place it gives to women. *Vimānavatthu* contains 50 poems about women, of which two are anthologies of 36 and four stories, while only 35 poems are about men.[75] The women's stories are also more varied in structure and in content than are the men's.[76] Most stories in which persons attain high levels of spiritual attainment are about women: the three persons said to join the Nimmānarati deities are women (Vv II.3, III.6, and IV.6), as is the person said to reach the Brahmaloka (Pv II.13). The persons said to attain the path are all women (Vv I.16, I.17, IV.3, and IV.12), while one female and one male aspire to nirvāṇa (Vv III.9 and VII.7). Unfortunately, the author of the story of the woman who reaches the Brahmaloka includes the misogynistic comment that she attains this goal after having set aside the mind of a woman (*itthicittaṃ virājetvā*, Pv II.13.19). For the most part, however, these stories valorize women and their religious attainments.

On the other hand, these texts downplay the religious life as an option for women. Both texts always represent the recipients of *dāna* as male, and they rarely mention nuns.[77] In a number of *Vimānavatthu* stories, goddesses count obedience to their husbands among their past good deeds. Vv III.4.8–11 provides a good example of how these texts teach women to fulfill their domestic role with the hope of a better future. A group of goddesses proclaims that women should practice the Dharma with regard to their husbands (or, that they should fulfill their dharma / duty to their husbands) in order to gain heaven, and concludes as follows:

> As a lion whose domain is a mountain ridge,
> Dwelling on a mountain,
> Overwhelming and killing other four-footed beasts,
> A meat-eater, devours mere deer,
> Just so here, a faithful noble female disciple
> Dependent on her husband, obedient to her lord,
> Having slain anger, having vanquished avarice,
> That one who practices Dharma rejoices in heaven.[78]

Here the faithful and obedient housewife's success in exercising self-discipline is compared, in an ironic and startling simile, to a lion's killing its prey. The home is here envisioned as an arena for rigorous ascetic practice, and appropriately so, for it is more difficult to overcome the taints while in the world than while removed from it. Vivid illustrations of the difficulty of practicing the Dharma at home are given by three stories of women who are struck dead by their mothers-in-law for giving *dāna* without permission.[79] *Vimānavatthu* and *Petavatthu* thus discourage women from pursuing monastic life while simultaneously stressing that fulfilling one's duties and making merit within the domestic sphere lead to the highest goals in the next life. As Nancy Auer Falk has argued, the Theravādin texts' opposition to female monasticism seems to derive less from a belief in the spiritual incapacity of women than from a belief in their inability to perform the ritual role of priest.[80]

Representations of giving and of other meritorious acts also suggest questions about the purpose of these texts. Why do the majority of stories depict a single act, rather than a lifetime of good or bad behavior? If the purpose of *Vimānavatthu* were to encourage lay support for the Saṅgha, we would expect the stories to depict regular and generous giving. Why are the actors almost always individuals rather than groups? Even in descriptions of great donative operations, the lion's share of the merit goes to the person who actually hands out the food (Vv VI.10, VII.10). Most puzzling, why are these stories so repetitive in both structure and language? A number of verses appear dozens of times, and many verses add no new information to a story.[81] Often two *Vimānavatthu* stories differ only in a single detail, such as the name of the deity in its past life (Vv II.8 and 9), the words used to describe a gift of cake (Vv I.13 and 14), or whether the deity's *vimāna* is compared to the sun or to the moon (Vv VI.4 and 5). Some stories, like Vv II.10 and 11, and VI.1 and 2, are identical. Vv III.5 contains 36 dialogs of eight verses in length, most of which vary only in the name of the gift given in the previous life.

These stories display these features because their purpose is not primarily to impart new information about how specific acts correlate with specific rebirth effects, but to dramatize ideals that hearers can affirm and appropriate. Most stories focus on individual acts of giving in order to draw attention to the intentions that inform them. These stories therefore present these actions not as routine or ritualized, but as spontaneous and unique gestures. When monks preach sermons containing stories such as these, they present meanings and motivations that donors can ascribe to the act of giving or dedication that they have just performed, as well as afterlife goals to which donors can aspire. Some *Vimānavatthu* stories state that one should not only give gladly, but that one should anticipate and recollect one's acts of giving, for the intention to give is more important than the act itself. *Petavatthu* encourages donors to dedicate dakṣiṇā with an attitude of detachment and compassion. Even non-donors can enjoy these repetitive tales because each telling gives a chance to identify with a good intention or to reject an evil one; the very act of hearing becomes a chance to make merit and perhaps to aspire to nirvāṇa.[82] By dramatizing individual deeds, these stories suggest purposes that may inform a lifetime of actions.

CHAPTER FOUR

The Commentaries' Karmic Retelling of the *Vimānavatthu* and *Petavatthu* Narratives

Theravādins regard the commentaries (*aṭṭhakathās*) written in Sri Lanka in the middle centuries of the first millennium CE as the authoritative guides to the *Tipiṭaka*. Distilling centuries of interpretation, these commentaries present a reading of the canonical texts as a coherent and unified body of teachings.[1] In matters of action and rebirth, the commentaries are thoroughly grounded in karmic theory; however, their faithfulness to the authoritative texts keeps them from excluding sacrificial themes entirely. For example, *Visuddhimagga*, the great compendium of commentarial doctrine organized around the theme of the path of purification leading to nirvāṇa, makes little use of sacrificial discourse. *Visuddhimagga* presents *dāna* as an act not of devotion, but of generosity and freedom from avarice.[2] Nonetheless, in presenting the Saṅgha as an object for recollection, *Visuddhimagga* states that the Saṅgha purifies an offering for making great fruit, and that, with the Saṅgha as its support, merit (or meritorious acts) grows.[3] Even from *Visuddhimagga*'s remarkable synthesis of Buddhist practice as a single path of karmic purification the sacrificial discourse is not entirely excluded.

In this chapter I examine the commentarial project of exegesis and doctrinal systematization by considering the sections of *Paramatthadīpanī* that comment on *Vimānavatthu* and *Petavatthu*. The commentator, traditionally identified as Dhammapāla, gives a measure of uniformity to the stylistically and doctrinally heterogenous contents of these texts.[4] He comments on each dialog by narrating the story of how the verses were first spoken and by glossing words from the verses. Each story ends with the Buddha retelling the verses as a sermon. This device establishes the authority of both canonical verses and commentarial story as *buddhavacana*, words of the Buddha (Pv-a 2, Vv-a 26); it also places the various dialogs of the two texts within the master narrative of the life of the Buddha. When not specified otherwise in the verses, Vv-a identifies the interlocutor as the Buddha's disciple Moggallāna and sets the stories in the *devaloka*, and so the motif of the cosmic journeys of Moggallāna further unifies the narrative. In matters of doctrine, Dhammapāla retells the stories within a strongly karmic framework, and ties meritorious actions more closely to the attainment of nirvāṇa. At the same time, he also maintains characteristic elements of the sacrificial discourse.

Meritorious and demeritorious acts

Paramatthadīpanī uses the trope of sacrifice less frequently than do the texts, and it explains sacrificial passages with karmic terminology. For example, *Paramatthadīpanī* glosses *puñña* as *sucarita* and *kusalakamma*, and gives for an etymology of *puñña* that it purifies (*punāti*) the mental continuum in which it arises.[5] A move away from sacrificial models is also evident in discussions of stories that give as the only cause of a person's birth as a ghost his or her failure to give and thereby to make merit. The commentary tells of positive faults, such as disrespect, selfishness, and wrong view, shifting emphasis from ritual omission to impure mental action (Pv-a 54, 67, 201, 269).

Paramatthadīpanī nonetheless follows the texts in treating *dāna* as the paradigmatic meritorious deed. Like the verses, it presents the qualities of both donor and recipient as conditioning rebirth effects, and views the qualities of the gift itself as being of little or no importance. The introduction to Vv-a tells that Moggallāna once thought to himself,

> "At this time, even when there is no excellence of the object [to be given], by excellence of the field and of mental devotion, and by doing various meritorious acts, human beings arise in the *devaloka* and experience the attainment of that which is excellent."[6]

Moggallāna sees that even a small item can produce great results because of the fecundity of the Buddha and his Saṅgha as fields for merit.

Paramatthadīpanī develops this emphasis on donor and recipient in the story commentary to Vv I.1 (Vv-a 5–7). This story tells that when Pasenadi, Anāthapiṇḍika, and Visākhā made great gifts of alms to the

Buddha and his Saṅgha, people began to ask whether a gift made by relinquishing great wealth was of greater fruit than a gift made by relinquishing wealth in accordance with one's means. Hearing of this, the Buddha proclaims that a gift will become more fruitful not by the excellence of the thing to be given (*deyyadhammasampattiyā*), but by the excellence of (the donor's) thought and of the field (*cittasampattiyā ca khettasampattiyā ca*).[7] Even the smallest gift, established with a devoted mind in a person worthy of dakṣiṇā (*vippasannena cetasā dakkhiṇeyyapuggale patiṭṭhāpitam*) will be of great fruit. The text then describes an exemplary act of giving:

> At that time a certain elder who was wandering [in search of] alms in a manner inspiring devotion, whether approaching or leaving, whether looking forward or back, whether bending or stretching, with downcast eyes and of good deportment, reached a certain house near meal time. When a daughter of the family who was endowed with faith saw the elder, esteem and reverence were born in her and she gave rise to great joy and happiness. She brought him into the house, saluted him with the fivefold prostration, covered her own seat with a yellow cloth and gave it to him. When the elder was seated there, she, thinking, "This greatest field for merit has appeared for me," with a devoted mind served him food in accordance with her means and, taking a fan, fanned him. When the elder finished his meal, he gave a discourse on Dharma concerning the gift of a seat, food, and so forth, and departed. Contemplating her own gift and that discourse on Dharma, the woman's body became completely permeated with joy; this is how she gave the seat to the elder.[8]

The donor of this modest gift is consequently later reborn as a goddess. As in the sacrificial discourse, this text emphasizes the personal qualities of the donor – especially her joy and devotion – and of the recipient – notably his modest demeanor. This emphasis on the qualities of the individual donor and recipient are characteristic of the commentary as a whole.[9]

This description subtly suggests, however, that it is the woman's perception of the monk, rather than his innate qualities, that makes the act meritorious. His salient feature is that he *inspires* devotion, and the author throughout draws attention to her thoughts and feelings, including her recollection of the gift, as constitutive of the act. Other stories also place a large emphasis on the thoughts of the donor. Persons are said to recollect deeds, to establish them in their minds, to make them an object of meditation (*ārammaṇa*), and thinking of them to become joyful, happy, and devoted.[10] Pv-a 133 explains that the successful performance of the sacrifice (or of meritorious action) consists in the volitions (*cetanā*) before, during, and after giving, held with happiness and accompanied by belief in the fruit of actions.[11] Nonetheless, one story excludes any thoroughly psychological interpretation of meritorious action. At Pv-a 67–68, a group of girls physically force their companion to salute the elder Sāriputta, and the merit from this involuntary action causes her to be reborn as a ghost rather than in hell!

Eschatology and cosmology

Dhammapāla recognizes and develops the various rebirth mechanisms employed in the texts. He conceptualizes as a general principle the resemblance of acts to effects (*kammasarikkhatā*, Vv-a 6), and in places develops these correspondences in greater detail than do the texts. For example, in the commentary to Vv I.1, the donor's joyful impulse (*vega*, also meaning speed) produces swiftness in her *vimāna*, her acting in accordance with her mind's desire causes the *vimāna* to move according to her desire, and her attainment of devotion (*pasāda*) causes it to be bright (*pāsādika*).[12] The commentary also attributes to speech acts, especially aspirations (*patthana*, *paṇidhi*), considerable power to shape the effect of a meritorious act. In Vv-a 32, the wise men of Rājagṛha say that a meritorious act is like a wish-granting gem or a wish-granting tree, for when there is attainment of a field and a devoted mind, then whatever one wishes for comes into being.[13] In addition to the aspirations described in the verses, Dhammapāla presents people wishing for such diverse things as long, beautiful hair (Pv-a 47), golden garlands (Vv-a 270), authority over the donor's current mistress (Vv-a 207), or a celestial elephant, house, and couch (Vv-a 33). Donors also aspire to become a chief disciple of the Buddha (Vv-a 3) and to share in the Dharma (Vv-a 64). Dhammapāla also states that beings are sometimes reborn together because of the power of their love for each other (Pv-a 271; see also 21, 152, 192).

Paramatthadīpanī asserts that karma can drive people to cooperate in their own punishment. According to Pv-a 152, a *vimānapetī* lets herself be devoured by a dog every night because she is urged on by the power of her own evil actions (*pāpakammabalacoditā*). By the same logic, Dhammapāla would presumably say that Yama's servants are compelled by the force of their own past deeds to inflict punishment on the denizens of hell, and thereby to accumulate more bad acts.[14] This idea that one's past actions condition one's present actions follows easily from the Theravādin understanding of karmic potential as a *saṅkhāra*, or mental formation.

In *Paramatthadīpanī* some actions do not slowly ripen to yield results in a future birth, but quickly produce their effects. In Pv-a 178, a man who insults a pratyekabuddha is instantly overcome by intense heat, dies, and goes to hell. In Vv-a 65, a farmer's wife gives his meal to the elder Sāriputta, and the next day the farmer's field is covered with gold. Vv-a 221 tells of a man who donates a hall to Buddha and Saṅgha. As soon as he pours the water of dedication, there arises for him in the Tāvatiṃsa realm an enormous celestial palace made of jewels and attended by a thousand celestial maidens. These maidens later send word through Moggallāna to the donor urging him to come because they have become impatient waiting for him![15] Vv-a 156–159 is the story of a girl who, having made a gift for the construction of the stūpa of the Buddha Kassapa, still possesses great merit (*mahāpuññā*) when she is reborn at the time of Gotama Buddha. In this story, a man's trove of money and gems turns to stones through the power of (an unspecified) action (*kammabalena* or *kammaphalena*). When the girl looks at these stones they immediately, and without her knowledge or intention, again become gold and jewels through the eminence of her merit (*puññavisesena*). Dharmapāla thus attributes to the karmic process the immediacy of cause and effect that *Petavatthu* describes in accounts of dakṣiṇā dedication.

On the other hand, this story of a girl of great merit also shows that in *Paramatthadīpanī* many acts take unimaginably long periods of time to produce their effects. Passages such as Vv-a 156–157, Vv-a 207, Vv-a 331, and Pv-a 20–21 link acts performed at the time of a past buddha with their fulfillment during the dispensation (*sāsana*) of Gotama. The intervening eon is cursorily described as a time of transmigrating (*saṃsarantī*). This motif dramatizes the necessity of performing meritorious action now while the Buddha's relics, Dharma, and Saṅgha are still in the world.

Dhammapāla also standardizes the varied accounts of the afterlife in *Vimānavatthu* and *Petavatthu* by classifying them within the systematic eschatology and cosmology of the karmic discourse. Vv-a assigns every god and goddess to a class of deity that corresponds to a named heaven; when the text does not specify otherwise, Dhammapāla writes that a deity has arisen in the Tāvatiṃsa heaven. Where the texts present *vimānas* as discrete spheres of control unrelated to any larger cosmic hierarchy, the commentary tells that they are normally located in a named heaven. Dhammapāla frequently depicts *vimānas* as mobile, and also refers to the vehicles or mounts possessed by some deities as *vimānas*, collapsing these two categories. Dhammapāla also defines *petas* as a distinct birth and class of being. In *Petavatthu*, the term *peta* maintains its etymological sense of a being that has 'departed' from human existence. In Pv-a, however, *petas* constitute a distinct *gati*, the *petayoni*.[16] Consequently, birth as a *peta* need not follow a human birth, but in several stories follows birth in a hell (Pv-a 14, 21, 178, 263, 284). Dhammapāla imposes some cognitive order on the stories of *petas* who enjoy a degree of happiness by labeling them as *vimānapetas*.[17]

Stories of actions ripening over incomprehensibly long periods of time provide a temporal frame that matches the spatial and ontological ordering of the cosmos in which the commentators engaged. Unlike the earth-centered cosmology of the sacrificial-purificatory discourse, the classical karmic cosmology sees the earth as only one world among many. We are insignificant in comparison to the great expanses of space and time; the time and place we occupy are important only because a buddha recently appeared here, and because his relics, teachings, and monastic community remain present among us. Dhammapāla similarly relativizes the importance of human birth by claiming that merit may be made by those in non-human destinies, possibly even by those in hell. Humans are most able to make merit because only the human state combines dissatisfactoriness (*dukkha*), which causes one to seek a better existence, with the wide availability of the conditions for meritorious action (Vv-a 20). Nonetheless, we read of a *vimānapetī* who does a meritorious deed and thereby avoids rebirth in hell (Pv-a 53), and of a ghost who gives *dāna* to Buddha and Saṅgha and later arises among the Tāvatiṃsa deities (Pv-a 260). According to Dhammapāla, all destinies are, at least potentially, places of both action and karmic fulfillment.[18] This contrasts with the sacrificial discourse, according to which one makes merit and demerit in the human world, and experiences their effects elsewhere. Thus in regard to time, space, and eschatology, the karmic discourse as developed by the commentators dethrones humanity from the central place it occupies in the late Vedic worldview.

The dedication of dakṣiṇā and the dedication of merit

In their treatments of dakṣiṇā dedication, the commentaries fundamentally reinterpret this rite, taking the basis of its efficacy to be not the item given, but the act itself. In addition to the reference to merit in *Aṅguttara* IV 63–67, two other important Theravādin texts anticipate this development. *Kathāvatthu* 346–349 offers two conflicting responses to the question of whether *petas* live on what is "given from here." Of the three arguments in the affirmative, two appeal to the authority of *Tirokuḍḍa Sutta* and *Aṅguttara* III 43–44, while the other cites the *petas*' response to the donor as evidence of the efficacy of the gift:

> Is it not the case that ghosts cause the one giving a gift for [their] own sake to rejoice? That they gladden [the donor's] mind, cause joy to arise, and obtain happiness?[19]

These three arguments are all based on an understanding of dakṣiṇā dedication as a transfer of substance that fosters relationships between the living and the dead. The argument offered in the negative is that dakṣiṇā dedication would violate the principle that actions cannot be transferred: "Does one act for another? Does one do an act, whether pleasant or unpleasant, and another experience it?"[20] The proponent of this view rejects dakṣiṇā dedication because he understands it as the dedication of merit.

Milindapañha 294–297 adopts elements of both positions: although it treats the act of giving rather than the material gift as the basis for the dedication, it accepts this practice as orthodox. This passage employs some of the same terminology as *Tirokuḍḍa*,[21] but it refers to an offering as *dāna* rather than as *dakkhiṇā*, thereby perhaps deliberately avoiding the sacrificial connotations of that term. According to *Milindapañha*, when a gift is dedicated, donor and beneficiary share a good action, both obtain the result of the action, and both experience its fruit.[22] These phrases indicate that the dedication of gifts constitutes a dedication of a good action; unfortunately, they do not explain how actions are thus shared.

Like *Milindapañha*, the Pāli commentaries take dakṣiṇā dedication to be based on action, but they avoid canonical denials of the transferability of action by having the recipients generate their own merit. *Aṅguttara* III 41 states that one can share in merit by rejoicing over another's gift, and the commentators cleverly extend this possibility to the ghosts. As the *Petavatthu* commentary states, the donor "gives the attainment (*pattiṃ dadāti* or *sampattiṃ dadāti*)" to the recipient of the dedication, who then rejoices (*anumodati*) in the donor's act, thereby making merit and transforming his or her own condition:

> [One might say that] when "Let this be for our relatives" is said, the fruit of an act done by one person is given to another. To the contrary: when there is a dedication, the ghosts who are called recipients have the conditions for a good action. Therefore, in that place, at that very moment, a good, fruitful action is theirs.[23]

In other words, the donor gives neither the act nor the fruit, but the opportunity for the ghosts to make their own merit:

> Because of three factors – by the excellence of one worthy of an offering, by dedication to the recipients, and by rejoicing by the ghosts – an offering produces fruit at that moment.[24]

Dhp-a IV 122–123 compares this act of *pattidāna* to villagers lighting their lamps from a single lamp: the light is from the first lamp, but the villagers supply their own oil.

But if ghosts make merit by their own effort, what is the *patti*, or attainment, that is given? G. P. Malalasekere, Richard Gombrich, and Jean-Michel Agasse have all taken *patti* to mean merit,[25] but this interpretation only prompts the question of why the commentators would introduce the notion of "giving merit" when they also take pains to deny that any merit transfer takes place. Jean Filliozat connects *patti* with the Vaibhāṣika technical term *prāpti*, which signifies a mental *dharma* consisting in the acquisition of good dispositions or actions.[26] *Patti* would then refer to the attainment of merit or of a meritorious mental state.[27] Gombrich has also argued that *patti* has its origin in Sarvāstivādin ideas of *prāpti*, and that the Theravādins adopted this doctrine in order to make sense of widespread practices of merit transfer.[28] But as the Theravādins explicitly rejected the existence of *prāpti*,[29] it is unlikely that they would have turned to a heterodox concept in order to solve a theoretical problem. These difficulties are somewhat relieved when we consider that *dadāti* and *dāna* do not necessarily indicate a real transfer from one person to another. In Pāli and in Sanskrit, *dadāti* is often used figuratively, as in *okāsaṃ dadāti*, gives an opportunity, or *śokaṃ dadāti*, gives grief. *Pattiṃ dadāti* may therefore be understood as 'causes *patti* to arise.' Consequently, 'merit' and 'meritorious mental state' need not be ruled out as possible meanings for *patti*.

Regardless of the origins of this usage, we must look to the Pāli texts to see what meanings the Theravādins gave to it.[30] The commentaries use *pattiṃ dadāti* and related expressions to describe the dedication of dakṣiṇā in a few narratives, such as the story of Bimbisāra, which is told at both Dhp-a I 103–104 and Pv-a 19–31 in connection with the *Tirokuḍḍa Sutta*.[31] The commentary to *Macchuddāna Jātaka* (no. 288) explains a reference in the verses to a gift of dakṣiṇā by having the Bodhisattva give the remainder of his meal to some fish and give the *patti* to a river *devatā*. The *devatā* rejoices (*anumoditvā*) over the *patti* and thereby increases in celestial splendor. Most occurrences of *pattidāna*, however, do not refer to the dedication of dakṣiṇā to a ghost or a deity. [32] Instead, in each of these stories except Dhp-a II 4 the recipient of *patti* is a human being. One of these narratives is the commentary to *Vimānavatthu* IV.6, the story of a woman who rejoices over her companion's gift of a *vihāra* and is consequently reborn as a deity. This seems clear enough, as rejoicing over a good deed is itself meritorious, but the commentary explains that the woman rejoices after receiving from her companion *pattidāna* in connection with her gift. In Dhp-a I 197, a master gives *patti* in a gift of almsfood to the servant who delivers it. In Dhp-a I 270 and II 198, the suppliers of parts of larger offerings (lumber for the pinnacle of a hall and honey for a meal) demand and receive *patti* from the other donors. In Dhp-a IV 203, a man asks his uncle to give him *patti* and to let him assist in the construction of a perfumed chamber, but the uncle refuses, "I do not give [it], dear nephew, I will do [an act] not shared with others."[33]

These stories can hardly be understood as being about one person causing a meritorious mental *prāpti* to arise in another. In Dhp-a I 270, II 198, and IV 203, people desire to make merit before they ask the donors to give them *patti*; they are therefore in a state of mind to perform good action even before they obtain *patti*. Furthermore, the donors in these stories are portrayed as selfish, and are hardly the kind to instill meritorious thoughts in others. Rather, in these stories *patti* is about being included among the donors of gifts, and thereby sharing in the resulting merit. Remarkably, the principal donor can give or withhold *patti* as he or she pleases. *Pattiṃ dadāti* might therefore mean, 'gives the attainment [of merit]' in the sense of giving someone an opportunity to attain merit. Alternatively, what is attained is not the merit, but the factors of the gift: the object given and the monastic recipient.[34] In either case, *pattiṃ dadāti* must refer to giving another person the opportunity to make merit by participating in a donation.

In addition to redefining the mechanism of dakṣiṇā dedication, the commentaries give an entirely different significance to this rite. These shifts in emphasis are apparent in *Paramatthadīpanī*'s commentary on *Tirokuḍḍa Sutta*. While the verses describe the departed (*petā*) as having been relatives and friends of those now living, the *peta*s of the story commentary did their evil deeds during their last human existence–92 eons earlier (Pv-a 21)! In the verses people are moved to give by their fond memories of those who have died, while in the story the king is motivated by fear caused by the ghosts' wailing (22). Although the verses do not suggest that there is anything horrible about the dead, the gloss says that they are ugly, deformed, and terrible to behold. When verse 2 says that the departed are not remembered on account of their deeds (*kammapaccayā*), the context suggests that this phrase means that people do not remember the dead despite the good deeds that they did while alive. The commentary, however, imposes a heavy-handed karmic interpretation on this verse, taking it to mean that ghosts are forgotten as a result of their bad deeds (25).

This account does not represent dakṣiṇā dedication as a means of caring for the dead, nor does it emphasize the compassion of the donors. Rather, it presents dakṣiṇā dedication as a rite of exorcism. When Pv-a does comment on donors' motivations, it speaks of fear or agitation. Pv-a views *peta*s as miserable beings only distantly related to the living. Much as the *Tirokuḍḍa* commentary dissociates King Bimbisāra from the *peta*s, the story commentary concerning the *petī* who had been Sāriputta's mother specifies that she had been Sāriputta's mother only in their fifth prior birth (Pv-a 79), as if Sāriputta would be tainted by a closer relationship to such a being. In the human meaning it gives to dakṣiṇā dedication, Pv-a is of the canonical texts closest to the karmic prose *sutta Aṅguttara* V 269–272, which the *Tirokuḍḍa* commentary in fact quotes to explain how dakṣiṇā dedication produces its effects (Pv-a 27–28).

The social context of progress toward nirvāṇa

Although some verses in the texts posit a direct causal connection between acts of devotion and the future attainment of nirvāṇa, Dhammapāla does not develop this theme. Instead, he repeatedly shows that *dāna* and other acts of devotion become occasions for preaching the Dharma, and that by hearing the Dharma people progress toward nirvāṇa.[35] Although the preaching of the Dharma figures in relatively few stories of *Vimānavatthu* and *Petavatthu*, it becomes a central motif of *Paramatthadīpanī*.[36] In these stories, performance of a meritorious act may lead to hearing the Dharma both then and in future lives, and that act may also serve as the occasion for preaching a sermon to others. Hearing the Dharma may in turn give rise to further meritorious deeds, as well as to progress toward arhatship. Occasions for sermons may be grouped into four categories. First, in many stories the recipient of alms delivers a discourse after eating his meal. This discourse may in turn give rise to specific path attainments, including arhatship, or to further meritorious acts.[37] Second, sermons are sometimes delivered in response to other situations within the narrative. For example, a person may inquire about the Dharma, or the Buddha or an elder may sense that someone is ready to hear the teaching. This kind of preaching may likewise result in rebirth or path attainments.[38] Third, the Buddha or Moggallāna or another elder may preach a sermon to a deity who has just told his or her past life story. This sometimes results in path attainments for the deity, and in two cases for the deity's retinue as well.[39] Fourth, many Vv-a stories and almost all Pv-a stories end with the Buddha delivering a sermon in which he narrates the events just recounted.[40] The commentary usually simply says that the teaching was of profit (*sātthikā*) for the hearers,[41] but it often specifies rebirth and path attainments.[42] The hearers who progress toward nirvāṇa after hearing a sermon sometimes number 84,000, and in one case in the tens of billions!

These stories about preaching the Dharma give a new purpose to the texts. *Vimānavatthu* and *Petavatthu* encourage their hearers to develop meritorious mental states by praising good acts and condemning bad acts. *Paramatthadīpanī*, on the other hand, does not encourage imitating the donors in the text, nor identifying with them, in the hope of winning a *vimāna* of one's own. It instead uses these stories in order to show the nature of *saṃsāra* and to agitate[43] the hearer so that he or she gains insight into the Dharma and becomes established on the path to liberation. Dhammapāla places acts of giving and devotion low on the scale of efficacious action, as they usually lead to nothing greater than rebirth in the Tāvatiṃsa heaven, but hearing the Dharma and gaining insight into it lead to far greater rewards. Dhammapāla thus advocates an intellectual and detached attitude toward the stories of meritorious actions narrated in the texts.

As the accounts of crowds gaining insight into the Dharma indicate, this teaching is for women and laity as well as for monks. In four stories told by Dhammapāla, laywomen hear the Dharma and make progress toward nirvāṇa through meditation. In Vv-a 87–88, 92, and 98, women practice insight meditation (*vipassanā*) and attain the *sotāpatti* fruit, and in Vv-a 115 a woman develops her meditation subject (*kammaṭṭhānaṃ paribrūhantī*) and becomes a *sotāpannā*.[44] In these stories, the spiritual paths pursued by monks and by laity are not essentially different. However, by showing that women can attain spiritual goals at home, these passages imply that female monasticism is a redundant institution. Dhammapāla only twice mentions nuns, and then only briefly.[45] Instead, he encourages women to accept their place in the family. For example, in commenting on the story of a woman who gave a cake to Moggallāna and was consequently beaten to death by her mother-in-law, Vv-a 121 explains that the woman gave the cake only because she believed that her mother-in-law would approve of her action. Dhammapāla thereby removes from the meritorious act the hint of disobedience found in the text. Like the verses, the commentary offers women spiritual liberation only within the context of traditional roles.

CHAPTER FIVE

Giving as Sacrifice, Karma, and Heroic Generosity in *Sīhaḷavatthuppakaraṇa*

After the commentaries were completed, Theravādin Buddhists continued to produce anthologies of edifying stories on the effects of action, and especially of giving.[1] *Sīhaḷavatthuppakaraṇa*, a collection of 77 stories, is an important representative of this genre. We do not know the date of this text, although a work of its name is mentioned in a Burmese inscription of 1442. We also know little about the text's redactor, although he or she apparently exercised a light editorial hand, as the stories vary significantly in style and in content, and must be the work of multiple authors.[2] Unlike Dhammapāla, the redactor of *Sīhaḷavatthuppakaraṇa* does not reduce disparate story traditions to a single karma theory. Instead, *Sīhaḷavatthuppakaraṇa*'s stories of good deeds rewarded and bad deeds punished not only draw on karmic discourse,[3] but take *both* the devotional and ascetic understandings of religious action further than any of the texts I have discussed so far.

Meritorious acts and their fruits

Sīhaḷavatthuppakaraṇa is strongly informed by sacrificial themes. Giving to a buddha, a Buddhist monk, or another ascetic is by far the most common kind of meritorious action, being named in 35 stories. An additional five stories name other acts of service and devotion to a stūpa or an individual,[4] and a few verses recommend worship or service to the Three Jewels as a means of making merit.[5] References to other acts as meritorious are few: in five stories (3, 4, 7, 31, 77) persons hear the Dharma, and in three (4, 21, 48) they take the precepts and/or the Refuges. Only Sīh 50 presents as meritorious an action that is not specifically Buddhist, i.e. ruling righteously.[6] One story reiterates the traditional theme of the three elements of the successful gift as follows:

> It is not possible to measure any righteous gift
> Given by a person of pure mind to those of superior virtue.
> A gift given to those of superior virtue is of abundant fruit,
> Therefore the god who rejoices in the Dharma says, "It is incalculable."[7]

A number of stories employ the imagery of the field for merit,[8] and donors are usually concerned to give to worthy recipients. Typical is Sīh 82, in which a king who wishes to be delivered from a bad destiny travels five *yojanas* on foot to seek out an elder worthy of worship. In a number of stories, recipients of especially generous gifts attain arhatship before eating so that the donors will experience a greater reward.[9] In many of these stories, donors do not even know that the monks become arhats; it is therefore not the donor's perception of the recipient's status, but the recipient's status itself, that produces the augmented effect.

The stories express differing views about the item given. At least one tale makes the point often repeated in *Vimānavatthu* and *Paramatthadīpanī* that even a small gift can produce a great result. In Sīh 26, a monk gives his meal to a thief, who gives half of it back to the monk. Later, when the thief is at the verge of dying, the thief remembers this act and instead of going to hell is reborn among the gods. The narrator comments:

> Therefore even a small [gift] is to be given to those who are worthy of dakṣiṇā.
> There is no vehicle equal to a gift for all those going to good destinies.[10]

Many more stories, however, view the size of the gift as significant. In Sīh 43, a woman gives her only good garment to a monk, and in Sīh 69 a man gives away all his clothes to five monks. In Sīh 33, a couple sells their son into slavery in order to buy a cow whose milk they give to the Saṅgha. In Sīh 62, a slave girl borrows 60 *kahāpaṇas* against her future earnings from moonlighting and uses it to feed 60 monks, rather than to free herself. Some stories praise reckless and prodigal acts of giving prompted by the presence of a recipient and a lack of food to give. In Sīh 36 and 38, people cook their seed rice to feed some monks. In Sīh 43, a man happily exchanges a jewel worth 1000 *kahāpaṇas* for a single meal to give to a monk, and in Sīh 45, a man spends eight *kahāpaṇas* on a meal for a monk. Sīh 56 tells of a couple who work for years to earn the money to redeem their daughter from slavery. While journeying to free her, the man sees that no one has fed a monk who is among his fellow travelers. The man exchanges all his money and grain for a single meal and gives it to the monk.

In these stories, it is not the objective value of the gift that is praised and rewarded, but its cost to the donor. In Sīh 61, a girl works for three years in order to buy a gift for eight monks. The deity who resides in the king's parasol regards this righteous and difficult deed (*dukkaraṃ*) as more praiseworthy than the king's acts of giving. In Sīh 42, when King Duṭṭhagāmaṇī on his deathbed recalls all his great actions, he says that those done when he was king were not difficult, but those done when he was miserable were (vv. 16, 50). He regards as his most meritorious acts two gifts of food made to elders while he was in the forest on the run from his enemies. In Sīh 8, a king Saddhātissa who does not want to give a gift stained by violence decides to give a pure gift earned by his own labor. He harvests a field for a day, and with the proceeds, he and his wife prepare a meal for a single monk, an act recognized by an elder as difficult. In Sīh 57, a king and queen decide that while ruling they are not able to make a difficult gift, so they go in disguise to a village and work on the harvest. After a month their hands are so sore that they cannot continue, so they return home and with their earnings feed sixty monks. Clearly, these *Sīhaḷavatthuppakaraṇa* stories are inspired not by the sacrificial texts, which present the size of the gift as unimportant, but by *Vessantara Jātaka* and other stories that praise acts of giving for their difficulty. In particular, the gift of one's own children in Sīh 33 and 56 replicates Vessantara's gift of his children. Sīh 35 makes explicit this theme of ascetic giving by saying that a woman who sells her hair to buy food to feed some monks cuts off her hair with the joy of cutting off the defilements.[11]

One may ask, however, why stories of what may seem like immoral and insane acts committed against self and family appeal to Theravādin audiences. Perhaps Buddhists admire these donors but would not imitate them; it may also be that these stories fascinate because, by pitting two obligations against each other, they pose insoluble dilemmas. But these answers beg the question of why such acts are appealing at all, and why Buddhists do not rather trust in the easy path set out by the sacrificial texts. Apparently the sacrificial ideology's promise of easy merit struck many as less plausible and satisfying than the idea that rewards will be proportional to effort expended. The history of Christianity shows that ideas of salvation by works can be very compelling even when a doctrine of free grace is preached. As Kierkegaard observes, the promises of the Christian gospel offend against common sense and ordinary experience.[12] Ann Gold and Jonathan Parry describe a similar tendency among Hindu pilgrims in North India to trust their own efforts rather than promises of easy salvation.[13] Gold reports that most of the Rajasthani pilgrims she interviewed denied the claims made in authoritative texts that visiting pilgrimage sites is inherently meritorious. Instead, pilgrims most often credited the disbursement of money to pay for the costs of the journey, including the exorbitant fees demanded by priests, with producing the "loosening of bonds" and self-realization that is the pilgrimage's greatest spiritual benefit.[14] Parry presents as widely held the belief that while on pilgrimage one should give freely, without calculation, and to the extent of one's capacity, in order to purify one's soul.[15] Thus, according to Gold and Parry, a belief in the power of ascetic virtue supplements and even displaces belief in the power of holy sites. In a similar manner, these *Sīhaḷavatthuppakaraṇa* stories find it unproblematic to affirm that the efficacy of a gift is a function of the generosity of the donor as well as the virtue of the recipient.

In many *Sīhaḷavatthuppakaraṇa* stories, kings and deities reward good actors. This narrative element is also apparently drawn from *Jātaka*, but *Sīhaḷavatthuppakaraṇa* introduces an important difference: in *Jātaka* the gods act as free agents, as when Sakka rewards Vessantara for giving away his wife, while *Sīhaḷavatthuppakaraṇa* identifies people and deities as agents of karmic retribution. In at least twenty stories, a king, a deity, or a group of deities benefits a person who has performed some meritorious deed, usually in the immediate past, or, sometimes, in a previous existence.[16] For example, in the story of the couple who sell their son and use the proceeds to give *dāna* (Sīh 33), the king rewards the couple with gifts. The narrator indicates that the king's action should be understood as a result of merit:

> People obtain fruits of meritorious and demeritorious action in this life,
> Therefore one should do meritorious action, which is dear to those
> whose joy is the Dharma.[17]

Similarly, when deities plant and raise a crop for a donor, the text comments that the crop grows "by the majesty of the gods and yakṣas and by the power of his merit."[18] When a *nāga* king provides food and shelter for an elder, the king's followers ask, "Of what deed is this the fruit?" and the elder tells of a gift the king gave in his previous life.[19] In Sīh 7, a prince wonders whether his prosperity is the result of his own merit or that of another.[20] He determines that the former is the case by going to various remote locations, and finding that wherever he goes people or deities appear bearing abundant gifts.

Sīh 49 begins with some deities secretly leaving a quantity of meat for a youth named Sālikumāra, who, on seeing the gift, deduces that deities have brought it. The rest of the story is as follows:

> 8 Seeing the wondrous power of his own merit, he became joyful and happy.
> Knowing merit and the result of merit, he made this utterance:
> 9 "Gods and *nāgas* (and yakṣas) who desire great worship!
> Good is to be done continually toward an unsurpassed field for merit.
> 10 Beings who do meritorious deeds with a satisfied mind
> Experience heavenly and human happiness.
> 11 It must therefore be the case that the youth made a great gift in the past;
> Gods and humans give as a result of that meritorious deed.
> 12 Wild and domesticated beasts, birds, (deities, and humans)
> Who see (a man who possesses merit) are always in his power.
> 13 Whatever a person does has an effect for him,
> For that meritorious deed is not destroyed even in difficulty or in doubt."[21]

In this remarkable passage, the youth simply assumes that his unforeseen good fortune must be the result of his own past deed, and that the deities were acting to reward his own merit. He also assumes that his meritorious deed was an act of giving, showing that for many Theravādins giving and merit-making were virtually synonymous. Sālikumāra describes meritorious deeds as sources of wondrous power, and states that a person with merit exercises power over others.[22] Just as kings and deities respond to the merit of ordinary people, so, according to verse 12, do animals, deities, and humans respond to the merit of a ruler.

These stories thus construct a vision of the world as a web of karmic connections, in which actions not only produce effects, but are themselves the effects of actions performed by oneself and by others. Although the stories do not deny that beings have agency, they present the actions of beings as somehow automatically fulfilling the karmic destinies of others. While it may be possible to show that this complex account of reality is coherent, the authors of *Sīhaḷavatthup-*

pakaraṇa do not attempt to do so, any more than they explain how their overdetermination of giving as sacrifice and as heroic generosity fits with karmic theory. Unlike the commentators, the authors of these stories do not trouble themselves over the philosophical problems they raise.

Sīhaḷavatthuppakaraṇa also differs from the commentaries by shifting its frame of reference from the vast temporal and spatial expanses of the classical karmic cosmology to a focus on the here and now. As the large number of stories about gods and kings as karmic agents indicates, *Sīhaḷavatthuppakaraṇa* usually presents the human world, and not the heavens, as the place in which persons experience the fruits of good action. Stories in which a person experiences the effects of an action in the same lifetime, in some cases instantly, provide the most dramatic examples of this pattern. As soon as monks eat an offering given by one girl, she becomes beautiful, surpassing human beings in appearance.[23] When a donor plants his rice field, it instantly becomes full of plants ready for harvest; for an artisan who feeds a monk, a leaf turns into a plate made of gold.[24] The gifts of some donors multiply themselves, thereby reaching a greater number of recipients and producing even more merit.[25] In two stories, the protagonists blame their poverty on their failure to give, and when they do give, their fortunes improve.[26] Several verses speak of actions producing effects both in the here and now and in the next world; for example,

> Thus, [giving] dakṣiṇā to those who possess virtue is an unthinkably meritorious action:
> After giving pleasure in the here and now, it ripens in the next world.[27]

In a number of stories persons do attain birth in the heavens, but *Sīhaḷavatthuppakaraṇa* shows little interest in those worlds. The text frequently does not even name the heaven in which the protagonist is reborn,[28] and the only heaven that it describes at any length is the Tusita, which it calls the best abode and supremely pleasing.[29] But Tusita is not a realm of personal enjoyment like the heavens envisioned in *Vimānavatthu* and *Paramatthadīpanī*; rather, Tusita derives its importance from its place in a cosmic soteriology. Tusita is the city of the bodhisattva Metteyya, "the liberator from existence for those who fear *saṃsāra*."[30] Those who reach Tusita dwell in Metteyya's presence, seeing him, hearing the Dharma, and desiring the welfare of the world.[31] They will eventually be reborn with Metteyya and attain final nirvāṇa with him (3.16–17). The inhabitants of Tusita experience joy akin to that of nirvāṇa, while anticipating the full attainment of nirvāṇa, as one story tells of a donor who "obtained immeasurable, unending, incalculable, supreme happiness."[32] *Sīhaḷavatthuppakaraṇa* shows an interest in Tusita that it does not show for other heavens because those born in Tusita participate in nirvāṇa, partially in the present, and fully in a future human birth.[33] This duality is paralleled in the status of Metteyya, who is called Sammāsambuddha, Sugata, and the best of victors, even though his attainment of buddhahood is also spoken of as a future event.[34]

The attainment of nirvāṇa

The stories of *Sīhaḷavatthuppakaraṇa* link a variety of actions to the attainment of nirvāṇa. Some persons, like the thief of Sīh 22, become arhats easily and with little or no preparation (also 68 and 70). By contrast, in tales like Sīh 64 and 66 monks attain arhatship after many years of intense effort.[35] But most often stories use the idiom of karma to show that actions ripen over the course of births to produce the attainment of nirvāṇa. In keeping with *Sīhaḷavatthuppakaraṇa*'s focus on the here and now, this process usually takes only a few lifetimes.

The actions most often said to initiate a karmic process culminating in awakening are acts of giving and devotion. In Sīh 54, a man reaches arhatship (*tevijjo jāto*) by performing *pūjā* to a shrine and reflecting on this act. The excellence of arhatship is said to be a fruit of that worship (*pūjāphalavisesaṃ*). In Sīh 59 and 61, women make gifts while aspiring that they will not long remain in *saṃsāra*.[36] Sīh 47 tells of a woman who gives half of her clothes to a monk that she is reborn in heaven and attaining nirvāṇa will cross the flood of existence.[37] The verses containing this prediction precede and follow a verse in praise of giving to worthy recipients, indicating that her attainments should be viewed as resulting from her gift. Sīh 46.35 says of those who reach Tusita through their meritorious acts that they will eventually gain the pleasure of non-dying (*amara*, i.e. nirvāṇa). Even the Bodhisattva is said to have attained perfect awakening through giving.[38]

A more immediate connection between devotion and awakening is presented by Sīh 6, in which Māra assumes the physical form of the Buddha, and brings the elder Phussadeva to the attainment of arhatship. A brief version of this story appears in *Visuddhimagga*, and similar stories appear elsewhere in Buddhist literature.[39] Buddhaghosa tells the story as follows:

> It is said that when the elder saw an image of the Buddha created by Māra, he thought, "This one appears so splendid even though he has lust, hatred, and delusion; how much more splendid did the Blessed One appear, he who was without lust, hatred, and delusion?" He obtained joy with the Buddha as its object, developed insight, and attained arhatship.[40]

In this account, devotion to the body of the Buddha leads indirectly to arhatship: the vision produces joy, which prompts the cultivation of *vipassanā* meditation, which in turn brings about the attainment of nirvāṇa. Buddhaghosa also stresses that Phussadeva is aware of the imperfections of the vision. In the *Sīhaḷavatthuppakaraṇa* account, by contrast, devotion is the immediate cause of the attainment of nirvāṇa. Phussadeva does not restrain himself when sees the image, and does not suggest that this vision in any way fails to represent the Buddha. The elder salutes the vision, his eyes fill with tears, his hair stands on end, and he pronounces 21 verses in praise of the Buddha and his 32 auspicious marks. Finally,

> In this way, the elder sees the form created by Māra.
> Having developed insight, he attained arhatship.[41]

Although the second of these lines is identical to a line from *Visuddhimagga* cited above, this version gives these words a very different meaning. The author uses the parallel between *vipassati* and *vipassanaṃ* to equate Phussadeva's vision with the insight meditation by which he attains nirvāṇa. The following verse indicates that Phussadeva is still viewing the image when he achieves the goal.

But devotion is not the only seed of awakening; in other stories ascetic renunciation begins the process. In Sīh 1, a tailor named Tissa decides that half of his body will be his and half will be his parents'; thereafter he gives all that he earns in the morning to the Saṅgha, and all that he earns in the afternoon to his parents. When his parents attempt to give him a wife "to tend his body,"[42] he delivers a speech on the disadvantages of married life. He attains fame for his celibate life, and is praised for "having divided his body."[43] Although Tissa lives a life of quiet, this-worldly asceticism, the language of dismemberment used here recalls the Bodhisattva's awesome gifts of his own body in *Jātaka*. After Tissa shares his action with all beings, the king gives him much wealth, and Tissa becomes a great donor.

After a happy death, he goes to Tusita, ensuring that he will eventually attain nirvāṇa.

Finally, a set of stories about child arhats presents devotion, insight, and hearing the Dharma as causes of the future attainment of nirvāṇa. In Sīh 20, a reprobate monk witnesses the birth of a child and becomes disgusted with the human body. He seeks instruction from an elder and becomes a forest dweller. In his next life, he is reborn spontaneously (avoiding the horrors of gestation and birth), and at the age of seven goes forth and promptly becomes an arhat. This realization is described as the result of karma (*kammavipāka*, v. 33). In Sīh 72, a traveler gives his food to a monk and consequently starves to death. In his next life he hears the preaching of the Dharma, goes forth at age twelve, and in seven days becomes an arhat. In Sīh 77, a fish hears the Dharma preached, is reborn as a human being, goes forth at age seven, learns the *Tipiṭaka*, and becomes an arhat. Finally, in Sīh 79, a monk plants a flowering shrub; consequently he is reborn in a family of householders and hears the Dharma preached seven times. In his next life, he attains arhatship at age seven while in the tonsure room, and the same day preaches a sermon heard as far away as the Brahmalokas.

Although *Sīhaḷavatthuppakaraṇa* uses the karmic discourse to tell that this variety of actions leads to the attainment of awakening, it does not present any one ethical value or causal factor, like mental purification, as the basis for the karmic soteriology. Different stories present devotion, heroic asceticism, and insight as ways to enlightenment. In addition, as mentioned above, some stories demonstrate that the qualities of the recipient affect the merit produced even when the donor has no knowledge of those qualities. This strong formulation of the sacrificial theme is incompatible with an understanding of mental purity as the sole determinant of karmic effects. These stories therefore do not, like the canonical prose and the commentaries, share an explicit karma theory; karma is here simply an idiom of act and ripening used to label a variety of causal relationships. This lack of concern for systematic thought allows these texts to represent a diversity of ways in which actions bear fruit in awakening.

Demeritorious acts and the dedication of gifts

Sīhaḷavatthuppakaraṇa primarily describes good actions, but it also presents diverse views of the effects of evil. A series of stories at Sīh

11–19 deals with the effects of demeritorious acts. In the first of these stories, a ghost who in a previous life committed (an) unspecified bad action (*pāpakammaṃ*) asks a layman to help him, and the layman dedicates a gift to him. The description of the dedication resembles those of Pv-a. The donor gives water and says, "As a result of this, let water arise for the ghost," and similarly dedicates a gift of food.[44] The ghost rejoices (*anumoditvā*), and obtains heavenly existence (*dibbattabhāvaṃ*), supreme happiness (*paramaṃ sukhaṃ*) and the form of a *devaputta*, although he is still called a *peta*. The ghost rewards the donor with treasure, telling him to enjoy himself, have fun, do meritorious deeds, and give *patti*.

The other stories of this group are very different in tone. Sīh 12, 13, 14, 16, 18, and 19 all tell of ghosts who in their previous lives committed acts against a buddha or his community by destroying property, moving a property marker, speaking disrespectfully, failing to provide a regular meal for visiting monks, blocking access to an alms hall, or misusing community assets. These stories never suggest that these ghosts might benefit from a dedicated gift, and 12, 13, 14, and 18 state that the ghosts will later go to hell. Instead, these tales dramatize the especially terrible effects that befall those who harm Buddha or Saṅgha, and thereby warn their hearers to respect the property and rights of the Saṅgha. Just as the virtue of the recipient magnifies the merit produced through giving, so also do wrongs committed against the virtuous produce great demerit. In Sīh 18, the ghost states that, "an offense against the highly virtuous brings woe,"[45] and goes on to caution that one must not damage anything used by the Saṅgha, not even a root of a tree. In Sīh 19, the wrongdoer has a premonition that he will soon die and become a ghost, and he warns his fellow monks:

> All you who have seen me, fear the property of the Saṅgha!
> Fearing, diligently exert yourself in the dispensation of the Buddha.[46]

Although he regrets his deed and knows his imminent fate, this monk does not try to perform a meritorious deed to balance his bad acts; his evil deed is too powerful to be counteracted. In Sīh 16, the most extreme of these stories, the elder of a monastery orders that food not be prepared at the monastery because the local people will be preparing a feast for the monks that day. Two traveling monks arrive at the monastery at mealtime, and go hungry. The elder dies, and although he possesses *sīla* and is very learned, he arises as a ghost. Appearing to a forest monk, the ghost explains that his fault was obstructing a gift to the Saṅgha. The monk asks how he can liberate the ghost and offers to worship the Three Jewels, but the ghost replies that he will not be free for an extremely long time (not until the earth rises to the level of the top of the mountain). The monk goes to the monastery and inspires those who hear the ghost's story to conduct themselves with diligence and to fear the property of the Saṅgha.

Sīh 15 and 17 tell of men who become ghosts after offending against the Three Jewels (17.21), but who are saved through the dedication of offerings. In Sīh 15, a learned monk endowed with *sīla* borrows a half-measure of the monastery's rice in order to make a meal for his father, and dies before he is able to replace it. In Sīh 17, a farmer keeps a banner that has blown off a stūpa and onto his field. Each of these ghosts is released from its suffering through a dedicated gift, which is described with language like that of Sīh 11 and earlier stories, including *uddisi* and *pattiṃ adāsi,* and with a wish for the result to arise (*nibbattatu*). However, these two narratives differ significantly from earlier dedication narratives in regard to the items offered. In Sīh 15, the gift needed to liberate the ghost is rice enough to fill a line of carts stretching for three *gāvuta*s (five or six miles). In Sīh 17, the required offering is 1000 banners. The ghost is covered with 1000 burning hot iron plates, and with the gift of each banner one iron plate disappears. These offerings indicate that the authors understand the dedication of gifts in a fundamentally different way from canonical descriptions of dakṣiṇā dedication. In the canonical texts, the offerings are small, and correspond to the nature of the ghost's affliction: water for thirst, food for hunger, and so on. The gifts of Sīh 15 and 17 correspond instead to the original act: rice for rice, banners for a banner. The immense size of the gifts needed is a result of the offense having been committed against the Three Jewels.[47] These gifts show that the author of these tales understands the dedication of gifts as undoing the original action, and not as a transfer of sacrificial substance.[48]

Although these eight stories represent bad actions as being much more powerful than good, *Sīhaḷavatthuppakaraṇa* contains other views.[49] In Sīh 22, a thief disguises himself as a monk and attempts to steal an iron vessel from a monastery. Before he is able to take the vessel, he hears an elder's preaching and becomes an arhat. In Sīh 80, a man mocks a monk, but later regrets what he has done, becomes a believer and a possessor of *sīla,* and feeds the monk, helping him to become an arhat. Neither story suggests that these men who act against the Saṅgha have to undergo the terrible punishments that Sīh 12–19 would indicate.

Sīh 1, 34, 43, and 45 present another way of telling how a person may benefit from another's merit. In these stories, donors give a *bhāga*, meaning 'share' or 'portion,' of a good action or of its effect.[50] In the story of Tissa (Sīh 1), a king asks him for a share. Tissa replies that he gives a share to the king and to all beings,[51] and the king rewards him with great wealth. In Sīh 43, a king asks for a share in merit (or in the meritorious act, *puññabhāgaṃ*) from a man who has made a great gift. The man gives a share in merit to the king and to all beings, and the king rewards him with an office and wealth.[52] Similarly in Sīh 45, a great donor gives a share to a king and to all beings, and the king rewards him.[53] Sīh 34.37–38 presents a variation on this theme with this exchange between Sakka and a great donor:

> "What good you have done is yours, but what meritorious deed you will do,
> If you give me a share (in it), I will perform service."
> "A share is given to you and to other beings, king of the gods,
> Let it completely liberate *asuras* and humans from perdition."[54]

Sakka's statement alludes to the verse of *Aṅguttara* III 41 that says that one who assists in the performance of a meritorious action or rejoices over it will share in merit.[55] This allusion suggests that, as in the *pattidāna* doctrine, the donor gives another the opportunity to make merit by rejoicing over the donor's deed.

Curiously, however, none of these four stories indicates that the recipients rejoice in order to receive their share; these accounts thereby imply that the gift is successful apart from the response of the recipient. Similarly, in Sīh 39 a layman dedicates the benefit of feeding 500 monks to a man who is hostile toward him, but the narrator does not indicate whether the intended beneficiary is even aware of the dedication.[56] Two of the three stories about gift dedication (Sīh 15 and 17) likewise fail to state that the recipients rejoice over the gift. Perhaps in all of these stories it is to be understood that the recipients benefit only if they rejoice, but the impression that these stories would give an unlearned hearer is precisely the view that the commentators sought to deny: that merit is transferred. In contrast to the commentaries which stress that the recipients of *pattidāna* make their own merit by rejoicing over the gift, these *Sīhaḷavatthuppakaraṇa* stories place emphasis entirely on the salvific generosity of the donor, and neglect the action of the recipients.

This interpretation "of *pattidāna* as "giving merit" is made explicit in many Pāli texts. Agasse notes that in Southeast Asian Theravādin inscriptions, chronicles, and "apocryphal texts," the most common expressions for the dedication of gifts are (*mātāpitūnaṃ*) *atthāya puññaṃ karoti*, "to make merit for the sake of (one's parents or some other person)," and *dānaphalaṃ dadāti*, "to give the fruit of a gift."[57] Similarly, the expression, *pin dīma*, "give merit," is commonly used for the dedication of offerings in Siṅhala literature.[58] These postcommentarial traditions thus reassert the donative character of dakṣiṇā dedication despite the commentators' denials that this act involves any real transfer. More troubling from the perspective of the commentators, the thing transferred is here identified as merit. Ironically, the commentators may have inadvertently fostered such ideas of merit transfer by replacing 'dedicate' (*ā-* and *ud- disati*) with 'give' (*dadāti*), and '*dakkhiṇā*' with the ambiguous '*patti*.'

The social context of giving and of progress toward nirvāṇa

In *Sīhaḷavatthuppakaraṇa*, donors and those making progress toward nirvāṇa are of all social classes and of both genders. Although most people who attain arhatship are male, Sīh 60 and 70 tell stories of nuns becoming arhats. Given the traditional antipathy toward female monasticism, it may be that these stories represent female monasticism as a viable religious option only because the order of nuns had in fact died out by the time these stories were composed. Sīh 42 and 52 depict acts of giving to nuns, but neither story indicates that these nuns are to be thought of as efficacious fields for merit.

As in the older stories, acts of giving often provide the context for preaching; a number of stories reverse this scenario by having the donors help the recipients to attain arhatship. In some stories, monks become arhats because they are aroused by the donors' generosity.[59] In Sīh 32, an elder is so moved by the generosity of his lay supporters that he feels that he is unworthy of their gift, and becomes an arhat before consuming their offering (v. 13). In a number of stories, monks, motivated by compassion, become arhats before eating a donated meal in order to bring about a greater result for the donor.[60] These stories argue that monks do not attain arhatship out of selfish desire, as the Mahāyāna critique asserts. Rather, these monks attain nirvāṇa out of compassion for others, in order to be better fields for merit. Within a karmic framework, these stories assert the social complementarity of sacrificial and purificatory acts.

Sīhaḷavatthuppakaraṇa also demonstrates the continuing vitality of the storytelling tradition represented by *Vimānavatthu* and *Petavatthu*. Stories of these two texts draw on both sacrificial and karmic elements and do not present a uniform discourse and doctrine of karma. Their primary concern is to encourage their hearers to rejoice in and imitate good action and to reject bad acts. *Paramatthadīpanī*, on the other hand, frames these stories as Dharma talks delivered by the Buddha, and in so doing makes doctrinal instruction, rather than moral exhortation, its main purpose. The *Sīhaḷavatthuppakaraṇa* stories return to the dramatic and direct appeal exemplified by *Vimānavatthu* and *Petavatthu*. Setting aside philosophical speculation, these stories employ karmic discourse to describe a diversity of actions and causalities, including those of sacrifice and ascesis, and to encourage good actions, especially acts of giving and rejoicing over the gifts of others.

AFTERWORD

Doctrine and Narrative

This book tells a story of two incomplete doctrinal developments. First, practices for making merit and purifying the mind were rationalized within a unified karmic soteriology; however, the tradition has continued to include ideas incompatible with this karma theory, most notably the idea that the qualities of the recipient affect the merit produced by a gift. Second, dakṣiṇā dedication was reinterpreted as giving others the opportunity to make merit for themselves, but many Buddhists instead came to see this practice as giving merit to others. To these developments we could add a third: the Vedic vision of a universe centered around the earth and human beings was replaced by a cosmology in which human beings are rendered insignificant by unimaginable expanses of space and time. Although *Sīhaḷavatthuppakaraṇa* does not explicitly reject this worldview, it largely ignores it in favor of a cosmos more to human scale. All of these developments were part of a fundamental shift in Indic religions, from the Vedic vision of the world as constituted by sacrifice, to the classical view of the world as constituted by karma. Despite the efforts of the authors of the canonical discursive prose and the commentaries, Buddhists have not consistently applied karmic theory to all areas of life. In Theravādin literature we see deviations from karmic theory most clearly in narratives, and especially in accounts of giving and dedicating *dāna*. The capacity of acts to mean more than one thing has allowed these practices to retain their old sacrificial significance even as they have taken on new karmic meanings.

The overdetermination of these practices in narratives both represents and informs an overdetermination of these acts in life. Borrowing terms from James Fernandez,[1] we may ask how

Theravādins can display social consensus regarding giving and dedicating *dāna* while lacking cultural consensus regarding the meaning of these acts. Fernandez addresses a similar question concerning the diversity of explanations his informants provided for the purpose of a ritual:

> If we should ask how it is that cooperative participation continues in cult ritual despite a lack of consensus at this level, the obvious answer is that a cult rationale or charter is rarely explicitly stated, or if stated is phrased in such general terms as not to offend or exclude the particular purposes of various individuals. Secondly . . . the participants rarely discuss or debate the rationale and are content that it should be taken for granted. Only cult leaders concern themselves with such matters, in competition with other cult leaders for membership – and in discussion with the ethnographer.[2]

This description also characterizes the Theravādin situation. Doctrinal precision has been the concern of monastic elites, while Buddhist preaching has traditionally drawn more on story literature like *Sīhaḷavatthuppakaraṇa*. *Sīhaḷavatthuppakaraṇa*'s stories employ karmic discourse as well as the merit field doctrine without explaining how they are compatible; they likewise neglect to show explicitly that their accounts of dakṣiṇā dedication conform to the commentators' *pattidāna* doctrine. Stories like these allow readers to attach very different meanings to the acts these stories describe.

Just as they may mean different things to different members of Theravādin societies, these actions may also be overdetermined for individuals. How do those who hold to multiple understandings of these actions find them cognitively consonant? Again, a partial answer lies in the fact that these multiple explanations have been articulated less often as doctrines than as narratives. One may embrace more than one narrative account of a ritual without perceiving the contradictions that one would see in conflicting arguments. Indeed, by assigning multiple layers of meaning to these acts, these stories suggest a range of meanings and motivations that a ritual actor can impute to his or her actions. After hearing stories of Sāriputta who gives out of disinterested compassion, or of Bimbisāra who exorcises *peta*s by giving them an opportunity to make merit, a Theravādin can still give to his deceased parents a gift that is motivated by familial duty or affection. He may even, by thinking of the precedent of Sāriputta, attribute to his act not only filial piety, but also a more universal compassion. Alternatively, by thinking of Bimbisāra, he may find a socially sanctioned way of expressing feelings of fear or anger toward a dead parent. Similarly, a reader of *Sīhaḷavatthuppakaraṇa* may think of her *dāna* as an act of both meritorious worship and selfless asceticism. The multivalence of the narrative tradition, rather than creating cognitive dissonance, allows religious giving to express competing religious impulses.

Accommodating sacrificial explanations is only one way in which narratives make karma an idea by which people can live their lives. Karma theory presents a metaphysics and a psychology that contradict common sense notions of religious action. The discourse of *kamma, saṅkhāra,* and *vipāka* reduces human actions to the intentions that inform them; more broadly, Theravādin doctrine asserts the emptiness of all constructed things, including actors. Insofar as they draw on such doctrines, Buddhist narratives portray a strange kind of actor, one who views his or her own karmic development from the viewpoint of a spectator. This actor speaks of a deed as something that continues through time and has an identity and an effect upon the actor that are independent from the actor's subsequent intentions. As one goddess states:

> That I possessed *sīla* has not ripened for me,
> But my hope, lord of gods, is that I would be a once-returner.[3]

She describes mental purification leading to nirvāṇa not as something that she herself is doing, but as a discrete set of actions performed in the past that is producing its effect on its own. This is what it means for an agent not to be a self: the act is real, but the hoping ego is illusory. Although some narratives, such as Sīh 64 and 66, represent arhatship as the product of many years of intense effort, most tales of *Vimānavatthu* and *Sīhaḷavatthuppakaraṇa* present the attainment of nirvāṇa as the result of a specific act. These texts thus represent spiritual progress not as the formation of a moral agent, but as the performance of particular actions.

On the other hand, these stories combat the alienating implications of the doctrinal reduction of human activity to discrete, momentary volitions simply by virtue of their being stories. As Jerome Bruner observes, stories, like arguments, can be persuasive, but while arguments convince one of their truth, stories convince one of their lifelikeness.[4] Through repeated descriptions of individuals and the particular actions they perform, these Theravādin stories make the counterintuitive karma theory believable. By connecting actions to powerful emotions and experiences of bliss or suffering, these narratives give human meaning to the karmic process. In a number of stories, an actor continuously recalls and affirms her past acts; in this way she projects a sense of personhood in the face of a doctrine that denies the existence of an essential self. More generally, all of these stories present their characters not only as series of discrete and momentary mental phenomena,[5] but as agents with whom the hearers of the stories can empathize. These stories thereby make karmic discourse not only an analytic tool, but also a vocabulary for imagining how one should live in the world.

NOTES

Introduction

1 *Sīla* (Sanskrit *śīla*) is often translated as "morality;" I discuss the meaning of this term in chapter 1.

2 Melford E. Spiro demonstrates that Burmese Buddhists consider giving, or *dāna*, to be the primary means for acquiring merit. "When asked to list the ways in which merit can be achieved, the Burmese, almost without exception, mention *dāna* to the exclusion of anything else." *Buddhism and Society: A Great Tradition and Its Burmese Vicissitudes*. 2d ed. (Berkeley: University of California Press, 1982), 103. Stanley J. Tambiah makes this same point in regard to his Thai informants: "On the whole then we must conclude that merit-making through gift-giving is more valued than merit-making through the observance of Buddhistic precepts and the pursuit of Buddhistic ethical aims." *Buddhism and the Spirit Cults in North-east Thailand*, (London: Cambridge University Press, 1970), 148. Charles F. Keyes observes more broadly, ". . . the offerings made by the laity to the Sangha are defined in all Theravādin traditions as being the supreme moral acts through which the laity acquires merit. . . .." "Merit-Transference in the Kammic Theory of Popular Theravāda Buddhism," in *Karma: An Anthropological Inquiry*, ed. Charles F. Keyes and E. Valentine Daniel (Berkeley: University of California Press, 1983), 274.

3 Clearly, any reduction of an entire ethical tradition to one or two principles can only represent a theoretical ideal; human actions are normally, if not always, motivated by a variety of intentions and values. As Charles Hallisey has argued, Theravādin ethics is informed by a number of moral theories. Charles Hallisey, "Ethical Particularism in Theravāda Buddhism," *Journal of Buddhist Ethics* 3 (1996): 32–43. James Laidlaw similarly shows how Jainism, despite being "easily formulated as a set of metaphysical postulates," must in practice incorporate other values. *Riches and Redemption: Religion, Economy, and Society Among the Jains* (Oxford: Clarendon Press, 1995), 394.

4 Hammalawa Saddhatissa, *Buddhist Ethics*, third edition (Boston: Wisdom Publications, 1997), 4.

5 A reduction of *dāna* to the category of virtue or morality can be seen in translations of *dāna* as 'generosity' rather than as 'giving' (e.g.

Saddhatissa, *Buddhist Ethics*, 47). By contrast, canonical explications of *sīla*, *samādhi*, and *paññā* such as *Sāmaññaphala Sutta* (D I 47–86) and *Subha Sutta* (D I 204–210) do not name *dāna* among the practices comprising *sīla*.

6 Bhikkhu Bodhi, "Introduction," in *Dāna: The Practice of Giving, Wheel* 367/369, ed. Bhikkhu Bodhi (Kandy: Buddhist Publication Society, 1990), 2.

7 W. S. Karunatillake, "The Religiousness of Buddhists in Sri Lanka Through Belief and Practice," in *Religiousness in Sri Lanka*, ed. John Ross Carter (Colombo: Marga Institute, 1979), 20–21.

8 *Buddhism and Society*, 11–14, 31–139. Winston L. King makes a similar distinction in *A Thousand Lives Away: Buddhism in Contemporary Burma* (Cambridge, MA: Harvard University Press, 1964).

9 Ibid., 66–68.

10 Spiro, *Buddhism and Society*, 106–107.

11 Richard F. Gombrich, *Buddhist Precept and Practice: Traditional Buddhism in the Rural Highlands of Ceylon* (Delhi: Motilal Banarsidass, 1991), 289–290. The Saṅgha is the community of Buddhist monastics.

12 Ibid., 290.

13 Ibid., 292.

14 Charles Keyes has discussed social aspects of this relationship in "Merit-Transference in the Kammic Theory of Popular Theravāda Buddhism," 274. Torkel Brekke discusses this paradoxical quality of giving in Hinduism, Jainism, and Buddhism in "Contradiction and the Merit of Giving in Indian Religions," *Numen* 45 (1998): 287–320.

15 For example, Robertson Smith defines sacrifice as a meal given to deities, and he asserts that neither killing nor destroying the offering is essential to all forms of sacrifice. William Robertson Smith, *Lectures on the Religions of the Semites: The Fundamental Institutions*, 3d ed., (1927; reprint, [New York:] Ktav Publishing House, 1969), 214. For Durkheim, sacrifice consists of gift (or renunciation) and communion; Émile Durkheim, *The Elementary Forms of Religious Life*, tr. Karen E. Fields (New York: The Free Press, 1995) 347. Yerkes similarly argues that in Hebrew, Greek, and Roman traditions, sacrifice was an act of giving to the deities, and that killing was not an essential part of this act. Royden Keith Yerkes, *Sacrifice in Greek and Roman Religions and Early Judaism* (London: Adam and Charles Black, 1953), 5. Robertson Smith and Yerkes both note that while the worshipers may share in the meal, they frequently do not do so; Smith, 217; Yerkes, 26. Of course, this understanding of sacrifice as a meal for the gods is not universally accepted. Some interpreters, including Walter Burkert and René Girard, see killing and/or destruction as the essence of sacrifice; Walter Burkert, René Girard, and Jonathan Z. Smith, *Violent Origins*, ed. Robert G. Hamerton-Kelly (Stanford: Stanford University Press, 1987), 107, 174.

16 P. D. Premasiri, "Interpretation of Two Principal Ethical Terms in Early Buddhism," *Sri Lanka Journal of the Humanities* 2 (1976): 74. Premasiri defines his object of study as the "Pāli Nikāyas;" however, he does not consider texts generally considered relatively late, such as Pv and Vv.

17 Ibid., 72–73.

18 I translate *kamma* as 'karma' when it is used as an emic technical category as part of what I am calling karmic discourse. *Kamma* has many other meanings; see PED and CPD.

19 A debate on this question is presented in *Panels of the VIIth World Sanskrit Conference*, edited by Johannes Bronkhorst, vol. 2: *Earliest Buddhism and Madhyamaka*, edited by David Seyfort Ruegg and Lambert Schmithausen (Leiden: E. J. Brill, 1990). Richard Gombrich argues that the canonical texts present an accurate representation of Gotama's original teaching, while Lambert Schmithausen argues against this position. For other persuasive skeptical arguments, see Gregory Schopen's studies cited below.

20 Collins' statement continues, ". . . which remained remarkably stable in content throughout the traditional period, but which moved, as a developing whole, through various times and places within the premodern material-historical world." My point is not to imply that Collins does not recognize differences between and within Pāli texts, but that the concept of the Pāli imaginaire refers to the meanings that those texts do share. *Nirvana and other Buddhist felicities: Utopias of the Pali imaginaire* (Cambridge: Cambridge University Press, 1998), 41.

21 The term 'canonical' is used with caution, for as Collins points out, Theravādins have not had a sense of a closed canon similar to Christian understandings of canon. "On the Very Idea of the Pali Canon." *Journal of the Pali Text Society* 15 (1990): 89–126.

22 For a brief list of studies from the 1980s that employ historical-critical approaches, see J. W. De Jong, *A Brief History of Buddhist Studies in Europe and America* (Tokyo: Kosei Publishing Co., 1997), 96. See also titles by N. A. Jayawickrama listed in the bibliography, as well as Govind Chandra Pande, *Studies in the Origins of Buddhism* (Allahabad: University of Allahabad, 1957); Lambert Schmithausen, "An Attempt to Estimate the Distance in Time between Aśoka and the Buddha in Terms of Doctrinal History," in *The Dating of the Historical Buddha*, Part I, edited by Heinz Bechert, *Abhandlungen der Akademie der Wissenschaften in Göttingen, Philologisch-Historische Klasse Dritte Folge*, Nr. 189 (Göttingen: Vanderhoech & Ruprecht, 1991), 110–147; idem, "Preface" to *Panels of the VIIth World Sanskrit Conference*, edited by Johannes Bronkhorst, vol. 2: *Earliest Buddhism and Madhyamaka*, edited by David Seyfort Ruegg and Lambert Schmithausen (Leiden: E. J. Brill, 1990), 1–4; Gregory Schopen, "The Monastic Ownership of Servants or Slaves: Local and Legal Factors in the Redactional History of Two *Vinayas*," *Journal of the International Association of Buddhist Studies* 17 (1994): 145–173; and Jonathan S. Walters, "Suttas as History: Four Approaches to the *Sermon on the Noble Quest* (Ariyapariyesanasutta)," *History of Religions* 38 (1999): 247–284.

23 Gregory Schopen, "Two Problems in the History of Indian Buddhism: The Layman/Monk Distinction and the Doctrine of the Transference of Merit," *Studien zur Indologie und Iranistik* 10 (1987): 9–10.

24 "Two Problems," 14–15, 17; cf. idem, "Monastic Ownership," 146. The branching tree model which underlies this principle has been widely used by Buddhologists to describe the development of both textual traditions

and sectarian divisions. Note, for example, the neatly branching diagram of the "secessions" from Theravāda given at the beginning of *Points of Controversy, or Subjects of Discourse*, tr. Shwe Zan Aung and Caroline Rhys Davids. The weakness of this paradigm, as Schopen points out, is that it does not account for lateral influence. For a discussion of the tree model and its importance for earlier generations of Orientalists, see Thomas R. Trautmann, *Aryans and British India* (Berkeley: University of California Press, 1997), 7–9, 56–57.

25 Wilhelm Geiger, *Pāli Literature and Language*, trans. Batakrishna Ghosh, 2d ed. (Delhi: Oriental Books Reprint Corporation, 1968), 1–2; idem, *A Pāli Grammar*, trans. Batakrishna Ghosh, and ed. K. R. Norman (Oxford: The Pali Text Society, 1994), 1.

26 A. K. Warder cites L. De La Vallée Poussin, Lin Li-Kouang, J. Bloch, and even Geiger himself; *Pali Metre: A Contribution to the History of Indian Literature* (London: Pali Text Society, 1967), 10. N. A. Jayawickrama, "A Critical Analysis of the Pāli Sutta Nipāta Illustrating its Gradual Growth: General Observations and Conclusions," *University of Ceylon Review* 9 (1951): 122.

27 Warder, *Pali Metre*, v–vii. I confess that I lack the expertise to assess Warder's arguments.

28 K. R. Norman, *Pāli Literature*, Vol. VII, fasc. 2 of *A History of Indian Literature*, ed. Jan Gonda (Wiesbaden: Otto Harrassowitz, 1983), x. In *Studies in the Origins of Buddhism*, G. C. Pande gives a general stratification of the canonical texts, but this study is flawed by its lack of a clearly articulated methodology.

29 On this point, I should explain an ambiguity in my title. The doctrinal developments I discuss in the first half of this book probably occurred prior to the formation of the Theravāda as a distinct form of Buddhism. In fact, the term Theravāda only appears for the first time in inscriptions in the third century CE and in literary sources in the fourth century; Jonathan S. Walters, "Mahāyāna Theravāda and the Origins of the Mahāvihāra," *Sri Lanka Journal of the Humanities* 23 (1997): 105; idem, "Mahāsena at the Mahāvihāra: On the Interpretation and Politics of History in Pre-Colonial Sri Lanka," in *Invoking the Past: The Uses of History in South Asia*, ed. Daud Ali (New Delhi: Oxford University Press, 1999), 322–366; André Bareau, *Les Sectes Bouddhiques du Petit Véhicule* (Paris: École Française d'Extrême-Orient, 1955), 169. Even if we define Theravāda as the school of Buddhism for which the Pāli canon is authoritative, it is doubtful whether we can meaningfully speak of Theravāda prior to the Aluvihāra recension in the first century BCE. Nonetheless, I refer to Theravāda Buddhism in my title because I am primarily interested in doctrinal developments reflected in the scriptures considered authoritative by the Theravādin tradition and in how an understanding of these developments can help us better to understand these texts.

30 John Brough asserts on the basis of comparing different *Dharmapadas* that the early Buddhist poets drew on "a considerable treasure-house of versified tags," or orally transmitted quarter verses. *Gāndhārī Dharmapada* (London: Oxford University Press, 1962), xvii. Noritoshi Aramaki

argues that the oldest Buddhist literature draws on "the old stock of ascetic verses;" "A Text-strata-analytical Interpretation of the Concept "*pañcaskandhas*." *Jimbun* (*The Humanities*) [College of Liberal Arts, Kyoto University] 26 (1980): 1–36. (Aramaki in this article uses differences in how texts treat the topic of the *skandhas* to argue that we can distinguish between at least three stages of development in the Buddhist verse *suttas*, all of which predate the prose treatments of this topic. If we are able to develop a stratification of the Pāli canonical texts, such a project will probably be based on close studies such as these.) In the oral literature of ancient India, the *gāthā* was a common form of epigrammatic verse, which Ludwik Sternbach describes as follows, "Each *gāthā* forms a unity in itself and only in some cases two or three *gāthā*-*s* are combined to constitute a song. Not infrequently a *gāthā* forms an epigram or an aphorism expressing a certain truth in a few words and only rarely a *gāthā* contains well-rounded narrative verses borrowed from another poem or drama." Ludwik Sternbach, *Subhāṣita, Gnomic and Didactic Literature*, Vol. IV, Part 1 of *A History of Indian Literature* ed. Jan Gonda (Wiesbaden: Otto Harrassowitz, 1974), 12.

31 L. S. Cousins, "Pali Oral Literature," in *Buddhist Studies, Ancient and Modern*, ed. A. Piatgorsky and P. T. Denwood (London: Curzon Press, 1983), 1–11; Rupert Gethin, "The *Mātikās:* Memorization, Mindfulness, and the List," in *In the Mirror of Memory*, ed. Janet Gyatso (Albany: State University of New York Press, 1992), 149–172. Paul J. Griffiths, Joy Manné, and Mark Allon have similarly drawn attention to highly stereotyped prose passages that appear repeatedly in the canonical texts: Griffiths discusses short pericopes giving instruction in meditative techniques and Manné and Allon study narrative episodes. Griffiths argues that these passages must have originally been independent pieces of oral tradition, as they are combined in different ways in the *Tipiṭaka* to construct extended lessons in meditation. This may be the case; however, the high degree of similarity between these prose passages indicates that they were standardized while in written form. Griffiths, *Indian Buddhist Meditation-Theory: History, Development, and Systematization* (Ph.D. diss., University of Wisconsin, Madison, 1983); idem, "Buddhist Jhāna: A Form-Critical Study," *Religion* 13 (1983): 55–68; Manné, "Categories of Sutta in the Pāli Nikāyas and their Implications for Our Appreciation of the Buddhist Teaching and Literature," *Journal of the Pali Text Society* 15 (1990): 30–87; Allon, *Style and Function: A Study of the Dominant Stylistic Features of the Prose Portions of the Pāli Canonical Sutta Texts and Their Mnemonic Function*, Studia Philologica Buddhica, Monograph Series XII (Tokyo: The International Institute for Buddhist Studies, 1997).

32 On Sn, see Norman, *The Group of Discourses II*, xxviii; tradition classes the *Jātaka* prose entirely as commentary. On this issue see also Ludwig Alsdorf, "The Ākhyāna Theory Reconsidered," *Journal of the Oriental Institute, Baroda* 13 (1964): 195–207.

33 This list of texts is based on Norman, *Pāli Literature*.

34 N. A. Jayawickrama, "The Sutta Nipāta: Its Title and Form," *University of Ceylon Review* 6 (1948): 82–83.

35 Norman, *Pāli Literature*, 6.

36 This commentary is *Niddesa*. Norman, *Pāli Literature*, 67, 69, 84. J. W. De Jong argues that, despite their apparent antiquity, *Aṭṭhakavagga* and *Pārāyaṇavagga* do not necessarily represent an older form of Buddhist doctrine. Rather, he argues that these verses were shared with other ascetic groups, and "were incorporated much later into the *Khuddaka-nikāya*, the fifth and last collection of the Suttapiṭaka of the Theravādins." J. W. De Jong, *A Brief History of Buddhist Studies in Europe and America* (Tokyo: Kosei Publishing Co., 1997), 97–98. From the fact that some phrases appear in both Buddhist and Jain texts, Hajime Nakamura draws the opposite conclusion, that these expressions probably date from the pre-Aśokan period, when Jainism and Buddhism were not clearly distinct traditions. "Common Elements in Early Jain and Buddhist Literature," *Indologica Taurinensia* 11 (1983): 303–330.

37 "Otherwise than in Jainism where the influx of karma into the soul is the decisive cause of rebirth and suffering, according to the well-known formulas of early Buddhism, namely, the four Noble Truths (*ārya-satya*), suffering, invariably involved with rebirth, is conditioned by craving (*tṛṣṇā*), with no mention of karma. In a similar way, numerous other canonical texts, including passages in old verse collections like *Suttanipāta* (945, 740f) or *Dhammapada* (212–216), declare or presuppose craving, desire (*kāma*), etc. to be the root of misery. Such passages seem to disclose a view according to which karma had no essential, if any, function with regard to rebirth." Lambert Schmithausen, "Critical Response," in *Karma and Rebirth: Post Classical Developments*, ed. Ronald W. Neufeldt (Albany: State University of New York, 1986), 205, notes omitted. As I discuss in chapter 1, Schmithausen also observes that the Aśokan inscriptions contain no karmic language.

38 N. A. Jayawickrama, "A Critical Analysis of the Pāli Sutta Nipāta Illustrating its Gradual Growth: General Observations and Conclusions," *University of Ceylon Review* 9 (1951): 122.

39 Important proponents of this interpretation include: Gananath Obeyesekere, "The Rebirth Eschatology and its Transformations: A Contribution to the Sociology of Early Buddhism," in *Karma and Rebirth in Classical Indian Traditions*, edited by Wendy Doniger O'Flaherty (Berkeley: University of California Press, 1980), 137–164; Richard Gombrich, *Theravada Buddhism: A Social History from Ancient Benares to Modern Colombo* (London: Routledge, 1988), 66–69; idem, *How Buddhism Began: The Conditioned Genesis of the Early Teachings* (London: Athlone, 1996), 31 fn. 7, 51; K. R. Norman, "Theravada Buddhism and brahmanical Hinduism," in *Collected Papers* vol. IV (Oxford: Pali Text Society, 1990), 271, 276; Wilhelm Halbfass, *Tradition and Reflection: Explorations in Indian Thought* (Albany: SUNY Press, 1991), 292.

These positions resemble those expressed by A. B. Keith, Paul Deussen, and other scholars who held that the early *Upaniṣads* marked a radical shift from the view that rebirth is determined by ritual action to the view that morality determines rebirth. Herman Tull critiques this view and argues that the early *Upaniṣads*, like the *Brāhmaṇas*, view only ritual acts as determinative of rebirth. Herman W. Tull, *The Vedic*

Origins of Karma: Cosmos as Man in Ancient Indian Myth and Ritual (Albany: State University of New York Press, 1989), chapter 1. H. W. Bodewitz has responded by providing examples from Vedic literature of moral and immoral actions conditioning rebirth. H. W. Bodewitz, "Non-Ritual Karman in the Veda," in *Chowkhamba Sanskrit Series Office Centenary Commemoration Volume (1892–1992)*, edited by Sudhakar Malaviya (Chowkhamba Sanskrit Series 105, Varanasi: Chowkhamba Sanskrit Series Office, 1993): 221–230.

These scholars have not been incorrect in recognizing that when we compare, e.g., the *Brāhmaṇas* with the Pāli *suttas* we see a shift from a concern with actions that we would typically consider ritual to a concern with actions that we would typically consider ethical. However, these categories are not very helpful, as the opposition of ritual to ethics is a false dichotomy. An injunction that one should perform a certain ritual makes an ethical claim, and ritual performance conditions how one acts in less ritualized spheres. Although rituals may often be performed without thought given to their meaning, it is surely also often the case that the deliberate and intentional performance of ritual acts draws attention to their ethical significance. When Christians wash each other's feet on Maundy Thursday in imitation of Christ's deed, they intend that this rite will inform and transform the ways in which they act toward each other during the rest of the year. (Or at least, that is what Christian theologians would tell us is supposed to happen.) Similarly, as Maria Hibbets argues, almsgiving is an important locus for moral formation in Buddhist, Brahmanical, and Jain traditions, as texts from all of these traditions stress the attitude of esteem that the donor should feel toward the recipient. Maria Hibbets, "The Ethics of Esteem," *Journal of Buddhist Ethics* 7 (2000): 26–42; idem, "Saving Them from Yourself: An Inquiry into the South Asian Gift of Fearlessness," *Journal of Religious Ethics* 27 (1999): 437–469.

Chapter One

1 AV 7.17.4. Translation from Jan Gonda, *The Savayajñas. Verhandlingen den Koninklinjke Nederlandse Akademie van Wetenschappen afd. Letterkunde*, n.s. 71, no. 2 (1965), 186. Gonda states that all of these gods were like Agni thought of as *nidhípatis*, guardians of a treasury of rewards to be given to their supplicants.

2 H. W. Bodewitz, "Life after Death in the Ṛgvedasaṃhitā," *Wiener Zeitschrift für die Kunde Südasiens und Archiv für indische Philosophie* 38 (1994): 23–41; idem, "Yonder World in the Atharvaveda." *Indo-Iranian Journal* 42 (1999): 107–120; idem, "Pits, Pitfalls, and the Underworld in the Veda," *Indo-Iranian Journal* 42 (1999): 211–226.

3 Some texts identify the heaven enjoyed by the blessed dead as the world of the fathers (*pitṛloká*) ruled over by the god Yama. The underworld remains the destiny of those who fail to make sacrificial merits or who do evil. Only a few texts, notably, JB 1.42–44, ŚB 11.6.1.1–13, and AV 5.19.3, describe a place of torment as the destiny of evildoers. (See also the

discussion of the early *Upaniṣads* below.) Bodewitz, "Life after Death," "Yonder World," and "Pits, Pitfalls, and the Underworld in the Veda": 221; Paul Horsch, "Vorstufen der indischen Seelenwanderungslehre," *Asiatische Studien* 25 (1971): 111; Klaus Butzenberger, "Ancient Indian Conceptions on Man's Destiny After Death," *Berliner Indologische Studien* 9 (1996): 106.

4 E.g. AB 7.21, ŚB 13.1.5.6, Gonda, *Savayajñas*, 236–237; Charles Malamoud, "Terminer le Sacrifice," in *Le Sacrifice dans l'Inde Ancienne*, edited by Madeleine Biardeau and Charles Malamoud (Paris: Presses Universitaires de France, 1976), 165–166.

5 *sáṃ gachasva pitŕ̥bhiḥ sáṃyaména iṣṭāpūrténa paramé víoman / hitvā́ 'yāvadyám púnar ástam éhi sáṃ gachasva tanúvā́ suvárcāḥ* / ṚV 10.14.8.

6 *[átha yadvaṣáṭkṛte juhóti / eṣa vaí vaṣaṭkāro yá eṣa tápati sá eṣá mṛtyustádenamupáriṣṭānmṛtyoḥ sáṃskaroti tádenamáto janayati sá etáṃ mṛtyumátimucyate yajño vā́ asyātmā́ bhavati] tád yajñá evá bhūtvaìtán mṛtyumátimucyata eténo hāsya sárve yajñakratáva etám mṛtyumátimuktāḥ // átha yā́metāmā́hutiṃ juhóti / eṣā́ ha vā́ asyā́hutiramúṣmiṃloká ātmā́ bhavati sá / yadaìvaṃvídasmā́llokātpraityáthainameṣā́hutiretásya pṛṣṭhé satyā́hvayatyéhyayaṃ vaí ta'ihā̀tmā̀smī́ti [tadyádāhváyati tásmādāhutirnā́-ma]*.

Bracketed text is left untranslated.

7 For discussions of the *agnicayana*, see Paul Mus, *Barabuḍur: Esquisse d'une histoire du bouddhisme fondée sur la critique archéologique des textes* (Hanoi: Imprimerie d'Extrême-Orient, 1935), preface; Frits Staal, *Agni: The Vedic Ritual of the Fire Altar* (Berkeley: Asian Humanities Press, 1983); and Herman W. Tull, *The Vedic Origins of Karma: Cosmos as Man in Ancient Indian Myth and Ritual* (Albany: State University of New York, 1989), chap. 3.

8 6.1.2.17–19; 10.1.4.2–8. The text presents a number of apparently contradictory interpretations, thus we also find correspondences based on six seasons and 13 months in a year (6.4.2.10; 6.6.3.16 and 6.7.1.28).

9 *sá eténa kármaṇaitáyāvŕ̥taikadhā̀járamamŕ̥tamātmā́naṃ kurute* 10.1.4.1; cf. 10.4.2.31, and Jan Gonda, *Loka: World and Heaven in the Veda*, *Verhandlingen den Koninklinjke Nederlandse Akademie van Wetenschappen afd. Letterkunde*, n.s. 73, no. 1 (1966), 101.

10 See Gonda, *Loka*, 115ff. The opposites of these terms, *duṣkṛt-* and *duṣkṛta-*, are also attested.

11 On these uses of *puṇya*, see Gonda, *Loka*, 53, 120, 129–131, 148–9; Manfred Mayrhofer, *Etymologisches Wörterbuch des Altindoarischen* (Heidelberg: Carl Winter Universitätsverlag, 1986-), 2:139–140; Jean Filliozat, "Sur le domain sémantique de *puṇya*," in *Indianisme et Bouddhisme: Mélanges offerts à Msgr. Étienne Lamotte* (Louvain-la-Neuve: Institut Orientaliste, 1980), 101–116. *Pāpa* is used to refer to bad actors, acts, and effects.

12 Gonda, *Loka*, 133.

13 The only example of which I am aware is BĀU 4.4.6. Apart from its use of this term, this passage is typical of Vedic treatments of the effects of action, in that *karman* is here said to accompany the actor to heaven but not to condition his human rebirth.

14 . . . *ehy ehīti tam āhutayaḥ suvarcasaḥ sūryasya raśmibhir yajamānaṃ vahanti / priyāṃ vācam abhivadantyo 'rcayantya eṣa vaḥ puṇyaḥ sukṛto brahmalokaḥ*. *Brahmaloka*, or 'world of Brahman,' combines two multivalent terms. *Loka* has a wide range of meanings in Vedic as well as in Pāli, and can indicate a place or a status. Gonda defines *loka* in this context as "the sphere, situation, or plane of existence in which the religious, i.e. first and foremost the ritual, merits of the Aryan who strictly and punctually discharges his sacrificial obligations are accumulated, or which may be said to be produced by the continuous and dutiful performance of the rites which are incumbent upon him." *Loka*, 115. *Brahman* orginally denoted the power of Vedic ritual and of the Brāhmaṇ class which possesses it, and with the *Upaniṣads* came to signify the ultimate reality of the universe.

15 Patrick Olivelle, *Upaniṣads* (New York: Oxford University Press, 1996): xliv; J. C. Heesterman, "Reflections on the Significance of the *Dákṣiṇā*," *Indo-Iranian Journal* 3 (1959): 244. Cf. TS 6.1.3.6, MS 3.6.8, KS 23.4, and ŚB 9.4.1.11. This couple is in these passages presented as the parents of Indra. Dakṣiṇā is also presented as the mother of Agni at ṚV 3.58.1, 5.1.3, and 8.39.5.

16 *daívi pūrtír dákṣiṇā devayajyā́*.

17 ŚB 4.3.4.4; Jan Gonda, *Change and Continuity in Indian Religion* (The Hague: Mouton & Co., 1965), 203 gives several citations, including AV 5.11.11, TS 1.7.3.1, MS 1.4.6, ŚB 2.2.2.6–7. Brian K. Smith, *Classifying the Universe: The Ancient Indian Varṇa System and the Origins of Caste* (New York: Oxford University Press, 1994), 54 n. 51 also gives a number of references to Brāhmaṇs as gods.

18 Heesterman, *Broken World*, 35; ĀpŚS 10.1.13.

19 *dvayā vaí devā́ devāḥ / áhaivá devā átha yé brāhmaṇāḥ śruśruvā́ṃso 'nūcānāsté manuṣyadevāstéṣāṃ dvedhā́ vibhaktá evá yajña ā́hutaya evá devā́nāṃ dákṣiṇā manuṣyadevā́nām*; cited in Smith, *Classifying the Universe*, 34.

20 ŚB 4.3.4.32 (*táddevátāyā átidiśati*); see Julius Eggeling, trans., *The Satapatha Brâhmana According to the Mâdhyandina School* (Oxford: Clarendon Press, 1900; reprint, Delhi: Motilal Banarsidass, 1966), 2: 349, n. 1); TB 2.2.5.1 (*vyāvṛtya*); see also Heesterman, *Inner Conflict* 37.

21 Smith, *Classifying the Universe*, 34.

22 *tatra pitaro devatā brāhmaṇās tv āhavanīya-arthe*, ĀpDhS 2.16.3, Olivelle's translation, with modification of spelling. Cf. Manu 3.74.

23 The *śrauta* rites are the solemn rites believed to be enjoined by the Vedas, or *śrūti*. The *gṛhya* rites, by contrast, involved a single domestic fire and were considered part of *smārta* tradition: authoritative but not explicitly enjoined by the Vedas. On this distinction see Gonda, *The Ritual Sūtras*, Vol. I, fasc. 2 of *A History of Indian Literature*, ed. Jan Gonda (Wiesbaden: Otto Harrassowitz, 1975), 468, and Sheldon Pollock, "From Discourse of Ritual to Discourse of Power in Sanskrit Culture," *Journal of Ritual Studies* 4 (1990): 322–328.

24 ŚB 2.3.3.10; Patrick Olivelle, *The Saṃnyāsa Upaniṣads* (New York: Oxford University Press, 1992), 25; H. W. Bodewitz, *The Daily Evening and Morning Offering (*Agnihotra*) According to the* Brāhmaṇas (Leiden: E.

J. Brill, 1976), 125. The *agnihotra* was also identified with more elaborate sacrifices. The *gṛhya* rites included a version of the *agnihotra*, and so many not qualified to perform the *śrauta* rite performed a similar ritual.

25 *na rājanyasyāgnihotram, asya vratyo hi, sa hanti. vratam na vicchindyāt, paurṇamāsīṃ ca rātrīm amāvāsyāṃ ca juhuyāt, te hi vrataṃ gopāyato. yāny ahāni na juhuyāt tāny asya brāhmaṇāyāgre gṛha upahareyur, agnir vai brāhmaṇo, 'gnā eva taj juhoti, tad asya svaditam eṣṭaṃ bhavati.* KS 6.6.8. Translation based on Bodewitz, *Daily Evening and Morning Offering*, 116, and Navathe, 42–43. This passage is paralleled in MS 1.8.7 (Ibid., 116–117), but Bodewitz thinks that this passage is a careless reworking of the KS passage.

26 ŚB 1.1.1.1–11; Sukumar Dutt, *Early Buddhist Monachism* (revised edition, Bombay: Asia Publishing House, 1960), 82.

27 Cf. also ĀpDhS 1.3.43–44: "Almsfood is hailed as a sacrificial oblation at which the teacher plays the roles of the deity and the sacrificial fire." Patrick Olivelle, tr., *Dharmasūtras: The Law Codes of Ancient India* (Oxford: Oxford University Press, 1999), 11.

28 Richard Gombrich, *Theravada Buddhism: A Social History from Ancient Benares to Modern Colombo* (London: Routledge, 1988), 76; Melford E. Spiro, *Buddhism and Society: A Great Tradition and its Burmese Vicissitudes* (second edition, Berkeley: University of California Press, 1982), 46.

29 Although giving *dāna* and observing the Uposatha are the most important means of making merit, some didactic verses mention others. For example, a few *gāthās* recommend serving one's husband (e.g. A III 38).

30 *Juhāmi dakkhiṇeyy'aggiṃ, namassāmi Tathāgataṃ*. Thag 343cd. Tathāgata is a title of the Buddha. Similarly: *arahā dakkhiṇeyyomhi* Thag 296, 336, 516; *yassa te āsavā khīṇā, dakkhiṇeyyosi* Thag 629, 1179.

31 *āhuneyyo vedagu bhāvitatto / narānaṃ devānañca dakkhiṇeyyo* / S I 141.

32 *puññaṃ ākaṅkhamānānaṃ saṅgho ve yajatam mukhan / ti* // Vin I 246=M II 146= Sn 569b.

33 *Viceyyadānam sugatappasatthaṃ / ye dakkhiṇeyyā idha jīvaloke / etesu dinnāni mahapphalāni / bījāni vuttāni yathā sukkhette / ti* // S I 21, Ja III 472. 'Sugata' is an epithet of the Buddha.

34 "*. . . puññakkhettam anuttaraṃ / āyāgo sabbalokassa, bhoto dinna mahapphalan*" / Sn 486. Cf. S I 220, A II 35, III 36, 43, It 88, Thag 1177. When in this book I attribute words to the Buddha I mean only that a text attributes those words to the Buddha. It lies beyond the scope of historical study to determine what Gotama actually taught.

35 "*Sekho asekho ca imasmiṃ loke, / āhuneyyā yajamānānaṃ honti; / te ujjubhūtā kāyena, vācāya uda cetasā / khettaṃ taṃ yajamānānaṃ, ettha dinnaṃ mahapphalan*" *ti*. A I 63 CS.

36 *tuvaṃ h'etaṃ pajānāsi puññakkhettaṃ anuttaraṃ / amhaṃ pi ete samaṇā paṭigaṇhanti dakkhiṇaṃ / paṭiṭṭhito h'ettha yañño vipulo no bhavissati* / Thīg 287.

37 *Yajamānānaṃ manussānaṃ puññapekkhānaṃ pāṇinaṃ / karotaṃ opadhikaṃ puññaṃ saṅghe dinnaṃ mahapphalan / ti* // S I 233, A IV 293.

38 *ye naṃ dadanti saddhāya vippasannena cetasā* S I 32, 57, 58, 59; *saddho muttena cetasā* A II 44, III 337, IV 244.

39 Köhler, Hans-Werbin, Śrad-dhā- *in der vedischen und altbuddhistischen Literatur* (Wiesbaden: Franz Steiner Verlag, 1973); Jan Gonda, *Les Religions de l'Inde,* trans. L. Jospin (Paris: Payot, 1979), I:59; idem, "'Gifts' and 'Giving' in the Ṛgveda,'" 142–143; Stephanie W. Jamison, *Sacrificed Wife/Sacrificer's Wife: Women, Ritual, and Hospitality in Ancient India* (New York: Oxford University Press, 1996), 176–178.

40 *"Pubbeva dānā sumano, dadaṃ cittaṃ pasādaye; / datvā attamano hoti, esā yaññassa sampadā. / "Vītarāgā vītadosā, vītamohā anāsavā; / khettaṃ yaññassa sampannaṃ, saññatā brahmacārayo / "Sayaṃ ācamayitvāna, datvā sakehi pāṇibhi; / attano parato ceso, yañño hoti mahapphalo. / "Evaṃ yajitvā medhāvi, saddho muttena cetasā; / abyāpajjaṃ sukhaṃ lokaṃ, paṇḍito upapajjatī" ti.* A III 337 CS. In Pāli, *brahmacariya* and *brahmacārin* denote monastic life, especially celibacy. A IV 244 similarly states that one should give generously and without regret.

41 *vippasannamanā* A III 41; *cittaṃ pasādayaṃ* A III 354; *agge buddhe pasannānaṃ dakkhiṇeyye anuttare // agge dhamme pasannānaṃ virāgūpasame sukhe / agge saṅghe pasannānaṃ puññakkhette anuttare //* A II 35, III 36, It 88–89; *Saddhā hiriyaṃ* A IV 236; *mettaṃ cittaṃ bhāvayaṃ appamāṇaṃ* Sn 507; *medhāvī . . . paṇḍito* A II 44, III 337, IV 244; *sappaññā vadaññū vītamaccharā* A III 41; *Ettha patiṭṭhāya jahāti dosaṃ. / So vītarāgo pavineyya dosaṃ* Sn 506–507; *Dadāti seṭṭhasaṅkappo avyaggamanaso naro* A I 129; *sīlūpapannā* I 294, *sīlavā* A I 215, IV 255, 258 *aggamhi khettamhi pasannacitto, viññū pajānaṃ ko na yajetha kāle* It 98.

42 Almost all didactic *gāthā*s containing the word *puñña* are of the sacrificial type; I discuss the few exceptions to this generalization below and in chapter 2.

43 I have found only one didactic verse that describes acts themselves as *puñña*: S I 97 employs the compound *puññakammā*, 'those whose actions are meritorious;' this compound could also mean, 'those whose actions lead to merit' and 'those whose actions produce merit.'

44 *pekkha:* S I 167, 168, 173, 233, A IV 292, Sn 82, 463–466, 481, 487–489, 490–503, Dhp 108; *attho* Vin II 147, D II 355, A III 213, Sn 431, 487–489, Ud 30; *kāma:* Vin I 294, S II 198, V 402; *ākaṅkhā* Vin I 246 = M II 146 = Sn 569; (cf. S I 18, 20: see discussion below).

45 *Labhati:* Dhp 309–310; *puññavant-:* M II 131; *cīyate:* Sn 428, *upacita:* S I 92, Sn 697; *uccaya:* Dhp 118; *nicaya:* S I 72, 93; *sañcaya:* Sn 697; *nidhi:* Khp VIII; *patheyya:* Dhp 235; *dīpa:* Dhp 236.

46 S V 400, A II 55, A III 336, Dhp 196; Dhp 122.

47 S I 72; Dhp 220.

48 *upakāra* A III 32–34; *mitta* S I 37; *patiṭṭha* S I 18, 20, 32, 57, 58, 59, 72, 97, A III 41.

49 S I 2, 3, 55, 63; A I 155.

50 A I 161, Dhp 122.

51 Also *puññabhagin-* and *puññābhāgin*: D II 218, M III 72–74, S I 154, A III 41, 411, 412, 414. *Puññabhaga,* meaning 'fortunate,' corresponds to an older Vedic meaning of *bhaga*; cf. *dubbhaga,* It 90, and *bhagavān.*

52 S I 233 and A IV 292–293, It 19, 20, 78. O. H. Pind, "*opadhika,*" CPD I 736. Pind notes that *opadhika* has traditionally been understood to mean

merit leading to rebirth, but that "this interpretation is clearly contradicted by the canonical usage."

53 *agge buddhe pasannānaṃ dakkhiṇeyye anuttare // agge dhamme pasannānaṃ virāgūpasame sukhe / agge saṅghe pasannānaṃ puññakkhette anuttare // aggasmiṃ dānaṃ dadataṃ aggaṃ puññaṃ pavaḍḍhati / aggaṃ āyu ca vaṇṇo ca yaso kitti sukhaṃ balaṃ //* A II 35, III 36, It 88–89. Other passages which speak of merit growing include D II 136, III 58, 79, S I 33, A III 354, IV 285, 325.

54 *nirayaṃ, saggaṃ* It 59–60.

55 *nirayaṃ, bhaddakaṃ ṭhānaṃ* A I 129.

56 *apāyaṃ, sagge* A II 4–5.

57 *yamalokañ ca imaṃ sadevakaṃ*. The world of the Yāma deities which usually appears just above the Tāvatiṃsa deities in later lists of the heavens is a legacy of this positive evaluation of the Yamaloka as a celestial paradise.

58 Maurice Walshe finds it doubtful that *niraya* originally meant 'hell,' and Tilmann Vetter asserts that the earliest Buddhist belief included an idea of an underworld, but not of a hell. Walshe, *Thus Have I Heard: The Long Discourses of the Buddha* (London: Wisdom Publications, 1987), 558; Vetter, *Ideas and Meditative Practices*, 79. Some narrative verse texts, including *Kokāliya Sutta* (Sn III.10) and *Nimi Jātaka* (no. 541) develop within a sacrificial-purificatory framework a vision of the *niraya*s as places of torment.

59 *gabbhā gabbhaṃ tamā tamaṃ*.

60 ChU 5.10.8; BĀU 6.2.16 states that those who know neither the path of austerity nor of sacrifice are reborn as worms, insects, or snakes.

61 A II 35, A III 36, and It 88–89 discussed above; also S I 87, 89, A III 48–49, It 16.

62 At least three passages could be taken as exceptions to this generalization. At S I 154 a verse that refers to birth as an animal is followed by one that refers to merit, but this latter couplet also appears in a different context at D II 218. That this verse about merit is found elsewhere suggests that these two verses probably did not originally form a unit, but that the merit verse was incorporated into a later composition. Similarly, A III 354 contains a verse that refers to going to a womb, and another about merit, but the latter verse also appears elsewhere (A IV 285, 322, 325). A long set of verses at A III 213–214 contains references to merit and to birth in a family, but this set is also a composite, as the second half appears also at A I 162. In addition, this passage does not speak of human birth as a reward, but as a precondition for the attainment of nirvāṇa.

63 I refer here to the five *Upaniṣad*s that Olivelle claims are probably pre-Buddhist: he places *Bṛhadāraṇyaka* and *Chāndogya* at approximately one or two centuries before the Buddha, and *Taittirīya*, *Aitareya*, and *Kauṣītaki* about a century later. Patrick Olivelle, "Introduction," *Upaniṣads* (New York: Oxford University Press, 1996), xxxvi–xxxvii.

64 *yajñena dānena tapasā; lokān* BĀU 6.2.16; *iṣṭāpūrte dattam; pitṛlokam* ChU 5.10.3–4; translations by Olivelle.

65 Wilhelm Halbfass, *Tradition and Reflection: Explorations in Indian Thought* (Albany: SUNY Press, 1991), 325. KṣU 1.2 states that people

return to earth in the rain and are reborn according to their action and knowledge. It does not tell how souls reach the appropriate fathers but implies that the moon somehow directs this process. In this verse we can see the beginnings of the idea that past actions condition rebirth as a human being.

66 One Pāli narrative verse includes expressions found in the descriptions of the ultimate goal in both ChU and BĀU: "Having ascended to the way to the gods, the stainless great path, / Having abandoned desire and passion, he went to the Brahmaloka(s);" *so devayānam āruyha, virajaṃ so mahāpathaṃ, / kāmarāgaṃ virājetvā brahmalokūpago ahu,— /* Sn 139a-d. Although other Pāli passages present the Brahmalokas as heavens within *saṃsāra*, references in this verse to the "stainless great path" and to abandoning desire and passion suggest that Brahmaloka here designates the ultimate soteriological goal, as it does in BĀU.

67 A few examples from Dhp: *rāga* (passion) 99, 273, 369, 377; *ādāna* (attachment) 89, 421; *upādā* (clinging) 89, 414; *taṇhā* (thirst) 416; *ejā* (desire) 422; *dosa* (hatred) 369, 377; *kodha* (anger) 400; *raja* (defilement) 386; *āsavas* ('oozings') 89, 93, 226.

68 Steven Collins shows that the original sense of *nibbāṇa/nirvāṇa* is 'extinguishing.' *Nirvana and other Buddhist felicities: Utopias of the Pali imaginaire* (Cambridge: Cambridge University Press, 1998), chapter 2.

69 For this observation I am indebted to Schmithausen, "Critical Response," 205. See chapter 2 for discussion.

70 *pahāya* Sn 520, *puññapāpapahīnassa* Dhp 39; *bāhetvā* Dhp 267, *bāhitvā* S I 182. At Ud 21 we find similarly, *sabbakammajahassa bhikkhuno dhunamānassa purekataṃ rajaṃ*, "for a monk who rejects all 'karma' and shakes off the dust made in the past (or the dust of past deeds)." This verse is an exception to my generalization that *kamma* is not used to refer to the effects of past action in the didactic verse literature. Enomoto Fumio points out that Chinese and Tibetan versions of the parallel passage in *Udānavarga* indicate that their Sanskrit original read **sarvakāmajahasya*. Enomoto Fumio, "On the Annihilation of *Karman* in Early Buddhism," *Transactions of the International Conference of Orientalists in Japan* 34 (1989): 44. If the original version of this verse referred to *kāma* rather than *kamma*, then this anomaly would be explained.

71 *Yo 'dha puññañ ca pāpañ ca ubho saṅgam upaccagā, / asokaṃ virajaṃ suddhaṃ tam ahaṃ brūmi brāhmaṇaṃ. //* M II 196, Dhp 412, Sn 636, following Norman's translations. S I 182 = Dhp 267 are similar. A number of sacrificial verses appropriate the term *brāhmaṇa* as a designation for praiseworthy individuals. K. R. Norman discusses this and many more examples of appropriated Vedic terminology in Theravādin literature in "Theravāda Buddhism and brahmanical Hinduism," *Collected Papers* (Oxford: Pali Text Society, 1993), vol. IV, 271–280.

72 *Puṇḍarīkaṃ yathā vaggu toye na upalippati, / evaṃ puññe ca pāpe ca ubhaye tvaṃ na lippasi: /* Sn 547, translation by Norman.

73 *puññe ca pāpe anūpalitto attañjaho na-y-idha pakubbamāno.* Sn 790cd, translation by Norman.

74 Sn 714. Norman offers two alternative explanations for this verse, but neither of these seems to me persuasive. *The Group of Discourses II*,

285–286. Norman translates this verse as, "For high and low are the paths proclaimed by the ascetic. They do not go to the far shore twice; this is not experienced once." The expression *uccāvaca-* also appears at Sn 792, but this verse does not shed much light on v. 714.

75 The meaning of *muta* is not entirely clear; PED takes it to denote the senses of touch, taste, and smell. In any case, other Sn verses indicate that nirvāṇa cannot be *muta* (793, 812, 901, 914; cf. 798, 887, 1086, 1122).

76 *abhisaṅkhataṃ nirārambhaṃ yaññaṃ kālena kapiyaṃ / tādisaṃ upasaṃyanti saññatā brahmacariyā / vivattacchadā ye loke vītavattakālaṃgatī / yaññaṃ etaṃ pasaṃsanti buddhā puññassako vidā* / yaññe vā yadi vā saddhe bhavyaṃ* katvā yathārahaṃ / pasannacitto yajati sukhette brahmacārisu / suhutaṃ suyiṭṭhaṃ suppattaṃ dakkhiṇeyyesu yaṃ kataṃ / yañño ca vipulo hoti pasīdanti ca devatā / evaṃ yajitvā medhāvī saddho muttena cetasā / avyāpajjhaṃ sukhaṃ lokaṃ paṇḍito upapajjatī / ti //* A II 43–44. Translation based on that of F. L. Woodward. I follow Woodward in reading *havyaṃ* for text's *bhavyaṃ*, and *puññassa kovidā* for *puññassako vidā*. In reference to the second to last line, Woodward notes, "There seems to be a play on the words, contrasting *medha, medhāvī; saddha, shraddha*." The similarity between these words may be significant, but nothing in these lines suggests that these terms are being contrasted. Rather, these verses present sacrifice as congruent with faith and intelligence.

77 *yaññakāle* Sn 482; *kālena* A II 43–44, IV 244, Sn 490–503; *kāle* A III 41, It 98.

78 Cf. also S I 172–173, 174–175.

79 E.g., A I 165, Sn 647, and Dhp 423.

80 *Mā brāhmaṇa dāru samādahāno suddhim amaññi bahiddhā hi etaṃ / na hi tena suddhiṃ kusalā vadanti yo bāhirena parisuddhim icche / Hitvā ahaṃ brāhmaṇa dārudāhaṃ ajjhattam eva jalayāmi jotiṃ / niccagginī niccasamāhitatto arahaṃ ahaṃ brahmacariyaṃ carāmi. //* S I 169.

81 *kālena tesu havyaṃ pavecche, yo brāhmaṇo puññapekkho yajetha.* Sn 464cd, 465cd, 466cd; similarly 463cd.

82 *"Buddho bhavaṃ arahati pūraḷāsaṃ puññakkhettam anuttaraṃ / āyāgo sabbalokassa, bhoto dinnaṃ mahapphalaṇ" / ti. //* Sn 486.

83 *"Pucchām' aham bho Gotamaṃ vadaññuṃ / iti Māgho māṇavo / kāsāyavāsiṃ agihaṃ carantaṃ: / yo yācayogo dānapati gahaṭṭho / puññatthiko yajati puññapekho / dadaṃ paresaṃ idha annapānaṃ, / kattha hutaṃ yajamānassa sujjhe." // "Yo yācayogo dānapatī gahaṭṭho / Māghā ti Bhagavā / puññatthiko yajati puññapekho / dadaṃ paresaṃ idha annapānaṃ, / ārādhaye dakkhiṇeyyehi tādi."* / Sn 487–488, translation based on Norman's.

84 P. V. Kane, *History of Dharmaśāstra*, IV: 309–333. Similarly to this Sn passage, BDhS 1.10.4–8 argues that a sacrificer's *śraddhā* purifies his offering.

85 Sn 490–503. The refrain of these verses is the same as that of Sn 464–466.

86 *yo yajati tividhaṃ yaññasampadaṃ* Sn 509. The meaning of threefold here is unclear; the commentary states that it refers to the donor's thoughts before, during, and after giving.

87 *Pāṇaṃ na hane, na cādinnam ādiye, / musā na bhāse, na ca majjapo siyā, / abrahmacariyā virameyya methunā, / rattiṃ na bhuñjeyya vikālabhojanaṃ, // mālaṃ na dhāraye na ca gandham ācare, / mañce chamāyaṃ va sayetha santhate,— / etaṃ hi aṭṭhaṅgikam āh' uposathaṃ / Buddhena dukkhanta-gunā pakāsitaṃ.* // A I 214–215, IV 254, 257–258, Sn 400–401.

88 *Tasmā hi nārī ca naro ca sīlavā / aṭṭhaṅgupetaṃ upavass' uposathaṃ / puññāni katvāna sukhudrayāni / aninditā saggam upenti ṭhānan / ti.* // A I 215, IV 255, 258.

89 For a comparison of this list with another definition of *dasa sīla*, see chapter 2.

90 Hermann Jacobi, Introduction to *Jaina Sūtras: Part I* (Delhi: Motilal Banarsidass, 1964), xxii-xxiv. Jacobi points out that Weber and Windisch notice the close similarities between the vows undertaken by these three groups and establish that there must be a historical relationship between them.

91 For examples see "*Sīla*," PED, and ibid. s. v. *sīlabbataparāmāsa* (the third of the ten fetters (*saṃyojanāni*)) and *sīlabbatupādāna*. Stede writes, "The old form **sīlavata** still preserves the original good sense, as much as 'observing the rules of good conduct.'" Hajime Nakamura observes that other religious groups, including Jains, used *sīlabbata* to mean ascetic disciplines, and he argues that Buddhists stopped using this term when they adopted the term *pātimokkha*. "Common Elements in Early Jain and Buddhist Literature," *Indologica Taurinensia* 11 (1983): 314.

92 Durkheim, *Elementary Forms*, 347.

93 The practices discussed in these verses are often refered to as merit transfer, but this label is inaccurate because what is transfered is not merit, but the material offering. For references to secondary literature, see my discussion of this topic in subsequent chapters.

94 Another possible example is *Therīgāthā* 291–311, where a man leaving the mother of his child in order to go forth in the presence of the Buddha is asked by her to dedicate a gift in the presence of the Buddha, and does so. The phrases used are "*ādiseyyāsi dakkhiṇaṃ*," "*ādisissāmi dakkhiṇaṃ*," and "*Cāpāya ādisitvāna*" (307, 308, 311). This final phrase might be taken to mean that he dedicated the gift to Cāpā, but this elliptical phrase could also mean that he designated her gift, or that he designated a gift on her behalf.

95 Peter Masefield, Boris Oguibénine, Lambert Schmithausen, and David White have all noted the close similarity between Brahmanical sacrifice and the Buddhist dedication of dakṣiṇā. Peter Masefield, "Translator's Introduction," *Elucidation of the Intrinsic Meaning: so Named the Commentary on the Vimāna Stories (Paramattha-dīpanī nāma Vimānavatthu-aṭṭhakathā)*, translated by Peter Masefield, assisted by N. A. Jayawickrama (Oxford: Pali Text Society, 1989) xix-lvii; Boris Oguibénine, "La Dakṣiṇā dans le Ṛgveda et le Transfert de Mérite dans le Bouddhisme," in *Indological and Buddhist Studies: Volume in Honour of Professor J. W. de Jong on his Sixtieth Birthday*, edited by L. A. Hercus et al. (Canberra: Faculty of Asian Studies, 1982), 393–414.; Lambert Schmithausen, "Critical Response"; David Gordon White, "*Dakkhiṇa* and *Agnicayana*: An Extended Application of Paul Mus' Typology," *History of Religions* 26 (1986): 188–213.

96 *yasmiṃ padese kappeti vāsaṃ paṇḍitajātiyo / sīlavant' ettha bhojetvā saññate brahmacariye / yā tattha devatā āsuṃ tāsaṃ dakkhiṇam ādise, / tā pujitā pūjayanti mānitā mānayanti naṃ. / tato naṃ anukampanti mātā puttaṃ va orasaṃ, / devatānukampito poso sadā bhadrāni [sic] passatī / ti* // My translation is based on Masefield's translation of Ud 89.

The idiomatic phrase, "beholds auspicious things," "*bhaddāni passati*," is also found in Dhp 120: Even a good person sees evil as long as good does not ripen; if good ripens then he sees good things. *bhaddo pi passati pāpaṃ yāva bhadda na paccati / yadā ca paccati bhaddam bhaddo bhaddāni passati* // Dhp 119 is identical but with *bhadda* and *pāpa* reversed.

97 ŚB uses ā + √diś with dakṣiṇā (4.3.4.32) and oblations (1.1.2.18–19, 1.1.4.24) to denote the dedication of an offering for a particular deity; see also Schmithausen, "Critical Response," 225. The terms *ekoddiṣṭa* and *ekānudiṣṭa*, "dedicated to one," are names for a śrāddha rite performed for a recently deceased person.

98 Schopen cites Sanskrit Buddhist texts in which the dedication seems to be performed not by the donor but by the monks who chant verses (as a benediction or expression of appreciation). Schopen, "On Avoiding Ghosts," 30–31, note 43; idem, "The Ritual Obligations and Donor Roles of Monks in the Pāli Vinaya," *Journal of the Pali Text Society* 16 (1992): 101–102. This practice would actually conform better to the Vedic pattern, in which the recipient passes on the dakṣiṇā. (The expression *dakkhiṇā* + Ö*dis* also sometimes refers to the designation of certain monastics to receive a gift on behalf of the Saṅgha as a whole.)

99 *Khettūpamā arahanto dāyakā kassakūpamā / bījūpamaṃ deyyadhammaṃ etto nibattate phalaṃ. // Etaṃ bījaṃ kasī khettaṃ petānaṃ dāyakassa ca, / taṃ petā paribhuñjanti dātā puññena vaḍḍhati. // Idh' eva kusalaṃ katvā pete ca paṭipūjiya / saggañ ca kamati ṭṭhānaṃ kammaṃ katvāna bhaddakan / ti.* //

100 *1. Tirokuḍḍesu tiṭṭhanti sandhisiṅghāṭakesu ca / dvārabāhāsu tiṭṭhanti āgantvāna sakaṃ gharaṃ. // 2. Pahūte annapānamhi khajjabhojje upaṭṭhite / na tesaṃ koci sarati sattānaṃ kammapaccayā. // 3. Evaṃ dadanti ñātīnaṃ ye honti anukampakā / suciṃ paṇītaṃ kālena kappiyaṃ pānabhojanaṃ: / idaṃ vo ñātīnaṃ hotu sukhitā hontu ñātayo. // 4. Te ca tattha samāgantvā ñātipetā samāgatā / pahūte annapānamhi sakkaccaṃ anumodare. // 5. Ciraṃ jīvantu no ñātī yesaṃ hetu labhāmase / amhākañ ca katā pūjā dāyakā ca anipphalā. // 6. Na hi tattha kasī atthi gorakkh' ettha na vijjati / vaṇijjā tādisī natthi haraññena kayakkayaṃ, / ito dinnena yāpenti petā kālakatā tahiṃ. // 7. Unname udakaṃ vuṭṭhaṃ yathā ninnaṃ pavattati / evam eva ito dinnaṃ petānaṃ upakappati. // 8. Yathā vārivahā pūrā paripūrenti sāgaraṃ / evaṃ eva ito dinnaṃ petānaṃ upakappati. // 9. Adāsi me akāsi me ñātimittā sakhā ca me / petānaṃ dakkhiṇaṃ dajjā pubbe katam anussaraṃ. // 10. Na hi ruṇṇaṃ va soko vā yā c'aññā paridevanā / na taṃ petānam atthāya evaṃ tiṭṭhanti ñātayo. // 11. Ayañ ca kho dakkhiṇā dinnā saṅghamhi suppatiṭṭhitā / dīgharattaṃ hitāy' assa ṭhānaso upakappati. // 12. So ñātidhammo ca ayaṃ nidassito / petānaṃ pūjā ca katā uḷarā / balañ ca bhikkhūnam anuppadinnaṃ / tumhehi puññaṃ pasutaṃ anappakan / ti.* //

Stede holds that verses 10 and 11 appear to have been added to an older work. Wilhelm Stede, *Über das Peta Vatthu* (Inaugural diss., University of Leipzig, 1914), 63. Gombrich agrees, and further asserts that verses 1–10 contain no trace of Buddhism, and appear to have originally referred to food offerings given directly to the dead, rather than to *saddha* offerings mediated by the Saṅgha. Richard Gombrich, "Merit Transference in Sinhalese Buddhism: A Case Study of the Interaction between Doctrine and Practice," *History of Religions* 11 (1971): 212. However, the word *dakkhiṇā* in verse 9 clearly refers to giving to clergy thought of as sacrifice.

101 ŚB 2.4.2.19 gives the words, "This [is] for you," "*ásāv etát te*," as the *tyāga* formula for the *piṇḍapitṛyajña* rite. The general form of the renunciatory formula for sacrifice to the gods is, "This is for Agni, not for me" (*agnaye idaṃ na mama*); Frits Staal, *Agni: The Vedic Ritual of the Fire Altar* (Berkeley: Asian Humanities Press, 1983), I: 4–5, 41.

102 In this *sutta*, the word *peta* does not denote a distinct class of being, but simply means departed or dead. The departed are also called *kalakatā*, "dead," (literally, "[having] done [their] time"), and they are called "*peta*" even after receiving dakṣiṇā.

103 Schopen suggests that these usages may reflect "the influence of continental sources on canonical Pāli." Gregory Schopen, "On Avoiding Ghosts and Social Censure: Monastic Funerals in the Mūlasarvāstivāda-Vinaya," *Journal of Indian Philosophy* 20 (1992): 30–31, note 43.

104 A III 34, 43; other examples include A III 40, 41, 42, 44, 78, IV 244, and It 98. The composition and performance of such verses have a cultural precedent in the *dānastuti*, the Vedic poet's hymn in praise of a generous patron.

105 That Buddhists could have chosen another means of giving offerings to deities and to the dead is shown by references in canonical verse to offerings not mediated by monastics. In *Ratana Sutta* (Sn 223, Khp VI), the Buddha exhorts beings (*bhūtāni*) dwelling on earth and in the sky to protect and show lovingkindness (*metta*) toward human beings who day and night bring them *bali*. *Bali* cannot here mean dedicated gifts, as dakṣiṇā is normally given in the morning when monks and nuns make their rounds. *Bali* instead refers to offerings that are scattered and thereby offered directly to beings. *Bali* is given to the dead and to minor deities in both Buddhist and Vedic traditions. A II 68 and III 45 list five kinds of *bali* to be given by a householder: to kinsmen, guests, dead persons, kings, and deities. *Bali* given to human recipients is hospitality, taxes, and so forth, but the dead and deities are given scattered offerings. Kane discusses a number of Vedic texts that prescribe giving *bali*, including ŚB 11.5.61, TĀ 2.10, and ĀśvGS 3.1.1–4 (*History of Dharmśāstra* II 696ff.). Cf. also Manu 3.69–74. *Bali* offerings are still made by Sri Lankan Buddhists; see Michael M. Ames, "Ritual Prestations and the Structure of the Sinhalese Pantheon," in *Anthropological Studies in Theravada Buddhism*, ed. Manning Nash et al. (Yale University, 1966), 27–50; and Gombrich, *Precept and Practice*, 208, 212.

106 E.g. Sn 249, Thag 341. In D I 9 and 67, the *agnihotra* is included in a list of base arts (*tiracchanavijjā*). Animal sacrifice, by contrast, receives only

harsh censure in early Theravādin texts E.g. A II 42–43, IV 41–46. M III 167–168 presents a harshly satirical attack on animal sacrifice, stating that priests who run after the smell of offerings in search of food will be reborn as animals who follow the odor of dung to find their meals.

107 *aggihuttamukhā yaññā* Vin I 246, M II 146, Sn 568. Utt 25.16 similarly calls the *agnihotra* the best of the Vedas (*aggihuttamuhā veyā*).

108 As Patrick Olivelle has shown, in the *Dharmasūtras* of the last half-millenium BCE *brahmacariya* and the other three *āśramas* were not yet regarded as forming a sequence, but were considered alternative religious paths. See Olivelle, *The* Āśrama *System: The History and Hermeneutics of a Religious Institution* (New York: Oxford University Press, 1993), chap. 3.

109 E.g. M II 196, Dhp 412, Sn 636; S I 166–167, Sn 647, Dhp 423. For additional examples see K. R. Norman, "Theravāda Buddhism and brahmanical Hinduism." Some Jain texts, such as Utt 25, similarly appropriate Vedic terminology; see Hajime Nakamura, "Common Elements in Early Jain and Buddhist Literature," *Indologica Taurinensia* 11 (1983): 316–317.

110 *śākyājīvakādīn vṛṣalapravajitān devapitṛkāryeṣu bhojayataḥ śatyo daṇḍaḥ*. *Arthaśāstra* 3.20.16, cited in P. V. Kane, *History of Dharmaśāstra* I: 219. Other texts exclude Buddhist monastics from the rites without mentioning them by name. BDhS 2.15.5 asserts that when a person wearing ochre clothes makes a sacrifice or accepts a gift at a rite for gods or ancestors, the oblation does not reach its intended recipient. Manu 3.150–166 gives a long list of persons to be excluded from the śrāddha, including atheists, those who have not studied the Veda, those who have forsaken the fires, and those who revile the Veda.

111 Balkrishna Govind Gokhale, "The Early Buddhist Elite." *Journal of Indian History* 43 (1965): 395; idem, "Early Buddhism and the Brahmanas." In *Studies in the History of Buddhism*, edited by A. K. Narain (Delhi: B. R. Publishing Co., 1980), 74–75. If these data are unreliable, it is nonetheless significant that some monastic authors sought to represent the makeup of the Saṅgha as being relatively high-born.

112 Schopen, "Two Problems." 13ff; idem, "On Monks, Nuns, and 'Vulgar' Practices: The Introduction of the Image Cult into Indian Buddhism," *Artibus Asiae* 49 (1988/1989): 167–168.

113 Olivelle shows that this was a grave problem for Brahmanical renouncers as well, and they also devised theological solutions to compensate for their exclusion from śrāddha rites; *Saṃnyāsa Upaniṣads* 51, 72.

114 *Ye ca yaññā nirārambhā yajanti anukūlaṃ sadā.*

115 E.g. Thīg 271–290, S I 97 and 143.

116 *Ye tattha anumodanti veyyavaccaṃ karonti vā / na tesaṃ dakkhiṇā ūnā, te pi puññassa bhāgino. //* A III 41.

117 David M. Knipe, "*Sapiṇḍīkarana*: The Hindu Rite of Entry into Heaven," in *Religious Encounters with Death: Insights from the History and Anthropology of Religions*, ed. Frank E. Reynolds and Earle H. Waugh (University Park: Penn State University Press, 1977), 111–124.

118 Of course, this is only a textual representation that may not correspond to practice. Schopen remarks regarding Buddhism before the fourth

century CE that "nuns, indeed, women as a whole, appear to have been very numerous, very active, and, as a consequence, very influential in the actual Buddhist communities of early India"; "On Monks, Nuns, and 'Vulgar' Practices," 165.

119 J nos. 276 (*Kurudhamma J.*), 499, and 547. On the dates of the *Jātakas*, see Norman, *Pali Literature*, 80–82. On *Vessantara*, see Ludwig Alsdorf, "Bemerkungen zum Vessantara-Jātaka," *Wiener Zeitschrift für die Kunde Süd- und Ostasiens und Archiv für indische Philosophie* 1 (1957): 1–70; and Margaret Cone and Richard F. Gombrich, "Introduction," *The Perfect Generosity of Prince Vessantara: A Buddhist Epic* (Oxford: Clarendon, 1977), xv-xlvii.

120 *Biḷārikosiya Jātaka*, no. 450, is found at Ja IV 62–69. Nine verses appear in almost the same order in the two texts, and each passage contains one verse not found in the other. S I repeats some of these verses at 20, 32, and 57; two of these verses form J no. 180 (Ja II 86), and one appears in *Vessantara Jātaka* (Ja VI 571). The following *sutta* of *Saṃyutta*, S I 20–22, consists of verses that mostly express ascetic generosity and which correspond to J no. 424 (Ja III 469–474; two verses of this *jātaka* appear at S I 31).

121 *maccherā / macharī, pamādā*, and *bhīto / bhāyati*; similarly *malābhibhū*.

122 . . . *dukkaram hi karoti so, // Duddadaṃ dadamānānaṃ dukkaraṃ kamma kubbataṃ / asanto nānukubbanti, sataṃ dhammo durannayo. Dhamma* does not here signify the teaching of a buddha, but has the meaning of duty as it does in many Brahmanical texts.

123 I.e. a thousand gifts or a thousand coins.

124 Another set of verses about giving at S I 33 lends itself more easily to an interpretation in terms of generosity than of sacrifice. These verses say of those who establish groves, build bridges, dig wells, and give shelter that their merit grows both day and night, and that being established in the Dharma (or in righteousness) and accomplished in *sīla* they will go to heaven. Although it could be assumed that righteous ascetics are the intended recipients of these gifts, these verses do not specify that this is the case. Tilmann Vetter takes this verse to be an example of altruism in early Buddhist ethics (*The Ideas and Meditative Practices of Early Buddhism* (Leiden: E.J. Brill, 1988), 85).

125 *satañ ca dhammam aññāya, ko datvā anutappatīti.* Ja VI 552.31.

126 Ja VI 571; Sakka also cites the verse quoted in the previous paragraph. Sakka is the usual Pāli name for Indra, the king of the gods in Vedic mythology.

127 *Yā daliddī daliddassa aḍḍhā aḍḍhassa kittimā; / taṃ ve devā pasaṃsanti dukkaraṃ hi karoti sā.* Ja VI 508. Following Kern cited in PED, I read *tittimā* for text's *kittimā*.

128 Ja VI 494, 502.

129 The poet devotes three chapters to Jūjaka's journey to the forest: Ja VI 521–540.

130 At Ja VI 505 he twice refers to himself as a *yajamāno*, and at 502 ascetics call him *yajamāno*. J no. 450 and S I 18–19 discussed above also use sacrificial terminology but without the meaning of worship.

131 *yajissāmi, āhutiṃ, suyiṭṭhaṃ, suhutaṃ* Ja VI 527.

132 *mādisassa dhanaṃ datvā rāja saggaṃ gamissatīti* Ja VI 544.

133 Ja VI 488. Vessantara does, however, accept eight wishes from Sakka, and J no. 450 and S I 18 and 20 characterize the generous donor as *puññaṃ ākaṅkhamānena*, wishing for merit.

134 Sakka addresses Vessantara as "royal seer"; Ja VI 518. The term *rājisi* (Sanskrit *rājarṣi*), which also appears at VI 572, is rare in the *Tipiṭaka*, but is used often in *Mahābhārata*.

135 Ja VI 532–533, 542. Similar descriptions of the ideal forest-dweller appear in Brahmanical texts; e.g. VaDhS 9.1.7–8 reads, ". . . and when guests come to his hermitage, [the forest hermit should] honour them with almsfood of roots and fruits. He should only give and never receive. . . ." Translation from Olivelle, *Dharmasūtras*, 272.

136 *Avaruddh' ettha araññasmiṃ ubho sammatha assame / khattiyā gottasampannā sujātā mātupettito / yathā puññāni kayirātha, dadantā aparāparan ti.* Ja VI 572 with Cone and Gombrich's emendations.

137 *Ito vimuccamān' āhaṃ saggagāmī visesagū / anibbattī tato assam, atṭham' etaṃ varaṃ vare ti.* Ja VI 573.

138 Alsdorf, "Bemerkungen zum Vessantara-Jātaka," 46–49.

139 *teṣaṃ na punarāvṛttiḥ.* BĀU 6.2.15. BĀU and ChU also resemble VJ by making a king the spokesman for the ideal of the forest-dwelling ascetic, but of course these texts emphasize secret knowledge rather than giving.

140 Most scholars now favor a later date for the death of the Buddha, in the late fifth or early fourth century. Heinz Bechert, "Introductory Essay," in *The Dating of the Historical Buddha*, Part 1, ed. Heinz Bechert (Göttingen: Vanderhoech & Ruprecht, 1991), 15; idem, "Einleitung: Stand der Diskussion acht Jahre nach dem Symposion," in *The Dating of the Historical Buddha*, Part 3, 13.

141 Lambert Schmithausen, "Attempt to Estimate the Distance," 138, references omitted.

142 A version of this list of duties appears in seven edicts: Rock Edicts III, IV, IX, XI, XIII, Pillar Edict VII, and the Brahmagiri Rock Inscription, following Hultzsch's translations. The Third Rock Edict adds moderation in expenditure and possessions, and the Brahmagiri Rock Inscription includes speaking truthfully, but in general, for Aśoka, dharma consists in the fulfillment of particular social obligations. Aśoka presents his own acts of benevolence toward his citizens in the context of his particular debt to them, as he regards them as his children: Rock Edict V, First Separate Rock Edict. When quoting from the rock edicts I cite Hultzsch's edition of the Shāhbāzgaṛhī text.

143 In addition, Rock Edict X refers to *apuññaṃ* as dangerous.

144 The story that provides the preamble to VJ is very much like sacrificial discourse in its eschatology: the previous existence of Vessantara's mother in heaven comes to an end when her merit is exhausted (*parikkhīnaṃ*), and her past deeds do not condition her rebirth (Ja VI 482). In response to Vessantara's gift of his wife, Sakka cites the verse, "Therefore the way from here for good and evil is different: The evil go to a bad destiny; heaven is the destination of the good (*tasmā satañca asataṃ nānā hoti ito gati / asanto nirayaṃ yanti santo saggaparāyaṇā*); Ja VI 571. This verse expresses a view similar to the sacrificial under-

standing of heaven and a bad destiny as the two places in which the merit and evil are experienced. On the other hand, in other regards VJ and Aśoka differ significantly from the sacrificial-purificatory verses, notably in their descriptions of the ultimate soteriological goal.

The accounts of Sakka granting wishes to Vessantara and to his mother do not describe these acts as the result of merit or karma, but as actions freely done by Sakka. We should similarly understand *Sādhina Jātaka* (no. 494), in which Sakka informs Sādhīna, an inhabitant of the Tāvatiṃsa heaven, that his merits are exhausted, but tells him to remain in heaven by Sakka's divine power (*vasa devānubhāvena*, Ja IV 357). Although this command has been taken by the commentary and by modern interpreters as an offer to transfer merit to Sādhīna, the text presents Sakka's offer simply as an exercise of his divine power. E. Washburne Hopkins, "More about the Modifications of the Karma Doctrine," *Journal of the Royal Asiatic Society* 1907: 665–672; James Paul McDermott, *Development in the Early Buddhist Concept of Kamma/ Karma* (New Delhi: Munshiram Manoharlal, 1984), 45–47; idem, "*Sādhīna Jātaka*: A Case Against the Transfer of Merit." *Journal of the American Oriental Society* 94 (1974): 385–387.

145 Thomas Trautmann, *Dravidian Kinship* (Cambridge: Cambridge University Press, 1981), 282–283. A linkage between the Theravādin ethic of heroic generosity and Kṣatriya values is also suggested by a verse that likens giving by one who has little to a battle in which a few good men (*appāpi santā*) conquer many enemies (S I 20, Ja III 472).

146 The perceived dangers of unreciprocated giving have provided the basis for counter-Brahmanical gift theories, most notably the idea that the donor transfers his inauspiciousness or sin to the priestly recipient through the medium of the physical gift. Buddhists do not hold to this belief, and Mil 294–297 explicitly denies it. Historical and ethnographic studies of this pattern include: Nicholas B. Dirks, *The Hollow Crown: Ethnography of an Indian Kingdom* (Cambridge: Cambridge University Press, 1987); J. C. Heesterman, *The Inner Conflict of Tradition*, 26–28; idem, "Vrātya and Sacrifice," *Indo-Iranian Journal* 6 (1962): 20–27; Laidlaw, *Riches and Redemption*: 289–323; Jonathan P. Parry, *Death in Banaras*, (Cambridge: Cambridge University Press, 1994); idem, "*The Gift*, the Indian Gift, and the 'Indian Gift,'" *Man* (n.s.) 21 (1986): 453–473; idem, "On the Moral Perils of Exchange," in *Money and the Morality of Exchange*, edited by J. Parry and M. Bloch (Cambridge: Cambridge University Press, 1989), 64–93; Gloria Goodwin Raheja, *The Poison in the Gift: Ritual, Prestation, and the Dominant Caste in a North Indian Village* (Chicago: University of Chicago Press, 1988); Trautmann, *Dravidian Kinship*, 285–288.

147 *āsīnaṃ ca śayānaṃ ca pitā te pitaraṃ mama / stauti vandati cābhīkṣṇaṃ nīcaiḥ sthitvā vinītavat // yācatas tvaṃ hi duhitā stuvataḥ pratigṛhṇataḥ / sutāhaṃ stūyamānasya dadato 'pratigṛhṇataḥ //* MBh 1.73.9–10, text and translation from Trautmann, 285. Śarmiṣṭhā later gets her comeuppance when her father says that her criticisms do not apply to Devayānī's father, who is superior to the king.

148 Ja VI 528, 532–533, 542, 531.

149 Trautmann, 285. Against these contesting hierarchical ideologies, a mixed prose and verse passage at It 111–112 praises the reciprocity of the lay-monastic relationship. Laypeople supply monastics with their material needs, and monks teach the Dharma to laypeople; thus homeless and householders live the religious life in mutual dependence (*aññam-aññaṃ nissāya, aññaññanissitā* (PTS text reads *aññoññanissitā*)). Similar notions of reciprocity have no doubt played a much larger role in the attitudes of Buddhists than they do in textual ideologies.

150 Sāñcī Pillar Edict, Sārnāth Pillar Edict, and Bhabra Rock Edict.

Chapter Two

1 *āhuneyyo pāhuṇeyyo dakkhiṇeyyo añjalikaranīyo anuttaram puññakkhettam lokassa*, E.g. D II 94, III 5, 227, M III 137, S I 220, S IV 304, S V 343, 356, A I 208, 209, 222, 244–245, 245, 246, 284–285, II 34, 56, 113, 114, 117, 118, 171, 183, 250–251, 251–252. Roy Clayton Amore discusses this formula at length in the first chapter of *The Concept and Practice of Doing Merit in Early Theravāda Buddhism* (Ph.D. diss., Columbia University, 1970). The first two items likely refer to two types of Brahmanical sacrifice, *āhuta* (or *ahuta*) and *prahuta*. P. V. Kane, *History of Dharmaśāstra* (Pune: Bhandarkar Oriental Research Institute, 1930–1962), II 699. In this case *āhuneyyo* would indicate worthiness to receive *āhuta*, oblations (or possibly *ahuta*, non-oblation, meaning chanting and study) and *prahuta*, scattered offerings for terrestrial deities or the dead. The inappropriateness of the epithet *pāhuṇeyyo* suggests that this formula was created in a context in which the technical meaning of these phrases was unknown or disregarded. In any case, because of its inappropriateness or because its meaning was unknown, later interpreters gave this term the meaning, 'worthy of hospitality.'

2 In the karmic eschatology, existence as a *peta* is thought of not as a state of transition, but as a rebirth destiny in which beings experience the effects of bad actions. When *peta* or *petī* clearly indicate a rebirth destiny, I will translate these terms as 'ghost.'

3 Klaus Butzenberger, "Ancient Indian Conceptions on Man's Destiny after Death," *Berliner Indologische Studien* 9 (1996): 105.

4 PED and CPD give examples of the wide range of uses of *kamma*. Sn III.9 is an important discussion of *kamma* in which *kamma* does not imply the production of rebirth effects, but simply indicates normal causality. In fact, this passage opposes *kamma* to birth (*jāti*, 596). If vv. 653–654 are original to this *sutta*, and not interpolations, then this passage suggests that early understandings of *paṭiccasamuppāda* may have been informed by an understanding of *kamma* in terms of ordinary same-life causality.

5 Also *carati* and *samācarati*; see the article on *kamma* in the *Pāli Tipiṭakaṃ Concordance* for examples of these usages.

6 Padmanabh S. Jaini, "The Sautrāntika Theory of *Bīja*." *Bulletin of the School of Oriental and African Studies* 22 (1959): 236–249. According to Jaini, the Sautrāntikas found scriptural basis for their interpretation in A III 404–409, and Jaini reads this passage as being consistent with their interpretation. The three agricultural illustrations given in this passage are, however, simple parables on the sureness of cause and effect, and the elements of seed, field, and fruit do not have consistent allegorical meanings.

7 *mahāphalaṃ mahānisaṃsam*; a textual variant reads "of great fruit but not of great profit."

8 *Idha Sāriputta ekacco sāpekho dānaṃ deti, paṭibaddhacitto dānaṃ deti, sannidhipekho dānaṃ deti, 'imaṃ pecca paribhuñjissāmī' ti dānaṃ deti. So taṃ dānaṃ deti samaṇassa vā brāhmaṇassa vā annaṃ pānaṃ vatthaṃ yānaṃ mālāgandhavilepanaṃ seyyāvasathapadīpeyyaṃ.* A IV 60.

9 *Ijjhati bhikkhave sīlavato cetopaṇidhi visuddhattā.* This line is repeated frequently, and at the last repetition, *vītarāgattā* is substituted for *visuddhattā*.

10 *samaṇa-brāhmaṇa-kapaṇiddhika-vaṇibbaka-yācakānaṃ* D I 137; cf. II 354, III 76. Although *samaṇabrāhmaṇā* and similar phrases are never used to designate recipients of *dāna* in the didactic verse literature, this phrase is so used in the Aśokan edicts, and in *jātaka*s about generosity, such as no. 484.

11 Not surprisingly, the *kammpatha*s as a definition of *sīla* have in this century gained adherents among reformist laypeople in Sri Lanka, even though the *sikkhāpada* formulation has greater prominence in *Tipiṭaka*, and enjoys "centrality in Theravāda from an early period"; George D. Bond, "Theravāda Buddhism's Two Formulations of the *Dasa Sīla* and the Ethics of the Gradual Path," in *Pāli Buddhism*, edited by Frank J. Hoffman and Deegalle Mahinda (Richmond, Surrey: Curzon, 1996), 19, 26.

12 *Cetanāhaṃ bhikkhave kammaṃ vadāmi; cetayitvā kammaṃ karoti kāyena vācaya manasā.*

13 *Sañcetanikaṃ, āvuso Potaliputta, kammaṃ katvā kāyena vācāya manasā sukhavedanīyaṃ, sukhaṃ so vediyati. Sañcetanikaṃ kammaṃ katvā kāyena vācāya manasā dukkhavedanīyaṃ, dukkhaṃ so vediyati. Sañcetanikaṃ kammaṃ katvā kāyena vācāya manasā adukkhamasukhavedanīyaṃ, adukkhasukhaṃ so vediyati.* M III 209. Translation adapted from that of Ñāṇamoli and Bodhi.

14 For more thorough discussions of the term *saṅkhāra* and its various meanings, see Steven Collins, *Selfless Persons: Imagery and Thought in* Theravāda *Buddhism* (Cambridge: Cambridge University Press, 1982), 200–208, and Sue Hamilton, *Identity and Experience: The Constitution of the Human Being According to Buddhism* (London: Luzac Oriental, 1996), 66–81.

15 *Idha bhikkhave ekacco puggalo savyāpajjhaṃ kāyasaṅkhāraṃ abhisaṅkharoti savyāpajjhaṃ vacāsaṅkhāraṃ abhisaṅkharoti savyāpajjhaṃ manosaṅkhāraṃ abhisaṅkharoti. So savyāpajjhaṃ kāyasaṅkhāraṃ abhisaṅkharitvā savyāpajjhaṃ vacāsaṅkhāraṃ abhisakharitvā savyāpajjhaṃ manosaṅkhāraṃ abhisaṅkharitvā savyāpajjhaṃ lokaṃ upapajjati.* A I 122. A group of

parallel passages, including M I 390, make a similar distinction between formations that are dark, light, and both dark and light, adding a fourth category of neither dark nor light.

16 E.g. D III 234, 264, M I 73, A V 270 (discussed above), It 93. The *asuras* are the rivals of the gods, comparable to the Titans and giants of Greek and Norse mythology.

17 For examples, see *inter alia Bālapaṇḍita Sutta* (M III 163–178), *Devadūta Sutta* (M III 178–187), *Cūḷakammavibhaṅga Sutta* (M III 202–215), and S II 252–262.

18 *pāpakammaṃ dukkhavedanīyaṃ; kalyāṇakammaṃ sukhavedanīyaṃ; diṭṭheva dhamme vipākaṃ paṭisaṃvedeti upapajja vā apare vā pariyāye.* Translation by Ñāṇamoli and Bodhi. Although some sacrificial *gāthās* say that giving produces benefits for this life, these verses distinguish these effects from *puñña* (A II 35, A III 36, It 88–89). The karmic discourse, on the other hand, classes both kinds of effect as the results of the same cause, action.

19 E.g. D I 217, II 212, A I 210, A IV 239–241. On this cosmology, see also Collins, *Nirvana*, chapter 4. Sue Hamilton discusses the relationship between these worlds and meditative states in "The 'External World': Its Status and Relevance in the Pali Nikāyas," *Religion* 29 (1999): 73–90.

20 Discontinuity with subsequent tradition is generally considered to be the most reliable criterion for determining which Gospel traditions date from the time of Jesus, because later innovations presumably will reflect the practices at the time they arose. *The Anchor Bible Dictionary,* s.v. "Jesus Christ" by Ben F. Meyer.

21 Again, I am claiming not that sacrificial-purificatory discourse represents the actual teaching of the Buddha, but simply that sacrificial-purificatory passages predate karmic passages, and that some evidence suggests that sacrificial-purificatory discourse was well established by the time of Aśoka while karmic discourse was not.

22 Richard Gombrich translates and discusses this passage in "Recovering the Buddha's Message," *Panels of the VIIth World Sanskrit Conference,* ed. Johannes Bronkhorst, vol. 2, *Earliest Buddhism and Madhyamaka,* ed. David Seyfort Ruegg and Lambert Schmithausen (Leiden: E. J. Brill, 1990), 16–20. Gombrich argues that this metaphor is not merely a nice sermon illustration, but that this basic Buddhist formulation of the bad roots contains three items precisely because it was intended to parallel the three fires of the *agnihotra*.

23 The six directions are the east, the south, the west, the north, the nadir and the zenith. T. W. and C. A. F. Rhys Davids give textual citations for the Brahmanical rites described here, *Dialogues of the Buddha* (London: Pali Text Society, 1965), vol. 3, 170. Different groups of people are associated with the four cardinal directions in a number of Vedic texts, but this *sutta* does not conform to the usual Brahmanical associations. See Brian K. Smith, *Classifying the Universe*, 136–157.

24 *tividhaṃ yaññasampadaṃ soḷasaparikkhāraṃ.* The phrase *tividhaṃ yaññasampadaṃ* appears also in Sn 509, discussed in chapter 1.

25 Vin I 157, 158, 225, 352, II 216; M I 13; I 207; III 157.

26 The same exchange occurs at Sn p. 85 and S I 167, but these two passages do not concern themselves with the subsequent problem of disposing of the offering. In "La Transformation Miraculeuse de la Nourriture Offerte au Buddha par le Brahmane Kasibhāradvāja," in *Études Tibétaines Dédiées à la Mémoire de Marcelle Lalou* (Paris: Librairie d'Amérique et d'Orient, 1971), André Bareau follows Sp in taking *gāthābhigītaṃ* to mean "earned by chanting," as do PED, C. A. F. Rhys Davids, and I. B. Horner, but the definition offered by CPD and K. R. Norman, "sung over with verses" makes more sense in this context.

27 As Bareau points out ("Transformation Miraculeuse," 3), this phrase is similar to that used in the *Mahāparinibbāna Sutta* by the Buddha with regard to his final meal. In the *Mahāparinibbāna Sutta*, however, the problem with the meal is that it is poisonous.

28 Following Norman's translation of Sn.

29 *vighāsādā*, PED "one who eats the remains of food."

30 Pj II 154, cited in Bareau, "Transformation Miraculeuse," 4–5. Buddhaghosa's argument is actually more complex than I indicate here, as he describes various foods to be consumed by different types of beings.

31 Bareau, "Transformation Miraculeuse," 4. In this article, Bareau discusses only the Sn narrative.

32 Lioness: AB 6.35, ŚB 2.5.1.21; tigress: MS 4.8.3; female hyena: KS 28.4/ KapS 44.4, ĀpŚS 13.7.12. Gonda, *Change and Continuity*, 210; Heesterman, "Reflections on the Significance of the *Dákṣiṇā*," 244–245; Stephanie W. Jamison, *The Ravenous Hyenas and the Wounded Sun: Myth and Ritual in Ancient India* (Ithaca, NY: Cornell University Press, 1991), 92–96.

33 Idem, "Vedic *mení*, Avestan *maēni*, and the power of thwarted exchange." *Festschrift Paul Thieme. Studien zur Indologie und Iranistik* 20 (1996): 187–203.

34 Greg Bailey, "Problems of the Interpretation of the Data pertaining to Religious Interaction in Ancient India: The Conversion Stories in the Sutta Nipāta," *Indo-British Review* 19 (n.d.): 18.

35 Schopen argues in a similar vein that the Theravādin *Vinaya* appears to have developed in a social context not dominated by Brahmanical influence, i.e. Sri Lanka, while the Mūlasarvāstivādin *Vinaya* appears to have been shaped in response to an established system of Brahmanical law. "Monastic Law Meets the Real World: A Monk's Continuing Right to Inherit Family Property in Classical India," *History of Religions*: 35 (1995): 101–123; "The Monastic Ownership of Servants or Slaves: Local and Legal Factors in the Redactional History of Two *Vinayas*," *Journal of the International Association of Buddhist Studies* 17 (1994): 145–173.

36 Sacrificial verses in S are usually framed by a narrative without exegesis, while in A sacrificial verses are usually cited in order to praise or describe worthy recipients of gifts (e.g. A I 63, II 35, III 36, 213, 337, IV 244, and 292). The formula *āhuneyyo pāhuṇeyyo dakkhiṇeyyo añjalikaranīyo anuttaram puññakkhettam lokassa* is also usually cited in order to praise or describe recipients; see references given at the beginning of this chapter.

37 In A I 161, the Buddha says that feeding animals living in a cesspool will produce merit, much more so feeding a human being. Nonetheless, what

is given to a moral person produces great fruit, but not what is given to an immoral person. In A IV 404–408, the Buddha ranks gifts according to the worthiness of their recipients.

38 M III 255. Translation based on that of Ñāṇamoli and Bodhi.

39 A *sotāpanna* (stream-winner) is one who has attained the path leading to awakening; *sotāpatti* is attainment of the path.

40 In *Mātaṅga Jātaka* (no. 497) the Bodhisattva offers a different solution to the problem of laity evaluating the worthiness of recipients: he says that as a farmer sows on both good and bad soil, so in order to be sure of finding a worthy field a donor should give to all who ask.

41 These artless verses, which do not scan at all, repeat the points made in the prose using the same words and include a fifth stanza about a gift from an arhat to an arhat. The supposition that in this case the verses are dependent on the prose is supported by the observation that D III 231–232 and A II 80–81 contain this same prose passage but without the verses. A longer treatment of this scheme may be found at Kv 555–556.

42 *upakkiliṭṭhassa . . . sīsassa upakkamena pariyodapanā* A I 207.

43 *sāsavā puññābhāgiyā upadhivepakkā; ariyā anāsavā lokuttarā maggaṅga*. M III 72, translation by Ñāṇamoli and Bodhi.

44 *"Atthi dinnaṃ, atthi yiṭṭhaṃ, atthi hutaṃ, atthi sukaṭadukkaṭānaṃ kammānaṃ phalaṃ vipāko,. . . ."* M III 72. This formula also appears at M I 288, 291, 402 (x 2), III 23, 52, 71, S IV 348, 351, 355, A I 269, 270 (x 2), V 268, 285 (x 2), 291, 296, Nidd I 188.

45 *Puññam-eva so sikkheyya āyataggaṃ sukhindriyaṃ* / dānañca samacariyañca mettañca bhāvaye // ete dhamme bhāvayitvā tayo sukhasamuddaye / abyāpajjhaṃ sukhaṃ lokaṃ paṇḍito upapajjatī / ti //* I follow F. L. Woodward in reading *sukhudrayaṃ* for text's *sukhindriyaṃ*.

46 The expression *puññakiriyavatthūni* also appears at It 19, where *opadhikāni puññakiriyavatthūni* refers to material gifts.

47 Other texts do develop the theme of meditation as a means of making *kamma*; e.g. D I 249–251 presents cultivation of the four meditative states called *brahmavihāras* as a means to rebirth in the Brahmalokas.

48 *Avijjāgato ya bhikkhave purisapuggalo puññaṃ ce saṅkhāram abhisaṅkharoti, puññūpagaṃ hoti viññāṇaṃ; apuññaṃ ce saṅkhāraṃ abhisaṅkharoti, apuññūpagaṃ hoti viññāṇaṃ; āneñjaṃ ce saṅkhāram, āneñjūpagaṃ hoti viññāṇaṃ*. S II 82. These three *saṅkhāras* also appear at D III 217.

49 This *sutta* is a didactic verse text, but Khp is not generally considered to be among the earliest canonical literature.

50 This theme of *puññābhisandā kusalābhisandā* is the subject of S V 391–402 (six *suttas*), A II 54–7 (two *suttas*), A III 51–2, and A IV 245–7.

51 *Atha kho asaṅkheyyo appameyyo mahāpuññakkhandho teva saṅkhaṃ gacchati*.

52 *Yo puññakāmo kusale patiṭṭhito / bhāveti maggam amatassa pattiyā // so dhammasārādhigamo khaye rato / na vedhati maccurāja gamissatī / ti //* That the prose of these two *suttas* is nearly identical, but that the verses appear only in the second of them, shows that the prose was not composed as a commentary on the verses, and suggests that the verses were added to the prose.

53 Knipe similarly argues that Hindus continue to practice Vedic rites for the dead even though these rites are incompatible with "newer sentiments of saṃsāra and mokṣa"; "*Sapiṇḍīkaraṇa*," 112.

54 '*mayam assu bho Gotama brāhmaṇā nāma dānāni dema, saddhāni karoma: idaṃ dānaṃ petānaṃ ñātisālohitanaṃ upakappatu, idaṃ dānaṃ petā ñātisālohitā paribhuñjantū' ti.* A V 269.

55 The use of these terms, meaning 'relation,' 'and the donors are not without fruit,' and 'benefits,' indicates a literary relationship between these passages, either direct or through a common source. This paragraph also shares *paribhuñjati* with Pv I.1, and *dāyakā ca anipphalā* with Pv I.4.

56 *ātitheyyaṃ*; in Vedic ritual, *ātithya* is the name of a sacrifice to Soma: ŚB 3.4.1.

57 "*mama dakkhiṇaṃ ādiseyyāsi, etañ ca me bhavissati ātitheyyan,*" 64.

58 "*yad idaṃ bhante dāne puññaṃ hi taṃ Vessavaṇassa mahārājassa sukhāya hotū ti,*" 65. V.l. has *hitaṃ* for *hi taṃ*.

59 *Yaṃ idaṃ bho Gotama dāne puññañ-ca puññamahī ca taṃ dāyakānaṃ sukhāya hotūti.*

Yaṃ kho Aggivessana tādisaṃ dakkhiṇeyyaṃ āgamma avītarāgaṃ avītadosaṃ avītamohaṃ taṃ dāyakānaṃ bhavissati. Yaṃ kho Aggivessana mādisaṃ dakkhiṇeyyaṃ āgamma vītarāgaṃ vītadosaṃ vītamohaṃ taṃ tuyhaṃ bhavissatīti.

60 *tato bhagavatā pretasya nāmnā dakṣiṇā ādiṣṭā: ito dānādci yatpuṇyaṃ tatpretamanugacchatu. uttiṣṭatu kṣipramayaṃ pretalokātsudāruṇāditi. Avadānaśataka* 272.13–15, similarly 259.1–2, 264.13–14. In Sanskrit texts, either the donor or the monastic recipient may be said to dedicate dakṣiṇā (cf. 15.1).

61 *yad atra puṇyaṃ tad bhavatu,* Gregory Schopen, "Mahāyāna in Indian Inscriptions," *Indo-Iranian Journal* 21 (1979): 5–6, idem, "Two Problems," 41–42.

62 See Gregory Schopen's survey of this material in "Two Problems," especially 31–47. Most early inscriptions only name the donor and do not assign the benefits of the action to another party.

63 *aparimita-lokadatuya śatana śita-śukaye.* Senarat Paranavitana, *Inscriptions of Ceylon* ([Colombo]: Department of Archaeology, 1970-), vol. I, nos. 338–341. Inscriptions dating from at least as early as the second century CE express a desire that some person or persons, or all beings, would attain nirvāṇa. From the fourth century on, Mahāyāna inscriptions typically aspire that the gift will bring the attainment of unsurpassed knowledge by all beings. Schopen, "Two Problems," 31, 39–40, 42–3, 45; idem, "Mahāyāna in Indian Inscriptions," 4–7.

64 Although the practices described in this paragraph are often called "merit transfer," none of these involves the transfer of karmic potential to another person. Rather, these acts consist in directing some action, mental root of action, or merit to a particular named end, such as happiness or unsurpassed knowledge.

65 "*Yam kiñc' atthi kataṃ puññaṃ mayhañ c'eva pitu ca te / saccena tena kusalena ajaro tvaṃ amaro bhava.*" J no. 547, Ja VI 589. Steven Collins views this utterance as irony, as only nirvāṇa brings freedom from aging and death (*Nirvana*, 521), but I see no reason not to take Maddī's wish

literally as an aspiration that her children would attain nirvāṇa or eternal life in heaven. Vessantara's aspiration to buddhahood, discussed briefly in chapter 1, is another example of an aspiration for the benefit of another.

66 *iminā me adhikārena, katena purisuttame; / sabbaññutaṃ pāpuṇitvā, tāremi janataṃ bahuṃ* Bv IIA 56. As this example illustrates, the bodhisattva vow central to Mahāyāna practice has its origins in this practice of forming aspirations.

67 Bechert has characterized BAp as "a full-fledged Mahāyāna text" that was added to Ap probably in the first or second century CE. Heinz Bechert, "Buddha-field and Transfer of Merit in a Theravāda Source," *Indo-Iranian Journal* 35 (1992): 102, 104.

68 *Ye sattā saññino atthi ye ca sattā asaññino / kataṃ puññaphalaṃ mayhaṃ sabbe bhāgī bhavantu te. // Yesaṃ kataṃ suviditaṃ dinnaṃ puññaphalaṃ mayā / ye ca tattha na jānanti devā gantvā nivedayuṃ.//* BAp 45–46.

69 Also, in the preceding verses he stresses that all beings should witness his vision.

70 *Sabbe lokaṃhiye sattā jīvantāhārahetukā / manuññaṃ bhojnaṃ sabbaṃ labhantu mama cetasā.* BAp 47.

71 In *Avadānaśataka*, donors frequently wish that "by relinquishing this gift" (*deyadharmaparityāgena*) their actions would bear fruit in a future existence in awakening, and this phrase is also cited in inscriptions as the basis for dedications of merit. *Avadānaçataka : A Century of Edifying Tales Belonging to the Hīnayāna*, ed. J. S. Speyer (*Bibliotheca Buddhica* III, St. Petersburg: Imperial Academy of Sciences, 1906–1909; *Indo-Iranian Reprints* III, 'S-Gravenhage: Mouton & Co., 1958) 7, 12, 22, *et passim*. In inscriptions we find *d[e]yadharmaparityāgen[a]*, *deryadharmmaparītyāgen[a]*; see Schopen, "Two Problems," 31–32, 40–41.

Mahāyāna texts use the terms *pariṇāmayati* and *nāmayati* for attempts to direct the effect of good actions toward the attainment of awakening, whether by oneself or by others. For references and discussion see Har Dayal, *The Bodhisattva Doctrine in Buddhist Sanskrit Literature* (Delhi: Motilal Banarsidass, 1970), 192; Schopen, "Mahāyāna in Indian Inscriptions," 7–8; Joanna R. Macy, "Not to Escape, but to Transform: Enlightenment and the Concept of Parināmanā in the *Aṣṭasāhasrikā Prajñāpāramitā*," in *Buddhist Heritage in India and Abroad*, ed. G. Kuppuram and K. Kumudamani (Delhi: Sundeep Prakashan, 1992), 143–159. J nos. 524 and 545 use the term *pariṇāmaja* in the context of a discussion about karma.

Verbal dedications of merit can also be found in the colophons to all of the Pāli commentaries.

72 George Thompson, "On Truth-Acts in Vedic," *Indo-Iranian Journal* 41 (1998): 133, 142.

73 On this point, see my discussion at the beginning of chapter 3 of Jonathan S. Walters, "Stūpa, Story and Empire: Constructions of the Buddha Biography in Early Post-Aśokan India," in *Sacred Biography in the Buddhist Traditions of South and Southeast Asia*, ed. Juliane Schober (Honolulu: University of Hawai'i Press, 1997), 160–192.

74 These narratives contrast with numerous passages that identify the pursuit of nirvāṇa with monastic life (e.g. Sn I.3) and the pursuit of merit

with lay life and the enjoyment of wealth (e.g. Vin I 182, Vin III 16–7, M I 461, II 64, S IV 190–1, A III 374–5). In Vin III 13–14, for example, a man's parents and friends tempt him not to become a monk, saying, "enjoy yourself, eating, drinking, carrying on, enjoying pleasures, and making merit," *bhuñjanto pivanto paricārento kāme paribhuñjanto puññāni karonto abhiramassu.*

75 Alternatively, "I should do meritorious deeds." *So vat' ahaṃ puññāni kareyyaṃ.* D I 60–61.

76 A I 19–20, 21, 34, 69, 243–244.

77 *evam idaṃ puññaṃ pavaḍḍhati,* D III 58 and 79. The commentary glosses *puñña* here by distinguishing between this-worldly and transcendent fruits of merit (*lokiya-lokuttaram puññaphalam*): "Wholesome action is of two kinds: that which leads to rebirth and that which leads to nirvāṇa." *Tattha duvidhaṃ kusalaṃ vaṭṭagāmi ca vivaṭṭa-gāmi ca.* Sv 847–848. By this definition, the effects of all good acts are *puñña,* including even the attainment of the path, its fruits, and nirvāṇa (*maggaphalanibbānasamāpatti*).

78 *Mā bhikkhave puññānaṃ bhāyittha, sukhass' etaṃ bhikkhave adhivacanaṃ, [iṭṭhassa kantassa piyassa manāpassa,] yad idaṃ puññāni. Abhijānāmi kho panāhaṃ bhikkhave dīgharattaṃ katānaṃ puññānaṃ dīgharattaṃ iṭṭhaṃ kantaṃ piyaṃ manāpaṃ vipākaṃ paccanubhūtaṃ.* The bracketed section appears only in It.

79 To elucidate It's injunction not to fear merits, It-a 73–74 cites the discussions of *kamma* at S II 82 and A IV 241, as well as D III 58, and gives no indication that monks' merit-making might present difficulties of interpretation. The commentaries to most of the passages discussing merit-making by monastics do not explain the meaning of the term *puñña;* these include the commentaries to D I 60–61, II 28–29, A I 19–20, IV 88–89, V 75–76, Vin II 76, S V 146, A V 248–249, and A III 41.

Another indication that the question of whether monks should make merit was controversial is given by Kv 541–543, in which it is debated whether arhats accumulate merit (*puññūpacaya*).

80 Sacrificial verses commented on in this manner include A I 63, II 35, III 36, 213, 337, IV 244, and 292. Sacrificial verses in S are more often framed by a narrative and without exegesis. References to the formula *āhuneyyo pāhuṇeyyo dakkhiṇeyyo añjalikaranīyo anuttaram puññakkhettam lokassa* are given at the beginning of this chapter.

81 Patrick Olivelle, "Introduction," *Dharmasūtras: The Law Codes of Ancient India* (Oxford: Oxford University Press, 1999), xxvi–xxxiv. Olivelle (127) also judges BDhS 2.17 – 4.8 to be late additions, and I will not discuss them here.

82 Idem, *The Āśrama System,* 137.

83 Moriz Winternitz, *A History of Indian Literature,* trans. S. Ketkar (1931; reprint, New York: Russell and Russell, 1971), vol. 2, 432–433.

84 Schubring cited by Adelheid Mette in "The Synchronism of the Buddha and the Jina Mahāvīra and the Problem of Chronology in Early Jainism," in *The Dating of the Historical Buddha,* Part 1, ed. Heinz Bechert (Göttingen: Vanderhoech & Ruprecht, 1991), 132. Hermann Jacobi argues on the basis of meter that the oldest Jain texts were composed in

about the third century BCE, after the Pāli canonical texts, and he considers the first books of *Āyāraṅga* and *Sūyagaḍaṅga* to be among the older Jain texts; Hermann Jacobi, *Jaina Sutras, Part I*, Sacred Books of the East 22 (1884; reprint, New York: Dover, 1968), xli–xlii. Winternitz likewise considers the first books of *Āyāraṅga* and *Sūyagaḍaṅga* to be much earlier than the second; *History*, 437–438. Schubring reaches no firm conclusions about the dates of the texts; *The Doctrine of the Jains: Described after the Old Sources*, trans. of *Die Lehre Jainas*, revised ed., by Wolfgang Beurlen (Delhi: Motilal Banarsidass, 1962), 81–82. Paul Dundas dates the first books of *Āyāraṅga* and *Sūyagaḍaṅga* to the fifth or fourth century BCE or earlier and the second book of *Āyāraṅga* to the second or first century BCE, but provides no arguments in support of these dates; Paul Dundas, *The Jains* (New York: Routledge, 1992), 20. Jacobi shows that there is a high degree of similarity between Jain beliefs as represented in these texts and in the Pāli canon; *Jaina Sutras. Part II*, Sacred Books of the East 45 (Oxford: Clarendon Press: 1895; reprint, New York: Dover, 1968), xiv-xxxii. Mette argues that the Buddhist texts provide our most reliable guide to early Jain beliefs; "Synchronism," 137.

85 My interpretations of these Prakrit texts rely on Jacobi and Schubring's translations and on Śīlāṅka's commentary.

86 E.g., the misery of *saṃsāra*: Āyār 1.2.3.6, 1.2.6.5, 1.5.1.1, Utt 3.5–6, 7.18, 8.1, 8.15, 14.2 & 4, 19.10–16 and 45–46, 22.31, 25.40–41; repeated births and deaths: Sūyag 1.2.1.9, Utt 19.44–46 & 74; human birth a rare opportunity Utt 3.1, 10.4–27; immense spaces and periods of time: Āyār 2.15.2, Sūyag 1.1.3.16, 1.5.1.26, Utt 10.5–27, 33.19–23, 36, 58–63; karma producing rebirth in the four *gatis*: Āyār 2.15.26, Utt 3.3–4, 29.4; karma producing rebirth as a deity or in a hell: Sūyag 2.2; karma producing rebirth in high or low families: Utt 29.10; karma producing birth as a Tīrthaṅkar: Utt 29.43 (discussed below); hells as places of torment: Sūyag 1.5.1–2, Utt 19.47–73; classification of different kinds of deity / heaven: Āyār 2.15.7, 18, & 27, Utt 3.15, 7.16; past karma causing actions: Sūyag 1.4.1.23, 2.3.1; persons repeatedly reborn together: Utt 13.1–7.

87 *tataḥ parivṛttau karma-phala-śeṣeṇa jātiṃ rūpaṃ varṇaṃ balaṃ medhāṃ prajñāṃ dravyāṇi dharma-anuṣṭhānam iti pratipadyate* ĀpDhS 2.2.3a; *varṇāśramāḥ svasvadharmaniṣṭhāḥ pretya karmaphalam anubhūya tataḥ śeṣena viśiṣṭadeśajātikularūpāyuḥśrutacitravittasukham edhaso janma pratipadyante* GDhŚ 11.29.

88 *brahma-pūto brahma-bhūto brāhmaṇaḥ śāstram anuvartamāno brahma-lokam abhijayati* BDhS 2.7.22.

89 Ludo Rocher shows that this chapter combines five different karmic systems together with some additional miscellaneous rules; Rocher, "Karma and Rebirth in the Dharmaśāstras," in *Karma and Rebirth in Classical Indian Traditions*, ed. Wendy Doniger O'Flaherty (Berkeley: University of California Press, 1980), 61–89.

90 12.62, following Doniger's translation.

91 *te 'bhyāsāt karmaṇāṃ teṣāṃ pāpānām alpabuddhayaḥ / saṃprāpnuvanti duḥkhāni tāsu tāsv iha yoniṣu //* Manu 12.74, Doniger's translation.

92 *anantyaṃ phalaṃ svargya-śabdaṃ*, ĀpDhS 2.23.10–12.

93 *syāt tu karma-avayavena tapasā vā kaścit saśarīro 'ntavantaṃ lokaṃ jayati saṃkalpa-siddhiś ca syān na tu taj jyaiṣṭhyam āśramāṇām*, ĀpDhS 2.24.14, following Olivelle's translation.

94 GDhS 3.3 & 36, BDhS 2.11.9 & 27–34. VaDhS 8.14–16 further points out that everyone depends on the householder for material support.

95 K. K. Dixit "The Problems of Ethics and Karma Doctrine as Treated in the *Bhagavatī Sūtra*," *Sambodhi* 2 (1974): 1–2, 7. All action involves violence because simply by existing one causes other beings to suffer, as when one eats food (Suyāg 2.3, Laidlaw, *Riches and Renunciation*, 191–192). These texts sometimes uses phrases meaning 'bad karma' (e.g. *pāvagaṃ kammaṃ* Sūyag 1.8.10, *pāvakammī* Sūyag 1.13.5, *pāvayaṃ kammaṃ* Dasav 4.1–6, *pāvaṃ kammaṃ* Dasav 4.7–9), which could be taken to imply that there exists also good karma; however, the absence of references to good karma indicates that to the authors, all karma is *pāva* (*pāpa*).

Perhaps the most distinctive aspect of Jain karma theory is its conception of karma as a substance that adheres to the soul; however, this notion is only found in the texts under discussion here in Dasav 4–5. Dixit argues that we can see the beginnings of this idea in the *Bhagavatī Sūtra*; "The Problems of Ethics," 6.

96 Jacobi, *Jaina Sutras, Part II*, xvi–xvii. As Jacobi notes, in M I 372 Upāli states that Nātaputta (Mahāvīra) uses the term *daṇḍa* to mean karma.

97 *kamma-mūlaṃ ca jaṃ chaṇaṃ* (*yat kṣaṇaṃ*; *Ācārāṅgasūtraṃ Sūtrakṛtaṅgasūtraṃ ca*, 105–106).

98 Āyār 1.3.2, 1.7.8.2, 1.7.8.5; Sūyag 1.1.1.5, 1.1.2.12, 1.2.1.15, 1.6.7, 1.7.30, *et passim*.

99 Āyār 2.1.1.12 and 2.1.2.1; Sūyag 2.1.56.

100 Sūyag 2.6.29–45. Āyār 2.1.2.3 and 2.1.4.1 specifically forbid participation in śrāddha meals attended by many guests.

101 Notably, this passage never describes these acts as good karma or as merit.

102 Verses 6, 10–15, 18 of this *adhyayana* correspond to the first eight verses of *Mātaṅga Jātaka* (no. 497); the rest of both passages differ. As Utt 12:1–18 contains verses lacking in J 497.1–8, the *jātaka* is probably closer to the original version of this story, and the Jain redactor apparently added the device of the voice-throwing yakṣa in order to make this story acceptable to Jain sensibilities. The rest of Utt 12 also contains marked similarities to the conversion stories of Sn and S. On the other hand, the lesson drawn from the merit field metaphor, that one should give to all ascetics without discrimination, is atypical of Buddhist literature; we therefore cannot assume that this story was originally a Buddhist tale.

Despite its weak scriptural and doctrinal basis, the merit field idea has persisted as part of the Jain tradition, no doubt because it provides a rationale for giving to Jain ascetics. The problematic status of almsgiving in Jainism has received a good deal of attention in recent scholarship. See Torkel Brekke, "Contradiction and the Merit of Giving"; Maria Hibbets, "The Ethics of Esteem" and "Saving Them from Yourself"; James Laidlaw, *Riches and Redemption*, 289–323; John E. Cort, "The Gift of Food to a Wandering Cow: Lay-Mendicant Interaction among the

Jains," *Journal of Asian and African Studies* 34 (1999): 89ff.; Lawrence A. Babb, *Absent Lord: Ascetics and Kings in a Jain Ritual Culture* (Berkeley: University of California Press, 1996), 174–195.

103 Book one of Āyār and Sūyag do not address this problem. Sūyag 1.7.16 contrasts *kammamalaṃ* (the stain of karma) with *suhaṃ* (*śubhaṃ*, auspiciousness or merit); however, this verse characterizes the beliefs of non-Jains. In his translation of Sūyag 2.2.58–59, 69, and 74, Jacobi refers to merit leading to enlightenment, but merit is here a misleading translation of *dhammapakkhassa* (*dharmapakṣikasya*, subject to dharma).

104 For a discussion of how this ambivalent solution plays itself out in Jain practice, see Laidlaw, *Riches and Renunciation*, especially 26–31.

105 Dasav encourages acts that it calls meritorious (*puṇṇa*), but this term does not here seem to denote a form of karma.

Chapter Three

1 Norman, *Pali Literature*, 80–82. Although the *Jātaka* commentary identifies the protagonists of the stories as the Bodhisattva, they are only rarely so identified in the verses.

2 Wilhelm Geiger, *Pāli Literature and Language*, trans. Batakrishna Ghosh (2d ed. Delhi: Oriental Books Reprint Corporation, 1968), 20. Norman reaches similar conclusions regarding the dates of these texts; *Pali Literature*, 70, 71, 90, 94, 95, 42.

3 Jonathan S. Walters, "Stūpa, Story and Empire: Constructions of the Buddha Biography in Early Post-Aśokan India," in *Sacred Biography in the Buddhist Traditions of South and Southeast Asia*, ed. Juliane Schober (Honolulu: University of Hawai'i Press, 1997), 160–192.

4 Other sections of *Apadāna* tell about pratyekabuddhas and about the past lives of various arhats.

5 *caritaṃ . . . bodhipācanaṃ* I.1.1; *patthayiṃ* I.1.10, *manasā . . . patthitan* II.5.11; *pubbakammasamāyutto* III.11.3. What is meant by *carita* becomes apparent in the stories, which describe the acquiring of the perfections not as a process of mental purification, but as the performance of discrete actions.

6 Thus Cp uses the verb *cajati*, 'relinquishes,' to describe both Vessantara's perfection of giving in relinquishing his children and wife (I.9.48 & 52) and Yudhañjaya's perfection of renunciation in giving up sovereignty over the entire earth, relations, attendants, and fame (III.1.5). This range of meanings of *cajati* is found in other canonical texts. Lay people typically renounce their gifts: e.g. S I 215, 231–2, IV 250, 304, A II 66, III 34, 44. The objects of renunciation most often recommended to Buddhist monastics are thirst and a catalog of harmful mental states beginning with hatred, greed, and delusion: *taṇhā* Vin I 10, 49, 299, M I 6, S III 158, V 421, 426; *rāga, lobha, moha* etc. Vin IV 27, M II 224, A II 257, III 278, IV 349–350, 465, 466, V 310, 360–361. Other forms of mental bondage are named at M I 37, M I 486, M III 31, 245, S III 13, A II 41, V 31, and It 94. On monks and *cāga*, see also M I 465, 468, M III 239ff.

7 Bv and Ap also integrate sacrificial emphases into the karmic path of purification by showing that giving to worthy recipients eventually yields fruit in awakening.

8 Vv contains 85 dialogs and Pv contains 51; two dialogs, Vv V.2 = Pv IV.4 and Vv VII.10 = Pv IV.2, appear in both collections. The only organizing principles to which the collections conform seem to be that in Vv similar stories are sometimes grouped together, and that the 50 stories about females are given before the 35 stories about males. They are classed by their commentaries as *gāthā* (Pv-a 2, Vv-a 4), but Vv and Pv are mostly made up not of short didactic verses like those discussed in chapter 1, but of dialogs concerning specific events.

9 Many stories contain a verse identifying the person who speaks to the deity as Moggallāna, reflecting the tradition that Moggallāna was foremost of the Buddha's disciples in the possession of wondrous powers. Vv-a 21 states that these identifying verses were added by the redactors (*saṅgītikāra*), and sometimes these identifications conflict with other verses, as in III.5. Other persons sometimes identified as the interlocutor are Sakka (Vv I.17), a female deity (Vv III.4 and III.6), Gotama (Vv V.1), Vaṅgīsu (Vv V.11), a group unidentified in the text (Vv V.12), and a Brāhmaṇ speaking to his former son (Vv VII.9). The Pv stories usually do not identify the interlocutor, although he is identified as Nārada in Pv I.2, I.3.

10 Thirteen of these stories combine dialog with narration to describe the dedication of dakṣiṇā. Five of these stories consist of a dialog followed by narration in which the gift dedication is described (Pv I.10, II.1–4). Then follows in four of these stories another dialog in which the donor does not recognize the recipient who has been transformed by the gift, and asks about his or her identity and meritorious deed. The recipient replies that the donor's gift effected the change. Seven other gift dedication stories contain only one dialog, while another consists entirely of third person narration (Pv II.8, II.10, III.1, III.2, III.6, IV.1, Pv IV.12; no dialog: Pv IV.3).

11 Pv I.8, II.6, and II.13; Pv I.1, I.4, I.5, IV.6, IV.7; Pv I.12, IV.13–15; Pv II.10 and IV.3. The theme of not mourning for the dead also appears in a dialog with a *peta* at Vv VII.9.

12 Three of the Vv stories (Vv III.5, IV.2, and IV.7) contain some verses in the archaic *ārya* meter; Ludwig Alsdorf holds that this suggests that they may be relatively old. "Die Āryā-Strophen des Pali-Kanons," *Akademie der Wissenschaften und der Literatur in Mainz: Abhandlungen der Geistes- und Sozialwissenschaftlichen Klasse* 1967: 243–331. On the other hand, the sections of third person narration are self-evidently late. Most obviously, Pv IV.3, which consists entirely of third person narration, refers to Maurya hegemony over Surāṣṭra, and so cannot predate the Mauryan empire. Dhammapāla, the commentator, consistently attributes all third person narration to the redactors; Pv-a 144 says that Pv II.10 was added at the second council, and Pv-a 244, 257 attributes Pv IV.3 to the third council. Attributions of parts of the *vatthus* to the redactors are also found at Pv-a 49, 70, 81, 109, 136, 133–134, 137–138, 140, 142, 148, 162–163, 169–70, 179, 217, 233–240, 172–173, 196–197, 199–200, 203–204, and

245–250, and Vv-a 106, 108, 202, 224, and 332. Pv II.3.26–28 and the first *pāda* of Vv VII.9.7 are the only examples I have found of third person speech not attributed to the redactors.

13 Vv contains 85 poems. Vv III.5 and IV.7 tell very similar stories about 36 and 4 goddesses respectively, and I count each of these poems as a single narrative. As Vv III.6 and IV.6 each contrast the acts and resulting happinesses of two deities, I count each of these poems as two stories, making for a total of 87 stories. In some of these 62 acts, no item is offered. For example, an act may consist of an *añjali* salute, or rearranging a garland on a stūpa (Vv IV.11 and VII.9, VII.11). However, they are, like *dāna*, acts of worship directed toward a worthy individual. In one of these stories (Vv VII.3.6), the meritorious act is building a bridge and planting trees in gardens (*ārāmarukkhāni*). This could be considered an act of disinterested generosity, but I follow Vv-a 301 in assuming that Buddhist monastics are to be understood as the intended recipients.

Theravādin tradition understands acts of worship toward stūpas as acts of giving even though the relics themselves cannot receive gifts. This point is discussed at Mil 95–102, where Nāgasena argues that worship of the Buddha can be fruitful even though the Buddha, having attained parinirvāṇa, does not enjoy (i.e. receive) worship (*pūjaṃ sādiyati*): "Gods and men who make as their basis a relic-gem of the Tathāgata (who does not enjoy [worship]), and who practice rightly with the Tathāgata's gem of knowledge as their mental object, attain the three attainments." ". . . *asādiyantass' eva Tathāgatassa devamanussā dhāturatanaṃ vatthuṃ karityā Tathāgatassa ñāṇaratanārammaṇena sammāpaṭipattiṃ sevantā tisso sampattiyo paṭilabhanti*" (Mil 96, similarly at 96–97). The three attainments are identified at Mil 410 as the human world, the heavens, and nirvāṇa (*manussa-*, *devaloka-*, and *nibbāna-sampatti*). The text similarly states that the Tathāgata's relics and gem of knowledge are the condition (*paccaya*) for achieving the three attainments (96–97). Nāgasena also names relics, the *suttas* and the *Vinaya* (*dhammavinaya*), and the instruction as the condition for achieving the attainments (97–98). These formulations affirm the importance of particular objects, viz. the Buddha and his teaching, for attaining both a happy rebirth and nirvāṇa. Nāgasena presents a number of analogies for the role of the Buddha and his relics, including the *puññakkhetta* trope: although the earth does not actively receive seeds it still serves as the ground (*vatthu*) and condition (*paccaya*) for the growth of plants (99).

14 *Bahunnaṃ vata atthāya uppajjanti tathāgatā / dakkhiṇeyyā manussānaṃ puññakkhettānam ākarā / yattha kāraṃ karitvāna sagge modanti dāyakā / ti. //* Vv IV.12.31 Cf. Vv I.10.6.

15 *Karaṇīyāni puññāni paṇḍitena vijānatā / sammaggatesu buddhesu yattha dinnaṃ mahapphalaṃ. //* Vv V.6.6.

16 *niraggaḷaṃ / yaññaṃ yajitvā tividhaṃ visuddhaṃ* Vv V.14.31, cf. Sn 509. *āhuneyyānaṃ paramāhutiṃ gato / puññatthikānaṃ vipulapphalesinan / ti //* Vv V.14.33; my paraphrase of this unusual construction follows Masefield and Vv-a 285–286, which also considers an alternative reading with the same meaning.

17 *supatiṭṭhitaṃ* Vv II.3.6; *kāle*: Vv IV.1.40; *ujubhūtesu*: Vv II.2.6, II.6.6–7, IV.5.6, VII.3.1, Pv I.10.10; *sammāvimuttānaṃ santānaṃ brahmacārinaṃ* Vv I.5.11.

18 Sacrificial terms used include *yajitvā* v. 57; *yaññassa* v. 51; *yaññassa sampadā* vv.48–49, v.l. *puññassa sampadā*; *khattiyo* v. 55; *puññapekkhassa* v. 50.

19 *dakkhiṇeyyena* v. 67.

20 *Sā dakkhiṇā saṅghagatā appameyye patiṭṭhitā, / puggalesu tayā dinnaṃ na taṃ tava mahapphalan / ti. //* v. 15. We have seen this emphasis on giving to the Saṅgha rather than to individuals in *Dakkhiṇāvibhaṅga Sutta*.

21 *Tato maṃ avadhī gāvī thūpaṃ appattamānasaṃ / tañ cāhaṃ abhisañceyyaṃ bhiyyo nūna ito siyā. //* v. 6.

22 *Eso hi saṅgho vipulo mahaggato / es'appameyyo udadhīva sāgaro / ete hi seṭṭhā naravīrasāvakā / pabhaṅkarā dhamam udīrayanti. // Tesaṃ sudinnaṃ suhutaṃ suyiṭṭhaṃ / ye saṅgham uddissa dadanti dānaṃ / sā dakkhiṇā saṅghagatā patiṭṭhitā / mahapphalā lokavidūna vaṇṇitā. // Etādisaṃ yaññam anussarantā / ye vedajātā vicaranti loke / vineyya maccheramalaṃ samūlaṃ / aninditā saggam upenti ṭhānan / ti. //* Vv III.6.25–27 = IV.6.24–26.

23 Cited in chapter 1. Jayawickrama prefers *puññassa* for *yaññassa*. He also has *eso* for *esā*; I think he errs here.

24 Étienne Lamotte gives the following references: six *anussati*, D III 250, 280, A III 284–287, 312–313, 452, V 329–332; ten *anussati*, A I 30, 42. *La Traité de la Grande Vertu de Sagesse de Nāgarjuna (Mahāprajñapār-amitāśāstra)* (Louvain: Institut Orientaliste, 1970), 1329.

25 Paul Harrison, "Commemoration and Identification in *Buddhānusmṛti*," in *In the Mirror of Memory: Reflections on Mindfulness and Remembrance in Indian and Tibetan Buddhism*, ed. Janet Gyatso (Albany: State University of New York, 1992), 215–238.

26 Pv II.1.4.

27 *santesu deyyadhammesu dīpaṃ nākamha attano*, Pv III.6.4 and IV.10.4 and 10.

28 Pv II.3.17–18.

29 Pv I.11.11, II.7.11, III.1.9, IV.15.3; cf. Pv IV.6.4. The trope of making an island for oneself appears in Dhp 236.

30 In some stories the deity cites being without envy, meanness, or spite, possessing faith or exertion, or being diligent as part of his or her meritorious action. These virtues are, however, always cited in connection with some specific action.

31 *Appakam pi kataṃ mahāvipākaṃ / vipulaṃ hoti tathāgatassa dhamme /* Vv V.3.21; cf. v. 17.

32 *Tath' eva sīlavantesu guṇavantesu tādisu / appakam pi kataṃ kāraṃ puññaṃ hoti mahapphalan / ti. //* Pv II.9.72.

33 E.g. *anubhomi*: Vv I.5.11, III.2.7–8, IV.2.3–4, IV.10.7 & 8, V.10.18 (= Pv IV.4.18), Vv VII.10, Pv I.10.11; *vedanaṃ vedissa*: Pv II.7.16 & 18, *sukhuvedanīya* Pv II.11, *vedanīya* Pv III.3.7–8, IV.1.63, 73–74, & 81.

34 *kin nu kāyena vācāya manasā dukkaṭaṃ kataṃ / kissa kammavipākena . . .* For citations see Jayawickrama's Index of repeated stanzas, no. 24, Pv p. 97.

35 *Disvā ca sutvā abhisaddahassu / kalyāṇapāpassa ayaṃ vipāko / kalyāṇapāpe ubhaye asante/ siyā nu sattā sugatā duggatā vā. // No c'ettha kammāni kareyyuṃ maccā / kalyāṇapāpāni manussaloke / nāhesuṃ sattā sugatā duggatā vā / hīnā paṇītā ca manussaloke. //* Pv IV.1.26–27. Following Pv-a; Jayawickrama's text appears to be in error here.

36 Pv IV.1.62–63, 73–74, 80.

37 In 41 Vv stories a deity is said to possess a *vimāna* and in 14 stories a deity possesses a flying chair, elephant, or chariot. 16 stories describe the happiness of a deity solely in terms of his or her physical splendor.

38 Pv I.2–3; other stories of mixed results include Pv I.10, II.12, III.5, III.9, IV.1.

39 Manuscripts read variously *nihitaṃ*, *nataṃ*, and *nitaṃ*. This belief that one may attain rebirth in a particular heaven by directing the karmic effects of past acts is foundational to Pure Land practice.

40 *Abhikkhaṇaṃ Nandanaṃ sutvā chando me upapajjatha / tattha cittaṃ paṇidhāya upapanna 'mhi Nandanaṃ. // Nākāsiṃ satthu vacanaṃ buddhass' ādiccabandhuno / hīne cittaṃ paṇidhāya sāmhi pacchānutāpinī. //* Vv II.7.12–13. Nandana is the name of one of Sakka's gardens; alternatively, *nandana* here may simply mean 'pleasant.'

41 *Tiṭṭhante nibbute cāpi same citte samaṃ phalaṃ / cetopaṇidhihetu hi sattā gacchanti suggatiṃ. //* Vv IV.9.12.

42 Vv III.4; II.3, III.6, and IV.6; Vv III.1, Vv III.7, V.6–7. Other stories associate their deities with the Tāvatiṃsa but do not label them as Tāvatiṃsa deities. In Vv II.1 a goddess tells that she is an intimate (*āmantanikā*) of Sakka. Vv I.17 inverts the usual *vimāna* story by having a goddess arise in Sakka's *vimāna* and be greeted by him there. Other deities say that their *vimāna* is frequented by the gods of the Thirty (*devā Tidasagaṇā*, VII.8) or by their celestial maidens (*dibbā kaññā Tidasacarā*, VI.3, VI.8–9, VII.6). Some goddesses tell that they are under the protection of Sakka and the Thirty, and others delight in inhabiting Sakka's Nandana grove. Vv III.2 and IV.10; Vv II.1, II.5, IV.10, and IV.12. In other stories (II.7, IV.10, V.10, V.13), it is difficult to tell whether *nandana* should be taken as referring to Sakka's Nandana grove, as the commentary indicates, or whether *nandana* here simply means "pleasing." In the *vimāna* stories II.4, VI.7, and VII.4–5, the latter reading seems preferable. VII.4.12 includes the line, *vasaṃ vattemi nandane*, "I exercise control in Nandana" or "I exercise control in that pleasing place." Because the god is not Sakka, the second reading is clearly preferable. III.9 is similarly unclear as to whether *cittalatā* refers to Sakka's grove of that name or to another grove (cf. IV.1).

43 Most of the stories that specify the location of *vimāna*s place them in the air (*vehāsayaṃ* IV.6, VII.10, *antalikkhe* VI.1–2, 4–5, 10, VII.1–2), although *vimāna*s also appear in a grove (IV.1), on a mountain (VII.4), and in the third heaven (*Tidise* VI.3). One *vimāna* that appears in space (*ākāse*) near the earth is said to have come from the third heaven, Vv V.3; other mobile *vimāna*s include Vv I.16, II.4, IV.6a, V.3.

44 The commentary calls these *vimānapeta*s and *vimānapetī*s. The *yakkhabhūta*s (yakṣa-ghosts or yakṣa-demons) of Pv III.5 might be another example of a hybrid being.

45 Pv II.1–4, II.8, IV.1. In other stories, such as Pv III.1, after receiving the gift the being is still called a *peta*; see below.
46 hell: Vv V.2 = Pv IV.4; *petas*: *Yamalokika/-ā*: Pv I.6.2, I.7.2, II.1.2, III.6.2 & 7 & 10–11, II.7.2, IV.8.2, IV.16.2, III.2.2, III.2.6, IV.10.2; *Yamavisaya*: Pv II.8.2; *Yamassa ṭhāyino*: Pv I.11.9, *Yamapurisā*: Pv IV.3.6 & 8.
47 Dhammapāla writes that the ghost had formerly been cooked in the Avīci hell for many thousands of years (Pv-a 284).
48 "Translator's Introduction," *Vimāna Stories*, xxxiv.
49 Wilhelm Stede, *Über das Peta Vatthu* (Inaugural diss., University of Leipzig, 1914), 39, 53.
50 Vv I.16, IV.3, IV.12; I.17.
51 *Sāhaṃ avaṭṭhitā pemā dassane avikampinī / mūlajātāya saddhāya dhītā buddhassa orasā.* // Vv IV.12.22.
52 *Yan ca sīlavantī āsiṃ na taṃ tāva vipaccati / āsā ca pana me devinda sakadāgāminī siyan / ti.* // Vv III.9.13.
53 *Yañ ca me ahuvā hāso saddaṃ sutvāna bodhiyā / ten' eva kusalamūlena phusissaṃ āsavakkhayaṃ.* // Vv VII.7.24.
54 As the terms *kusalamūla* and *akusalamūla* usually refer to mental states, especially greed, hatred, and ignorance, or their opposites, the good root here is apparently Kanthaka's thoughts as he laughed. A wish incorporating the term *kusalamūla* is unusual in the Pāli canon; however, a good root, or root of goodness (Sanskrit *kuśalamūla*), is frequently named in the Sanskrit *avadāna* literature as the basis for making an aspiration. In particular, the use of the expression *kusalamūlena* in the Kanthaka story links it with Sanskrit *avadāna* texts in which donors make aspirations for the attainment of awakening on the basis of a *kuśalamūla*. In a story of *Avadānaśataka*, for example, a gardener who gives a lotus to the Buddha resolves to become a buddha "*kuśalamūlena cittotpādena deyadharmaparityāgena*": "by this good root, by the production of this thought, by the renunciation of this thing to be given" (*Avadānaśataka*, 40; similarly, 7, 12, 22, *et passim*). These terms point to an understanding of giving as an act of detachment and generosity, distinguishable from an understanding of giving as an act of meritorious sacrifice. See John S. Strong, "The Transforming Gift: An Analysis of Devotional Acts of Offering in Buddhist Avadāna Literature," *History of Religions* 18 (1979): 221–237. A version of the Kanthaka story that corresponds closely to the Vv account appears in the Sanskrit Buddhist text, *Mahāvastu* (II 191–195).
55 Pv I.10, II.1, 2, 3, 4, and 8, III.1, 2, and 6, IV.1, 3, and 12. In Pv II.10, a *petī* asks that dakṣiṇā be dedicated to her, but this story does not tell whether the request is granted.
56 These stories stress that gifts may not be given directly to the dead (e.g. Pv I.10, II.5, II.10), but only by making a gift to a worthy recipient and assigning the dakṣiṇā to the being. This usage is standard in these stories: Pv I.10.5 *dakkhiṇaṃ ādisa*; .6 *dakkhiṇaṃ ādisuṃ*; II.1.6 *ādissa*; .7 *dakkhiṇam ādisi*; .14 *dakkhiṇaṃ ādisi*; II.2.6 *uddisāhi*; .8 *dakkhiṇam ādisi*; II.3.25 *dakkhiṇam ādisa*; *dakkhiṇam ādisi*; II.4.8 *dakkhiṇam ādisa*; .10 *dakkhiṇam ādisi*; II.8.8 *dakkhiṇaṃ ādisa*; .9 *dakkhiṇam ādisittha*; .11 *anuddiṭṭhaṃ*; III.1 – ; III.2 *anvādisāhi*; .11, 15, 20, 24, 29 *anvādisi*; III.6.9, 13 *dakkhiṇaṃ anvādissatu*; 14 *dakkhiṇam adisi*; IV.1.51,52 *dakkhiṇāyo*;

IV.3 – ; IV.12 – . The recipient need not be a Buddhist monk: in Pv I.10 he is a lay follower, and in Pv III.1 he is a barber (and a lay follower, explains the commentary). In Pv II.8, gifts given to Brāhmaṇs by the deceased's daughter are ineffective while those given to the Saṅgha by a stranger reach the ghost.

Three of the stories cite the donor's words, including, "Let these dakṣiṇās go to that yakṣa," *yakkhass' imā gacchantu dakkhiṇayo* (Pv IV.1.51, 52). "Let this be for my relations; let my relations be happy," *idaṃ vo me ñātīnaṃ hotu sukhitā hontu ñātayo* (Pv III.2.11, 15, 20, 24, 29; cf. I.5.3). "My father has died, sir; let this benefit him," *pitā me kālakato bhante tass' etaṃ upakappantu* (Pv IV.3.45). Such statements stress the identity between the object given by the donor and the object received by the recipient.

57 The correspondences of offerings to results are as follows: I.10: garments→food, clothing, drink; II.1: food, cloth, water→food, clothing, drink; II.2: huts, food, water→clothing, food, pools; II.3: food→clothing, food, drink; II.4: food, drink, hard food, clothing, lodging, sunshades, scents, garlands, sandals→food, clothing, drink, ornaments; III.1: meal, food, clothes→ clothes; III.2: food, clothes, hut, water, sandal→food, clothes, houses, pools, chariot; IV.1: clothes→clothes; IV.3: water, cakes→water, cakes; IV.12: mango→mango grove. John Strong points out that in Sanskrit *avadānas*, the object given is immediately transformed into a glorious but similar object. This trope resembles descriptions of the transformation of dakṣiṇā in Pv, suggesting a historical relationship between these story traditions. John S. Strong, "The Transforming Gift: An Analysis of Devotional Acts of Offering in Buddhist Avadāna Literature." *History of Religions* 18 (1979): 233–234.

58 Category names applied to beings by themselves, others or the narrator before and after they receive dedicated gifts (a space indicates that no name was applied): Pv I.10: __ → *devatā*; II.1: *petī* → *devatā/devī*; II.2: *pettivisaya* → *devatā/devī*; II.3: *petaloka* → *devatā/devī*; II.4: *petaloka* → *devatā/devī*; II.8: *peta* → *yakkha*; III.1: *peta* → __; III.2: *peta* → __; III.6: *petī* → __; IV.1: *yakkha* → *yakkha*; IV.3: __ → *peta/yakkha/devatā*, is said to have the appearance of a *deva*, however, he denies that he is a *deva* or a *gandhabba*; IV.12: __ → __ .

59 Pv IV.1.58 and IV.3.51. These stories resemble accounts of present-day Hindu rites in which an unhappy ghost is appeased by enthroning it as a deity and worshiping it. C. J. Fuller, *The Camphor Flame: Popular Hinduism and Society in India* (Princeton: Princeton University Press, 1992), 49, 227–231. Fuller discusses ethnographies by Ann Grodzins Gold and David Knipe. By contrast, Gombrich relates that Siṅhala Buddhists treat exorcised *pretas* with contempt. *Precept and Practice*, 194.

60 Stede, *Über das Peta Vatthu*, 53; Masefield, "Translator's Introduction," *Vimāna Stories*, xxxiv.

61 Jean-Michel Agasse, "Le transfert de mérite dans le Bouddhisme Pāli classique," *Journal Asiatique* 266 (1978): 327, n. 69. Schmithausen favors Stede's reading to Agasse's: *Critical Response*, 212.

62 This story also tries to set some limitations on the miraculous results of the dedication of dakṣiṇā. Here a gift of the cakes and water produces a

supply of cakes and water that never runs out, but is otherwise identical to the original gift. This story is the one most clearly marked as late, as it consists entirely of narrative verse and is set in the time of the Mauryas.

63 I will discuss the commentarial interpretation in the next chapter. Modern scholars who have seen in this text a transfer of merit include: G. P. Malalasekere, "Transference of Merit in Ceylonese Buddhism," *Philosophy East and West* 17:87; Agasse, "Le transfert de mérite," 316; Gombrich, "Merit Transference," 213; Holt, "Assisting the Dead," 15–19; Schmithausen, "Critical Response," 212; White, "*Dakkhiṇa* and *Agnicayana*," 201–202.

Stede does not explain these passages in terms of merit (see "Über das Peta Vatthu," 51–54). Neither does Masefield: "Thus we may say that the expression 'transfer of merit' in such contexts is at best misleading and that it is always the divine counterpart of alms offered that is assigned." "Translator's Introduction," xl.

64 *Samanantarānudiṭṭhe vipāko upapajjatha / bhojanacchādanapānīyaṃ, dakkhiṇāya idaṃ phalan. //* Pv I.10.7, II.1.8, II.2.9, II.3.27, II.4.11, III.2.12, 16, 21, 25, & 30; similarly IV.3.46.

65 The theme of immediacy appears in other Pv descriptions of dakṣiṇā dedication: *ṭhānaso* Pv I.4.4, I.5.11, *ṭhāne* III.1.4.

66 White, "*Dakkhiṇa* and *Agnicayana*," 201.

67 Pv I.10.11–15, II.7.12–17, IV.3.35–40.

68 Pv II.1 & 2. In III.2 the elder Poṭṭhapāda collects food from his fellow monks and then gives it back to them as a gift, dedicating it to his relatives; he then collects rags and gives them, and so forth.

69 Pv IV.3 describes how a pious Buddhist gave alms to a monk who had entered her village, and wished that her gift would benefit her recently deceased father (vv. 41–46).

70 Relation: II.2 (mother), II.3 (co-wife), II.4 (wife), III.2 (brother and parents); stranger: I.10, II.1, II.8, III.1, III.6, IV.1. In III.6 the ghost asks her interlocutor to tell the ghost's mother to give *dāna*. In IV.12 a deity relates that his daughter gave on his behalf.

71 *anukampo*, II.1.7 and II.2.7, *anukampāya* III.1.5, *anukampassu kāruṇiko* III.2.8, *anukampāya* III.2.10, *anukampito* III.2.30. In IV.1.51, the donor is motivated by agitation (*saṃvegam*) caused by the sight of the yakṣa.

72 The donors in these stories are: Pv I.10 traders; II.1 Sāriputta; II.2 Sāriputta; II.3 woman (former co-wife); II.4 layman (former wife); II.8 king; III.1 chief minister; III.2 *thera* Poṭṭhapāda; III.6 laywoman (former mother); IV.1 layman Ambasakkhara; IV.3 former daughter; IV.12 former daughter.

73 It is, of course, difficult to draw from these representations any conclusions about the actual practices of monks and nuns. Schopen has demonstrated on the basis of textual and inscriptional evidence that Buddhist monks and nuns did act as donors. (On Buddhist monastics as donors in *Vinaya* texts, see Schopen, "The Ritual Obligations"; page 92, note 1 contains references to Schopen's studies of inscriptions.) Pv III.2 sheds some light on a question suggested by Schopen's studies, that of how monks and nuns would have had the financial resources to make large donations. In this story, the elder collects from his fellow monks the alms they have just received and then gives them back to them as dedicated

gifts. Monks and nuns may have similarly made gifts of articles previously donated to them, or, as Walters suggests, they may have acted on behalf of groups of donors; "Stūpa, Story and Empire," 169–171.

74 A similar validation of persons of low status is given in Pv I.10 and Vv VII.10.39–47, in which the only *upāsaka* in a company of traders is the barber. In Pv I.10 the barber is able to receive *dāna* from his comrades, while in Vv VII.10 a yakṣa saves the company for the sake of the barber.

75 Pv contains about equal numbers of stories about males and females.

76 For example, Vv III.7 contains the finest poetry in either collection, and III.6 and IV.6 compare the results of two different acts.

77 In Pv II.13 a woman goes forth into the homeless life, and in Vv III.5.55 monks and nuns are said to exemplify Dharma.

78 *Sīho yathā pabbatasānugocaro / mahiṃdharaṃ pabbatam āvasitvā / pasayha hantvā itare catuppade / khudde mige khādati maṃsabhojano, // Tath' eva saddhā idha ariyasāvikā / bhattāraṃ nissāya patiṃ anubbatā / kodhaṃ vadhitvā abhibhuyya maccharaṃ / saggamhi sā modati dhamma-cārinī / ti. //* Vv III.4.10–11.

79 III.1, 2 and IV.10; other daughter-in-law stories are I.13,14 and III.3,7.

80 Nancy Auer Falk, "The Case of the Vanishing Nuns: The Fruits of Ambivalence in Ancient Indian Buddhism," in *Unspoken Worlds: Women's Religious Lives in Non-Western Cultures*, ed. Nancy A. Falk and Rita M. Gross (San Francisco: Harper & Row, 1980), 207–224.

81 E.g. the trio of verses at Vv.I.1.2, 4, and 6 appears dozens of times yet are usually (as here) redundant. See the indices to N. A. Jayawickrama's edition for additional examples.

82 In Vv IV.3, IV.12, I.17, and VII.9, people hear the words of the Buddha after performing acts of devotion toward him. In Vv IV.2, a deity regrets that after giving to the Buddha she did not remain to hear him preach the Dharma.

Chapter Four

1 The commentaries were composed on the basis of an older Siṅhala commentarial tradition, which was in turn probably based on older Indian traditions. Norman, *Pāli Literature*, 118–119. Buddhaghosa maintains that these commentaries go back to the First Council (Sv I, 15–18=Ps I 1, 21–24=Spk I 1, 17–20=Mp I, 1, 18–21, cited in Ibid.). Dhammapāla refers to earlier commentaries at Vv-a 1 and at Pv-a 1 and 287.

2 Vism 223–224. This passage, from a discussion of objects for recollection (*anussati*), uses the word sacrifice (*yāja-*, *yajana-*) but without giving it the meaning of worship. Vism 325 similarly observes that buddhas give to all without discrimination.

3 *mahapphalakaraṇatāya visodhenti; saṅghaṃ nissāya lokassa nānappakār-ahitasukhasaṃvattanikāni puññāni lokassāti.* Vism 218–221. The theme of purification is based on the interpretation given at M III 256–257, D III 231, A II 80–81, and Kv 555–556. Not surprisingly, the idea of the field for merit shows up in Buddhaghosa in the same context as in the

canonical prose: not in explanations of action and rebirth but in discussions of the recipients of gifts.

4 On Dhammapāla see Norman, *Pāli Literature*, 133–137. Norman tentatively dates Dhammapāla's works to the middle of the sixth century CE (137).

5 *yattha sayaṃ uppannaṃ, taṃ santānaṃ punāti visodhetī ti* Vv-a 19.

6 *Etarahi kho manussā asati pi vatthusampattiyā khettasampattiyā attano ca cittasampasādasampattiyā tāni tāni puññāni katvā devaloke nibbattā uḷārasampattiṃ paccanubhonti;* Vv-a 3. *Sampatti* and *patti* are used in various ways in Vv-a and Pv-a; I translate them both as attainment as these words have a similar range of meanings. *Vatthu* seems here to refer to the object to be given rather than to the object of worship as it does in Mil 99 (discussed in chapter 3).

7 Cf. also Vv-a 32: *khettasampattiyā cittasampattiyā*.

8 *Tena ca samayena aññataro piṇḍacāriko thero pāsādikena abhikkantena paṭikkantena ālokitena vilokitena samiñjitena pasāritena okkhittacakkhu iriyāpathasampanno piṇḍāya caranto upakaṭṭhe kāle aññataraṃ gehaṃ sampāpuṇi. Tatth'ekā kuladhītā saddhāsampannā theraṃ pasīditvā sañjāta-gāravabahumānā uḷārapītisomanassaṃ uppādetvā gehaṃ pavesetvā pañca-patiṭṭhitena vanditvā attano pīṭhaṃ paññāpetvā tassa upari pītakaṃ maṭṭhavatthaṃ attharitvā adāsi. Atha there tattha nisinne 'idaṃ mayhaṃ uttamapuññakkhettaṃ upaṭṭhitan' ti pasannacittā yathāvibhavaṃ āhārena parivisi bījaniñ ca gahetvā bīji. So thero katabhattakicco āsanadānabhoja-nadānādi-paṭisaṃyuttaṃ dhammakathaṃ katvā pakkami. Sā itthi taṃ attano dānaṃ tañ ca dhammakathaṃ paccavekkhantī pītiyā nirantaraṃ phuṭṭhasārīrā hutvā taṃ pīṭhaṃ pi therassa adāsi.* Vv-a 6, reading v.l. *passitvā* for text's *pasīditvā*.

9 Regarding the recipient, see e.g. Vv-a 46, 61, 101. Vv-a 152 comments briefly on the instruction in Vv III.6 to give to the Saṅgha rather than to individuals, but Vv-a generally presents donors as giving to individual monks.

10 Vv-a 40, 184, 257, 293, 294, 323, 353.

11 Furthermore, the physical presence of a recipient is of course not essential in the commentary's karmic ethics. Dhammapāla claims to have made merit by saluting the Three Jewels (Vv-a 1, Pv-a 1), and tells of two householders who do meritorious deeds designated (*uddissa*) for the Three Jewels (Vv-a 286). In describing the meritorious acts of taking the Three Refuges, Vv-a 233 tells that a youth recollected the virtues of the Three Jewels and established the formula for taking the Refuges in his heart.

12 Vv-a 6. Cf. also the list of correspondences at Vv-a 32. As this description indicates, *vimānas* are in Vv-a represented more as vehicles than as heavens.

13 I follow Masefield here in reading *karoti* for text's *karonti*.

14 The commentaries clearly indicate that birth as an attendant deity is desirable (Vv-a 131 and 149); presumably the tormenters of hell are real beings as well. The existence of the guardians of hell is a debated point in Buddhism; at Kv 596–598 it is debated whether beings in hell are tormented by beings or by their own actions. ADhKBh denies the existence of the *nirāyapālā*, III 59a-c, Pruden 458–9; Vasubandhu cites

the views of different schools on this question at *Vijñaptimātraviṃśaka* 4, cited in Pruden 534, note 409.

15 The meeting between Moggallāna and the *accharās* does not appear in all manuscripts. Vv-a 65 and 221 are both derived from Dhp-a; see Burlingame, *Buddhist Legends*, I, 57.

16 Literally, "*peta*-womb," Pv-a 9, 35, 36, 55, 78, etc. Pv-a 17–18 invokes the etymological sense of *peta*, referring to *pubbe pete*. In glossing the names of the six *gatis*, Pv-a 272 defines *petā* as *khuppipāsādibhedā petā*, "hungry and thirsty ghosts, and so forth." This is apparently an allusion to Mil 294's four classes of *petas*. Dhammapāla does not systematically apply this typology to the verses, probably because it does not fit them, as I explain below.

17 Pv-a 47, 145, 152, 186, 204, 244, 271. Similarly we find *vimānadevatā* Vv-a 229, Pv-a 92, 190, and *rukkhadevatā* Pv-a 5, 43. Pv-a 92 accounts for any passages in which the term *peta* is applied to someone who does not seem to belong to this distinct class by saying that *peta* can refer to anyone who has left the human state. Similarly, Vv-a 333 broadly defines *yakkha* as a deity to be worshiped by human beings and some deities, and thereby accounts for references to Sakka and the Four Great Kings as *yakkhas*. Nonetheless, Dhammapāla does not eliminate all classificatory ambiguities in the texts. One being is called both a terrestrial deity (*bhummadevatā*) and a *peta* of great wondrous power (Pv-a 216, 217, 232). Another being is called a *vimānapeta*, but he does not seem to suffer in any way: he can travel as high as the realm of the Four Great Kings, and he is addressed as *yakkha* and *devatā* (Pv-a 271). Another story introduces a problem not found in the verses, as it refers to a being both as *vimānapetī* and *vimānadevatā* (Pv-a 186–190).

18 While Vv and Pv speak only in passing of past actions determining the qualities of human birth, notably at Pv III.1.13–18, this theme appears often in the commentary. Vv-a 32, for example, lists a number of correspondences between different gifts and their results in a future human birth. At Vv-a 289, a gardener gives a mango to the elder Moggallāna with the expectation of great fruit, in both the here and now and in the next world (*diṭṭhadhammikasamparāyikaṃ*). In addition to the heavenly reward described in the verses, the commentary adds that the man received a village and clothing from the king. A perhaps unintended consequence of this focus on this world as a place of karmic fulfillment is that beings are affected by the fruit of other's actions. In Vv-a 156–159, for example, when the girl turns stones to gold and jewels, her great merit reverses the effect of the man's bad action, and so he enjoys the fruit of her action. Although such phenomena might seem to violate the principle that action is inalienable (e.g. A V 292, 297, 300, Sn 666), if action determines not only rebirth, but also the vagaries of human existence, then people will inevitably be affected by the results of each other's actions.

19 *nanu petā attano atthāya dānaṃ dentaṃ anumodenti, cittaṃ pasādenti, pītiṃ uppādenti, somanassaṃ paṭilabhantīti?*

20 *añño aññassa kārako parakataṃ sukhadukkhaṃ añño karoti, añño paṭisaṃvedetīti?*

21 Mil describes the dedication of dakṣiṇā with phrases like *ime dāyakā dānaṃ datvā pubbapetānaṃ ādisanti: idaṃ tesaṃ pāpuṇātūti* and terms like *saramānā* that seem to echo *Tirokuḍḍa Sutta*. Nāgasena asserts that there are four classes of *petas*, of which only one, those who live on what is given by others (*paradattūpajīvino*), receive the result of a dedicated gift. This name suggests a condition of ongoing dependence on human beings for food, a state like that suggested by *Tirokuḍḍa*. In contrast with the Mil authors' apparent familiarity with *Tirokuḍḍa*, they seem either not to know the individual dedication stories of Pv, or to reject their authority. The state of ongoing dependence on the part of the dead for offerings does not fit the twelve Pv dedication stories in which a single gift produces a definitive transformation in the status of the deceased. The four categories map onto the Pv rather poorly in other ways. For example, Pv II.2.2 describes a *petī* who later receives a dedicated gift as *khuppipāsasamappitā*, endowed with hunger and thirst, but *khuppipāsino* is one of Nāgasena's three classes of *petas* who cannot receive dedicated gifts.

22 *kusalaṃ saṃvibhajituṃ*, Mil 295, *vipākaṃ paṭilabhanti, phalaṃ anubhavanti* Mil 294.

23 *Yasmā idaṃ vo ñātinaṃ hotū ti vutte pi aññena katakammaṃ aññassa phalaṃ dinnaṃ hoti kevalaṃ pana tathā uddissa dīyamānaṃ vuttapetānaṃ kusalakammassa paccayo hoti, tasmā yathā tesaṃ tasmiṃ vatthusmiṃ tasmiṃ yeva khaṇe phalanibbattakaṃ kusalaṃ kammaṃ hoti*. Pv-a 26.

24 *Petānaṃ hi attano anumodanena dāyakānaṃ uddissanena dakkhiṇeyyasampattiyā vā tīhi aṅgehi dakkhiṇā taṃ khaṇ' aññe'va phalanibbattikā hoti*. Pv-a 27.

25 Malalasekere, "Transference of Merit," 85–90; Gombrich, "Merit Transference," 203–219; Agasse, "Le transfert de mérite," 311–331. Gombrich and Agasse provide very helpful discussions of the commentarial theory of *pattidāna*.

26 Filliozat, "Sur le domain sémantique de *puṇya*," 116.

27 On *prāpti* see *Abhidharmakośabhāṣyam*, tr. by Leo M. Pruden from Louis de la Vallée Poussin's version (Berkeley: Asian Humanities Press, 1991) II: 179–195, Jaini, "The Sautrāntika Theory of *Bījā*," 238–239, Étienne Lamotte, *History of Indian Buddhism: From the Origins to the Śaka Era*, tr. Sara Webb-Boin (Louvain-la-Neuve: Institut Orientaliste, 1988), 606–607 <672>.

28 Gombrich, *How Buddhism Began*, 57.

29 Lamotte, 606–607.

30 In "Le transfert de mérite," Agasse discusses the following examples: Ja no. 190, 288; Dhp-a I 103–104, 197, II 4, 198, III 63, IV 122–123, 200–201, 203. Ja and Dhp-a were both used as sources by the author of Pv-a. For literary history, see Eugene Watson Burlingame, tr., *Buddhist Legends* [translation of Dhp-a], Harvard Oriental Series (Cambridge: Harvard University Press, 1921), 3: 52–57; and K. R. Norman, *Pāli Literature*, 134–135.

31 In the Pv-a version *patti* is replaced by *sampatti*; more on this below. *Pattidāna* is also used to gloss *dakkhiṇā* at Pv-a 9 and 88.

32 Dhp-a I 197, I 270, II 4, 198, III 63, IV 122–123, 200–203, Vv-a 188, 289.

33 *'Na demi tāta, aññehi asādhāraṇaṃ karissāmī' ti.*

34 Pv-a's version of the Bimbisāra story (19–31) seems to support this reading when it replaces the *patti* of Dhp-a I 103–104 with *sampatti*, the term Pv-a uses for the excellence of the result of giving, as well as of the three factors of the gift: a worthy field, a devoted mind, and a thing to be given (Vv-a 3, 5–7, and 32 and Pv-a 27). This reading fits nicely with the argument at Vv-a 20 that non-human beings have difficulty attaining the conditions of meritorious action.

35 As discussed above, another way in which Vv-a links giving to nirvāṇa is that donors aspire to become a chief disciple of the Buddha (Vv-a 3), or to share in the Dharma (Vv-a 64).

36 This theme appears in five Vv stories. In Vv IV.3, IV.12, I.17, and VII.9, people hear the words of the Buddha after performing acts of devotion toward him. In Vv IV.2, a deity regrets that after giving to the Buddha she did not remain to hear him preach the Dharma.

37 Vv-a 66: three become *sotāpannas*; 69: one attains *sakadāgāmi* fruit, three attain *sotāpatti* fruit, 501 become *sotāpannas*; 77–78: one becomes an arhat, 84,000 attain insight into the Dharma; 181: one attains *sotāpatti* fruit. Pv-a 38 and 66: one attains *sotāpatti* fruit, 171–177 and 195–196, 84,000 attain insight into the Dharma. Others: Vv-a 98, 109, 115, 179, 187, 208–209, 246, 254, 270–271, Pv-a 23–24, 178–179, 208. On acts giving rise to additional acts, see e.g. Vv-a 6 discussed above.

38 Vv-a 208, Pv-a 99, 168, 282: persons attain *sotāpatti* fruit; Vv-a 217–219: frog becomes *devaputta* and then attains *sotāpatti* fruit, 84,000 gain insight into the Dharma; Pv-a 54: monks attain arhatship; Pv-a 141, 233: people are converted and take up meritorious acts, leading eventually to attainment of *sotāpatti* fruit and becoming *sotāpanna* respectively. Others: Vv-a 87, 92, 230, 297, 319, 322, Pv-a 17–19, 54–55. In Vv-a 114 and Pv-a 140 the Buddha preaches *Abhidhamma* (*Abhidhammapiṭaka* in Vv-a 114) to the gods in heaven for three months.

39 Vv-a 50, 286: deity established in *sotāpatti* fruit; 53: deity with her retinue attain *sotāpatti* fruit; 99: deity attains *sakadāgāmi* fruit; 197: four goddesses with their retinues become *sotāpannās*. Others: Vv-a 176, 178, 187, 266, 305, 322, 354.

40 Stories that take place after the death of the Buddha are usually not retold, but in Pv-a 270 Mahākaccāna retells the story. That the Buddha retells the stories creates the paradox of the telling of the definitive version of the story being an event within the story itself! This trope appears in other Indian texts, notably *Mahābhārata* and *Rāmāyaṇa*.

41 Vv-a 91, 97, 104, 108, 114, 165, 176, 178, 187, 195, 243, 254, 286, 305, 354, Pv-a 12, 16, 35, 46, 53, 61, 78, 82, 92, 168, 194, 204, 244, 263, 269, 277, 278; similarly, Pv-a 207.

42 Vv-a 53–54, 89, 105, 111, 144, 150, 273, Pv-a 159, 186, 191, 260, 271, 286: people are inspired to perform meritorious deeds; Vv-a 86: a monk becomes an arhat; Pv-a 42, 266, 279: many attain *sotāpatti* fruit; Vv-a 330, Pv-a 9, 31 84,000 attain insight into the Dharma; Pv-a 140: countless thousands of *koṭis* attain insight into the Dharma; Pv-a 259 people are established in the precepts and Refuges.

43 *saṃvigga-* Pv-a 31 *et passim.*

44 Despite asserting that women can progress in meditation, Vv-a 96 incongruously glosses woman (*itthikā*) as "one whose understanding is as thick as two fingers" *dvaṅgalabahalabuddhikā* or *dvaṅgalabahalabuddhikā*.

45 Vv-a 158 and 286. The latter passage states that nuns receive gifts, but says nothing about the efficacy of such gifts.

Chapter Five

1 Norman, *Pāli Literature*, 153–156.

2 For example, stories 20–24 all begin with the same formulaic praise of the land of Surāṣṭra and are characterized by a light tone unlike that of most other stories. Stories 8, 20, and 50 identify their author, but his name and home have not been conclusively identified with any known person or place. See Norman, *Pāli Literature*, 154, and Jacqueline Ver Eecke, ed. and trans., *Sīhaḷavatthuppakaraṇa*, (Paris: École Française d'Extrême-Orient, 1980), iii.

3 Of course, Sīh also employs many of the same mechanisms linking act and effect presented in Vv, Pv, and Pd, including acts producing effects similar to them (5, 67), mixed good and bad acts producing mixed effects (7, 24), aspirations shaping the effects of actions (3, 5, 7, 8, 46, 59, 61), groups of people being reborn together (6, 82), and recollection of gifts producing merit (8, 16, 22, 26, 31, 42, 46, 47).

4 Acts said to be meritorious: giving to buddhas or Buddhist monastics: Sīh 1, 2, 3, 5, 7, 8, 26, 31, 32, 33, 34, 35, 36, 37, 39, 40, 41, 42, 43 (x2), 44 (x2), 45, 46 (also took refuge but gift emphasized), 47, 49, 56, 57, 58, 61, 62, 68, 69, 72, 75, 76, 79; giving / worship to stūpa: 3, 67; service to an elder by an elephant: 23; mental devotion (*cittapasāda*): 6 (toward a yogin), 38 (toward an elder). Acts of giving are also represented in stories 38, 51, and 52, but no reward is stated. (Unless otherwise indicated, references are to story and verse numbers. References by page number are to Ver Eecke's edition.)

5 *Pūjā*, Sīh 16.15, 43.60–61, *adhikāra*, 17.21, unspecified (*te karonti bahuṃ puññaṃ*) 33.5.

6 Like the *Jātaka*'s stories of righteous kingship, this story is set in the interim between the Buddha Kassapa and our Buddha, a time when one could not practice specifically Buddhist forms of merit making. The *dhamma* that forms the tale's main theme is not the Buddhist Dharma, but the righteousness that kings must possess if they are to bring prosperity to their realms. Although the righteous king of the story does go to heaven after he dies, the text does not describe this event in terms of *puñña* or *kamma*.

7 *yaṃ kiñci dhammikaṃ dāṇaṃ suddhacittena jantunā / guṇādhikesu dinnaṃ vā parimetuṃ na vaṭṭati // guṇādhikesu yaṃ dinnaṃ taṃ dānaṃ vipulapphalaṃ / tasmā dhammapīti devo asankheyyanti bhāsati //* Sīh 41. 20–21.

8 Sīh 37.29–31, 38.8, 46.35, 47.21, 49.9.

9 Sīh 35, 36, 43 (x2), 45, 56, 62.

10 *tasmā appampi dātabbaṃ dakkhiṇeyyesu tādisu / natthi dānasamaṃ yānaṃ sabbasuggatigāminaṃ //* Sīh 26.19. Alternatively, "*-gāminaṃ*" could be taken as an accusative singular in apposition to *yānaṃ*. In Buddhism as in other South Asian traditions, one's thoughts at the time of death are thought to have a powerful effect on one's rebirth, consequently when near death Theravādins often review their past meritorious deeds. Collins, *Selfless Persons*, 245. Cf. also the story of Duṭṭhagāmaṇī below.

11 *sirasmiṃ kese chinditvā kilesacchedatuṭṭhiyā* Sīh 35.19cd.

12 Søren Kierkegaard, *The Sickness unto Death*, trans. Edward V. Hong and Edna H. Hong (Princeton: Princeton University Press, 1980), 83–87 [XI 194–199].

13 Ann Grodzins Gold, *Fruitful Journeys: The Ways of Rajasthani Pilgrims* (Berkeley: University of California Press, 1988); Jonathan P. Parry, *Death in Banaras* (Cambridge: Cambridge University Press, 1994).

14 Gold, 63, 263–264, 291–292.

15 Parry, 120–121, 142, 147.

16 A king rewards an actor in 31, 32, 33, 35, 36, 39, 40, 43, 45, 56, 61, and 68; a king and an elder in 76; Sakka in 34, 43, 58, and 68, a *nāga* king in 72, a group of deities in 49, people and gods in 7 and 67. In 67, 72, and perhaps 49 the reward is for an act done in a prior existence. Other stories, such as 1 and 30 should perhaps also be listed here. Similar to these stories is 64, in which a god rewards a monk for his *tejas*. In addition to these episodes, in a number of stories gods appear to take a person to heaven, thereby helping to bring about a karmic effect. Conversely, karma may prevent a deity from helping people. In 65, arhats seek Sakka's help during a famine, but he says that he can do nothing because the famine is a result of the actions of beings (*sattānaṃ kammavipākena*).

17 *puññapāpaphalaṃ loke labhanti diṭṭhadhammikaṃ / tasmā puññaṃ hi kātabbaṃ piyaṃ taṃ dhammapītino //* Sīh 33.31.

18 *devayakkhānubhāvena tassa puññabalena ca* Sīh 34.17.

19 *kissa kammassa phalanti* Sīh 72. A *nāga* is a serpent-like being; 'dragon' is perhaps the closest English term.

20 *kassidaṃ puññavipākaṃ mama puññassa vā idaṃ* 7.20cd.

21 8. *puññiddhiṃ attano disvā somanassena pīṇito / puññaṃ puññavipākañ ca ñatvā vākyam udīrayi //* 9. *devā nāgā ca (yakkhā ca) ye icchantatipūjanaṃ / kattabaṃ kusalaṃ niccaṃ puññakkhette anuttare //* 10. *puññāni sattā ye keci karonti tuṭṭhamānasā / dibbaṃ mānusakam ceva sukham anubhavanti te //* 11. *kumārohi tato pubbe mahādānam adāsi so / tena puññavipākena denti devāpi mānusā //* 12. *pasūpi migapakkhīpi (devatāpi ca mānusā / puññāvantaṃ naraṃ) disvā vase vattanti sabbadā //* 13. *yaṃ yaṃ karoti puriso taṃ taṃ tassa samijjhati / na nassati hi taṃ puññaṃ api duggepi sankate // ti*

There is no indication of a change of speaker after verse 10; so in the text as it stands Sālikumāra speaks of himself in the third person in verse 11. Ending the quotation at the end of verse 10 would create a more natural break.

22 This does not necessarily amount to a theory of the karmic right of kings. In 75 the people overthrow an unjust king and replace him with a man who displays greater merit.

23 *bhuttamatteva āhāre surūpā āsi dārikā / appatvā dibbavaṇṇañ ca atikkāmesi mānusaṃ* Sīh 35.23.

24 *taṃ khaṇaṃ* 36.23; 40.16.

25 E.g. Sīh 8, 61, 69. Strong discusses similar transformations in the Sanskrit *avadānas* in "The Transforming Gift."

26 Sīh 35.6, 36.9. Their good fortune comes in the form of gifts from the king; see below.

27 *evam acintiyaṃ puññaṃ guṇavantesu dakkhiṇā / sandiṭṭhikaṃ sukhaṃ datvā samparāye ca paccati* // Sīh 40.27. Also, Sīh 32.40–41, 36.29, 39.16, cf. 40.25, 43.58.

28 *Sagga* Sīh 7, 23, 26, 31, 48, 50, 58, 61, 75; *devaloka* 7; *sugati* 62; *devakāyūpagā* 43. Some specific references are to *Tāvatiṃsa* 4, 6, 36, 47; *Akiṇiṭṭha* gods 69; primary queen of Sakka 69.

29 Tusita is named in Sīh 1, 2, 3, 5, 8, 31, 42, and 46, is called *nivāsaseṭṭhaṃ* in 46.32 and *ratikaravaram uttamaṃ surammaṃ* in 46.34.

30 Tusita is called a city in Sīh 1, 5, 8, and 46; Metteyya states "*saṃsārabhayabhītānaṃ bhavāmi bhavamocako,*" in 3.17.

31 *metteyyasammāsambuddhassa dassanaṃ*, Sīh 3.16, hearing Dharma, 31.30, 46.31, *jagatīhitesinaṃ* 46.31.

32 *aparimitaṃ anantaṃ appameyyaṃ paramasukhaṃ sukhaṃ sukhadāyako alattha* Sīh 8.26ab.

33 See especially Metteyya's discourse at 3.17–29.

34 *sammāsambuddha* 3.16, *sugata* 1.23, *jinavara* 1.23 & 25; future buddhahood 3.33.

35 Most people who attain arhatship are monastics. Stories of monastics attaining arhatship include Sīh 32, 35, 36, 43, 45, 56, 57, 58, 60, 62, 70, 80.

36 *mā me ciraṃ saṃsaranam ahosi* 59.1d, 61.1d.

37 *nibbutimpi gamissati* 47.20d; *sā pāpuṇissati bhavattaya oghatiṇṇaṃ* 47.22d.

38 *dānā sambodhisampattaṃ* Sīh 11.1.

39 Kevin Trainor, *Relics, Ritual, and Representation in Buddhism: Rematerializing the Sri Lankan Theravāda tradition* (Cambridge: Cambridge Univ. Press, 1997), 183–184, and John S. Strong, *The Legend of King Aśoka: A Study and Translation of the* Aśokāvadāna (Princeton: Princeton University Press, 1983), 185–198.

40 *so kirāyasmā mārena nimmitaṃ buddharūpaṃ disvā "ayaṃ tāva sarāgadosamoho evaṃ sobhati, kathaṃ nu kho bhagavā [na] sobhati, [so hi] sabbaso vītarāgadosamoho" ti buddhārammaṇaṃ pītiṃ paṭilabhitvā vipassanaṃ vaḍḍhetvā arahattaṃ pāpuṇīti.* Vism 228. "*Na*" and "*so hi*" appear in some mss. and not in others.

41 *mārena nimmitaṃ rūpaṃ evaṃ thero vipassati / vipassanaṃ vaḍḍhetvāna arahattam apāpuṇi*// v. 37.

42 *sarīraṃ jagganatthāya*, v. 1.

43 *sasarīraṃ* [sic] *vibhajitvā*, v. 14.

44 *iminā vipākena petassa udakaṃ nibbattūti uddisi.*

45 *evaṃ dosāvahaṃ hoti aparādho guṇādhike* Sīh 18.16. Filliozat discusses the disproportionate effect of actions against worthy recipients at "Sur le domain," 241.

46 *mamaṃ disvāna sabbe te bhāyatha saṅghasantakā / bhāyitvā appamādena ghaṭetha buddhasāsane* // 19.13.

47 Sīh 15.8–9 contain comments similar to those cited above on the great effect of acts committed against the Saṅgha.
48 This reading is supported by the author's use of transmigration language. For example, one *peta* states, "I would be completely liberated from this *peta* birth" (*parimuccāmi imaya petayoniyā* 15.12), and after the dedications the two *petas* are called *deva* and *devaputta* respectively.
49 Mil 83–84 and 290–294 argue that the effect of good actions greatly outweighs that of evil acts.
50 At 81, "*bhante theriyā bhāgaṃ gaṇhathāti*," "obtain a share for the old woman," seems to mean, "give her the opportunity to make merit." The term *bhāga* is also used to refer to the effects of good or bad action for the actor in at least two places in *Sīhaḷavatthuppakaraṇa*. In Sīh 82, *akusalabhāgī* refers to a person who does a bad act. At 40.29, "*ettha bhāgaṃ karitvāna*" refers to merit making. *Bhāgadāna*, in 42.47–48, is a different usage, referring to the gift of a share of food.
51 *demi deva tuyhaṃ bhāgaṃ sabasattānañ cāti*; p. 2.
52 *tuyhañ ca sabbasattānaṃ puññabhāgaṃ dadāmahaṃ/* Sīh 43.51ab.
53 *tuyhañ ca sabbasattānaṃ demi bhāgaṃ narādhipa/* Sīh 45.34 ab.
54 *yaṃ kataṃ kusalaṃ tuyhaṃ yaṃ puññaṃ pana kāhasi / mama bhāgaṃ dadeyyasi veyyāvaccaṃ karissahaṃ // bhāgo dinno devarāja tuyhañ ca aññapāṇīnaṃ / apāyā parimuccantu asurā mānusā ca te //*
55 See chap. 1, cf. discussion of BAp 45 in chap. 2.
56 Neither does the story indicate whether the donor's enemy benefits from the gift. The words of dedication used here are, "let this be for his welfare and happiness" (*tassa hotu hitaṃ sukhaṃ* Sīh 39.12d).
57 Agasse, "Le transfert de mérite," 315–316, n. 25.
58 Elizabeth Bopearachchi, "Le don dans le littérature singhalese," in *Donner et recevoir*, ed. Flora Blanchon (Paris: Presses de l'Université de Paris-Sorbonne, 1992), 265.
59 Sīh 57 (*saṃviggamānasā*), 58 (*saṃviggo*), 80 (*saṃvega*).
60 Sīh 35, 36, 43 (x2), 45, 56, 62.

Afterword

1 James W. Fernandez, "Symbolic Consensus in a Fang Reformative Cult," *American Anthropologist* 67 (1965): 913.
2 Ibid., 907.
3 *Yañ ca sīlavantī āsiṃ na taṃ tāva vipaccati / āsā ca pana me devinda sakadāgāminī siyan / ti. //* Vv III.9.13.
4 Jerome Bruner, *Actual Minds, Possible Worlds* (Cambridge, MA: Harvard University Press, 1986), 11.
5 Collins, *Selfless Persons*, 234–261.

BIBLIOGRAPHY

Editions and translations of primary texts

Unless otherwise indicated, citations are from the following editions and translations are mine. Citations marked 'CS' are to the Chaṭṭha Saṅgāyana [Burmese recension] CD-ROM, Version 3, Dhammagiri, Igatpuri, India: Vipassana Research Institute, n.d.

Abhidharmakośabhāṣya. Edited by Dwarikadas Shastri. *Abhidharmakośa and Bhāṣya with Sphuṭārtha Commentary of Ācārya Yaśomitra*. 4 vols. Varanasi: Buddha Bharati, 1970.

——. Translated by Leo M. Pruden from Louis de la Vallée Poussin's version. 4 vols. Berkeley: Asian Humanities Press, 1991.

Aṅguttara Nikāya. Edited by R. Morris, E. Hardy, et al. 6 vols. London: Pali Text Society, 1885–1910.

——. Translated by F. L. Woodward and E. M. Hare. *Gradual Sayings*. 5 vols. London: Pali Text Society: 1932–1936; reprint, Oxford: Pali Text Society, 1995–1996.

Apadāna. Edited by M. E. Lilley. 2 vols. London: Pali Text Society, 1925–1927.

Āpastambha Dharmasūtra. Edited by Yasuke Ikari. *Thesaurus Indogermanischer Text- und Sprachmaterialien*. October 19, 1999. <http://titus.uni-frankfurt.de/>.

——. Translated by Patrick Olivelle. *Dharmasūtras: The Law Codes of Ancient India*. Oxford: Oxford University Press, 1999.

Aśoka. Inscriptions. Edited and translated by E. Hultzsch. *Corpus Inscriptionum Indicarum, Volume I: Inscriptions of Asoka*. Second edition. Delhi: Indological Book House, 1969.

——. Edited and translated by N. A. Nikam and Richard McKeon. *The Edicts of Asoka*. Chicago: University of Chicago Press, 1959.

Avadānaśataka. Edited by J. S. Speyer. *Avadānaçataka: A Century of Edifying Tales Belonging to the Hīnayāna*. *Bibliotheca Buddhica* III. St. Petersburg: Imperial Academy of Sciences, 1906–1909; *Indo-Iranian Reprints* III. 'S-Gravenhage: Mouton & Co., 1958.

——. Translated by Léon Feer. *Avadāna-çataka: Cent Légendes (Bouddhiques)*. *Annales du Musée Guimet* 18. Paris: Ernest Leroux, 1891.

Āyāraṃga. Edited by Yumi Ousaka and Moriichi Yamazaki. <http://www.sendai-ct.ac.jp/~ousaka/>.

——. *Ācārāṅgasūtraṃ Sūtrakṛtaṅgasūtraṃ ca*. *Niryukti* by Bhadrabāhu and commentary by Śīlāṅka. Edited by Sāgarānandasūri and reedited by Jambūvijaya. New Delhi: Motilal Banarasidass, 1978.

——. Translated by Hermann Jacobi. *Jaina Sutras. Part I*. Sacred Books of the East 22. Oxford: Clarendon Press: 1884; reprint, New York: Dover, 1968.

Baudhāyana Dharmasūtra. Edited by Masato Fujii and Mieko Kajihara. *Thesaurus Indogermanischer Text- und Sprachmaterialien*. October 19, 1999. <http://titus.uni-frankfurt.de/>.

——. Translated by Patrick Olivelle. *Dharmasūtras: The Law Codes of Ancient India*. Oxford: Oxford University Press, 1999.

Buddhavaṃsa and *Cariyāpiṭaka*. Edited by N. A. Jayawickrama. London: Pali Text Society, 1974.

——. Translated by I. B.Horner. *The Minor Anthologies of the Pali Canon. Part III*. London: Pali Text Society, 1975.

Daṣavatthuppakaraṇa. Edited and translated by Jacqueline Ver Eecke. Paris: École Française d'Extrême-Orient, 1976.

Dasaveyāliya. Edited by Ernst Leumann and translated by Walther Schubring. In *Kleine Schriften*, by Walther Schubring, edited by Klaus Bruhn, 109—248. Wiesbaden: Franz Steiner Verlag GMBH, 1977.

Dhammapada. Edited by Sūriyagoḍa Sumaṅgala Thera. London: Pali Text Society, 1914.

——. Translated by John Ross Carter and Mahinda Palihawadana. Oxford: Oxford University Press, 1987.

——. Translated by K. R. Norman. *The Word of the Doctrine*. Oxford: Pali Text Society, 1997.

Dhammapadaṭṭhakathā. Edited by H. C. Norman. 5 vols. London: Pali Text Society, 1906–1915.

——. Translated by Eugene Watson Burlingame. *Buddhist Legends*. 3 vols. Harvard Oriental Series. Cambridge, MA: Harvard University Press, 1921.

Dharmapada. Edited by John Brough. *Gāndhārī Dharmapada*. London Oriental Series, vol. 7. London: Oxford University Press, 1962.

Dīgha Nikāya. Edited by T. W. Rhys Davids and J. E. Carpenter. 3 vols. London: Pali Text Society, 1889–1910.

——. Translated by Maurice Walshe. *Thus Have I Heard: The Long Discourses of the Buddha*. London: Wisdom Publications, 1987.

——. Translated by T. W. and C. A. F. Rhys Davids. *Dialogues of the Buddha*. 3 vols. London: Pali Text Society, 1965.

Gautama Dharmasūtra. Edited by Nobuyuki Watase and Yasuke Ikari. *Thesaurus Indogermanischer Text- und Sprachmaterialien*. October 20, 1999. <http://titus.uni-frankfurt.de/>.

——. Translated by Patrick Olivelle. *Dharmasūtras: The Law Codes of Ancient India*. Oxford: Oxford University Press, 1999.

Itivuttaka. Edited by Ernst Windisch. London: Pali Text Society, 1889.

——. Translated by F. L. Woodward. *The Minor Anthologies of the Pali Canon. Part II*. London: Oxford University Press, 1948.

Itivuttakaṭṭhakathā. Edited by M. M. Bose. London: Pali Text Society, 1934.

Jaiminīya Brāhmaṇa. Partial translation by H. W. Bodewitz. *Jaiminīya Brāhmaṇa I, 1–65: Translation and Commentary with a Study, Agnihotra and Prāṇāgnihotra*. Leiden: E. J. Brill, 1973.

Jātaka and *Jātakaṭṭhakathā*. Edited by V. Fausbøll. 7 vols. London: Pali Text Society, 1877–1897.

——. Translated by E. B. Cowell et al. *The Jātaka or Stories of the Buddha's Former Births*. Six volumes published as three volumes. London: Pali Text Society, 1973.

——. *Vessantara Jātaka*. Translated by Margaret Cone and Richard F. Gombrich. *The Perfect Generosity of Prince Vessantara: A Buddhist Epic*. Oxford: Clarendon, 1977.

Kathāvatthu. Edited by Arnold C. Taylor. 2 vols. London: The Pali Text Society, 1894–1897.

——. Translated by Shwe Zan Aung and Caroline Rhys Davids. *Points of Controversy, or Subjects of Discourse*. London: The Pali Text Society, 1979.

Karmasiddhiprakaraṇa. Chinese and Tibetan texts, translation and introduction by Étienne Lamotte. "La traité de l'acte de Vasubandhu, Karmasiddhiprakarana." *Mélanges Chinois et Bouddhiques* 4 (1936): 15–288.

Khuddakapāṭha. Edited by Helmer Smith. *The Khuddaka-Pāṭha, Together With Its Commentary, Paramatthajotikā I*. London: Pali Text Society, 1959.

Mahābhārata. Translated by Pratāpa Chandra Rāy. *The Mahabharata of Krishna-Dwaipayana Vyasa Translated into English Prose*. Calcutta: Bhārata Press, 1970.

——. Partially translated by J. A. B. van Buitenen. *The Mahābhārata*. Chicago: University of Chicago Press, 1973–1978.

——. Partially translated by J. A. B. van Buitenen. *The Bhagavadgītā in the Mahābhārata: a Bilingual Edition*. Chicago: University of Chicago Press, 1981.

Mahāprajñapāramitāśāstra.

——. Translated by Étienne Lamotte. *La traité de la grande vertu de sagesse de Nāgarjuna (Mahāprajñapāramitāśāstra)*. Louvain: Institut Orientaliste, 1970.

Majjhima Nikāya. Edited by V. Trenckner and R. Chalmers. 4 vols. London: Pali Text Society, 1888–1925.

——. Translated by Bhikkhu Ñāṇamoli and Bhikkhu Bodhi. *The Middle Length Discourses of the Buddha*. Boston: Wisdom Publications, 1995.

Māleyyadevattheravatthu. Edited by Eugène Denis S.J. "*Braḥ Māleyyadevattheravatthuṃ*." *Journal of the Pali Text Society* 18 (1993): 19–64.

——. Translated by Steven Collins. "The Story of the Elder Māleyya." *Journal of the Pali Text Society* 18 (1993): 65–96.

Manorathapūraṇī (=Aṅguttaraṭṭhakathā). Edited by M. Walleser and H. Kopp. 5 vols. London: Pali Text Society, 1924—1957.

Manusmṛti. Edited by M. Yano and Y. Ikari. *Thesaurus Indogermanischer Text- und Sprachmaterialien*. October 21, 1999. <http://titus.uni-frankfurt.de/>.

——. Translated by Wendy Doniger O'Flaherty. *The Laws of Manu*. New York: Penguin,1991.

Milindapañha. Edited by V. Trenckner. London: Pali Text Society, 1962.

——. Translated by I. B. Horner. *Milinda's Questions*. Two volumes. London: Pali Text Society, 1963–1964.

Papañcasūdanī (=Majjhimaṭṭhakathā). Edited by J. H. Woods, D. Kosambi, and I. B. Horner. 5 vols. London: Pali Text Society, 1922–1938.

Paramatthadīpanī. See *Itivuttakaṭṭhakathā*, *Petavatthu-aṭṭhakathā*, and *Vimānavatthu-aṭṭhakathā*.

Paramatthajotikā. See *Khuddakapāṭha*.

Petavatthu. *Vimānavatthu* and *Petavatthu*. Edited by N. A. Jayawickrama. London: Pali Text Society, 1977.

——. For translation see *Petavatthu-aṭṭhakathā*.

Petavatthu-aṭṭhakathā. Edited by E. Hardy. London: Pali Text Society, 1894.

——. Translated by U Ba Kyaw, edited and annotated by Peter Masefield. *Elucidation of the Intrinsic Meaning: So Named the Commentary on the Peta-Stories (Paramattha-dīpanī nāma Petavatthu-aṭṭhakathā)*. London: The Pali Text Society, 1980.

Ṛg Veda. Edited by Barend A. van Nooten and Gary B. Holland. *Rig Veda: A Metrically Restored Text with an Introduction and Notes*. Harvard Oriental Series. Cambridge: Harvard University Press, 1994.

——. Translated by T. H. Griffith. *The Hymns of the Rigveda*. Third edition. Benares: E.J. Lazarus, 1926.

——. Partial translation by Wendy Doniger O'Flaherty. *The Rig Veda*. New York: Penguin, 1981.

Saddharmaratnāvaliya. Dharmasēna Thera. *Jewels of the Doctrine: Stories of the* Saddharma Ratnāvaliya. Translated by Ranjini Obeyesekere. Albany: State University of New York Press, 1991.

Saṃnyāsa Upaniṣads. Translated by Patrick Olivelle. *The Saṃnyāsa Upaniṣads*. New York: Oxford University Press, 1992.

Saṃyutta Nikāya. Edited by L. Feer. 6 vols. London: Pali Text Society, 1884–1904.

——. Translated by C. A. F. Rhys Davids and F. L. Woodward. 5 vols. London: Pali Text Society, 1917–1930.

Sāratthappakāsinī (= *Saṃyuttaṭṭhakathā*). Edited by F. L. Woodward. 3 vols. London: Pali Text Society, 1929–1937.

Śatapatha Brāhmaṇa. Mādhyandina Recension. Edited by Albrecht Weber, reedited by J. R. Gardner. *Thesaurus Indogermanischer Text- und Sprachmaterialien*. October 14, 1999. <http://titus.uni-frankfurt.de/>.

——. Translated by Julius Eggeling. *The Satapatha Brâhmana According to the Mâdhyandina School*. Sacred Books of the East, vols. 12, 26, 41, 43, 44. Oxford: Clarendon Press: 1900; reprint, Delhi: Motilal Banarsidass, 1966.

Sīhaḷavatthuppakaraṇa. Edited and translated by Jacqueline Ver Eecke. Paris: École Française d'Extrême-Orient, 1980.

Sumaṅgalavilāsinī (= *Dīghaṭṭhakathā*). Edited by T. W. Rhys Davids, J. E. Carpenter, and W. Stede. 3 vols. London: Pali Text Society, 1886–1932.

Sutta-Nipāta. Edited by Dines Andersen and Helmer Smith. London: Pali Text Society, 1913.

——. Translated by K. R. Norman. *The Group of Discourses. Volume II*. Oxford: Pali Text Society, 1992.

Sūyagaḍaṃga. Edited by Yumi Ousaka and Moriichi Yamazaki. <http://www.sendai-ct.ac.jp/~ousaka/>.

——. *Ācārāṅgasūtraṃ Sūtrakṛtaṅgasūtraṃ ca*. *Niryukti* by Bhadrabāhu and commentary by Śīlāṅka. Edited by Sāgarānandasūri and reedited by Jambūvijaya. New Delhi: Motilal Banarasidass, 1978.

——. Translated by Hermann Jacobi. *Jaina Sutras. Part II*. Sacred Books of the East 45. Oxford: Clarendon Press: 1895; reprint, New York: Dover, 1968.

Taittirīya Brāhmaṇa. "Taittiriya Brahmana of the Black Yajur Veda." *Bibliotheca Indica* 31. Osnabrück, W. Germany, 1981.

Theratherīgāthā. Edited by H. Oldenberg and R. Pischel. London: Pali Text Society, 1883.

——. Translated by K. R. Norman. *The Elders' Verses*. 2 vols. London: Pali Text Society, 1969, 1971.

Trai Phum Phra Ruang (=Traibhūmikathā), by Phya Lithai. Translated by Frank E. Reynolds and Mani B. Reynolds. *Three Worlds According to King Ruang: A Thai Buddhist Cosmology*. Berkeley: Asian Humanities Press, 1982.

Udāna. Edited by Paul Steinthal. London: Pali Text Society, 1885.

——. Translated by Peter Masefield. *The Udāna*. Oxford: Pali Text Society, 1994.

Upaniṣads. Edited and Translated by Patrick Olivelle. *The Early Upaniṣads: Annotated Text and Translation*. New York: Oxford University Press, 1998.

——. Translated by Patrick Olivelle. *Upaniṣads*. New York: Oxford University Press, 1996.

Uttarajjhāyā. Edited by Yumi Ousaka and Moriichi Yamazaki. <http://www.sendai-ct.ac.jp/~ousaka/>.

——. Translated by Hermann Jacobi. *Jaina Sutras. Part II*. Sacred Books of the East 45. Oxford: Clarendon Press: 1895; reprint, New York: Dover, 1968.

Vasiṣtha Dharmasūtra. Translated by Patrick Olivelle. *Dharmasūtras: The Law Codes of Ancient India*. Oxford: Oxford University Press, 1999.

Vimānavatthu. *Vimānavatthu* and *Petavatthu*. Edited by N. A. Jayawickrama. London: Pali Text Society, 1977.

——. For translation see *Vimānavatthu-aṭṭhakathā*.

Vimānavatthu-aṭṭhakathā. Edited by E. Hardy. London: Pali Text Society, 1901.

——. Translated by Peter Masefield, assisted by N. A. Jayawickrama. *Elucidation of the Intrinsic Meaning: So Named the Commentary on the Vimāna Stories (Paramattha-dīpanī nāma Vimānavatthu-aṭṭhakathā)*. Oxford: The Pali Text Society, 1989.

Vinaya. Translated by H. Oldenberg. 5 vols. London: Pali Text Society, 1879—1883.

——. Translated by I. B. Horner. *The Book of the Discipline*. 6 vols. London: Pali Text Society, 1938—1966.

Visuddhajanavilāsinī nāma Apadānaṭṭhakathā. Edited by C. E. Godakumbura. London: The Pali Text Society, 1954.

Visuddhimagga, by Buddhaghosa. Edited by C. A. F. Rhys Davids. 2 vols. London: Pali Text Society, 1920–1921.

——. Translated by Bhikkhu Ñyāṇamoli. *The Path of Purification*. 2 vols. Berkeley: Shambala, 1976.

Yajur Veda. Kāṭhaka Saṃhitā. Partial edition and translation by P. V. Navathe. *Agnihotra of the Kaṭha Sākhā*. Pune: University of Poona, 1980.

Yajur Veda. Taittirīya Saṃhitā. Edited by A. Mahadevasastri & K. Rangacharya. *The Taittirīya Saṃhitā of the Black Yajurveda*. Delhi: Motilal Banarsidass, 1986.

——. Translated by Arthur Berriedale Keith. *The Veda of the Black Yajus School, entitled Taittiriya Sanhita*. Cambridge: Harvard University Press, 1914.

Secondary literature

Agasse, Jean-Michel. "Le transfert de mérite dans le Bouddhisme Pāli classique." *Journal Asiatique* 266 (1978): 311—331.

Allchin, F. R. *The Archaeology of Early Historic South Asia: The Emergence of Cities and States*. Cambridge: Cambridge University Press, 1995.

Allon, Mark. *Style and Function: A Study of the Dominant Stylistic Features of the Prose Portions of the Pāli Canonical Sutta Texts and Their Mnemonic Function*. Studia Philologica Buddhica, Monograph Series XII. Tokyo: The International Institute for Buddhist Studies, 1997.

Alsdorf, Ludwig. "The Ākhyāna Theory Reconsidered." *Journal of the Oriental Institute, Baroda* 13 (1964): 195–207.

——. "Bemerkungen zum Vessantara-Jātaka." *Wiener Zeitschrift für die Kunde Süd- und Ostasiens und Archiv für indische Philosophie* 1 (1957): 1–70.

——. "Die Āryā-Strophen des Pali-Kanons." *Akademie der Wissenschaften und der Literatur in Mainz: Abhandlungen der Geistes- und Sozialwissenschaftlichen Klasse* 1967: 243–331.

——. "Das Jātaka vom weisen Vidhura." *Wiener Zeitschrift für die Kunde Südasiens* 15 (1971): 23–56.

Ames, Michael M. "Ritual Prestations and the Structure of the Sinhalese Pantheon." In *Anthropological Studies in Theravada Buddhism*, edited by Manning Nash, et al., 27–50. Yale University, 1966.

Amore, Roy Clayton. *The Concept and Practice of Doing Merit in Early Theravāda Buddhism*. Ph.D. diss., Columbia University, 1970.

Anusaranaśāsanakiarti, Phra Khrū, and Charles F. Keyes. "Funerary Rites and the Buddhist Meaning of Death: An Interpretive Text from Northern Thailand." *Journal of the Siam Society* 68 (1980): 1–28.

Aramaki, Noritoshi. "A Text-strata-analytical Interpretation of the Concept "*pañcaskandhas*." *Jimbun (The Humanities)* [College of Liberal Arts, Kyoto University] 26 (1980): 1–36.

Aronoff, Arnold L. *Contrasting Modes of Textual Classification: The* Jātaka *Commentary and its Relationship to the Pali Canon*. Ph.D. diss., University of Chicago, 1982.

Babb, Lawrence A. *Absent Lord: Ascetics and Kings in a Jain Ritual Culture*. Berkeley: University of California Press, 1996.

Bailey, Greg. "Materials for the Study of Ancient Indian Ideologies: *Pravṛtti* and *Nivṛtti*." Publicazioni di *Indologia Taurinensia* 19. Torino: 1985.

——. "Problems of the Interpretation of the Data pertaining to Religious Interaction in Ancient India: The Conversion Stories in the Sutta Nipāta." *Indo-British Review* 19 (n.d.): 1–20.

Bareau, André. "Étude du Bouddhisme." *Annuaire du Collège de France* 74 (1974): 44–475.

——. *Les Sectes Bouddhiques du Petit Véhicule*. Paris: École Française d'Extrême-Orient, 1955.

——. "La transformation miraculeuse de la nourriture offerte au Buddha par le Brahmane Kasibhāradvāja." In *Études Tibétaines Dédiées à la Mémoire de Marcelle Lalou*, 1–10. Paris: Librairie d'Amérique et d'Orient, 1971.

Bechert, Heinz. "Buddha-Feld und Verdienstübertragung: Mahāyāna-Ideen im Theravāda-Buddhismus Ceylons." *Académie Royale de Belgique Bulletin de la Classe des Lettres et des Sciences Morales et Politiques* 5e sér., 62 (1976): 27–51.

——. "Buddha-field and Transfer of Merit in a Theravāda Source." *Indo-Iranian Journal*. 35 (1992): 95–108.

——. "Einleitung: Stand der Diskussion acht Jahre nach dem Symposion." In *The Dating of the Historical Buddha*, Part 3, edited by Heinz Bechert, 1–13. *Abhandlungen der Akademie der Wissenschaften in Göttingen, Philologisch-Historische Klasse Dritte Folge*, Nr. 222. Göttingen: Vanderhoech & Ruprecht, 1997.

——. "Introductory Essay." In *The Dating of the Historical Buddha*, Part 1, edited by Heinz Bechert, 1—21. *Abhandlungen der Akademie der Wissenschaften in Göttingen, Philologisch-Historische Klasse Dritte Folge*, Nr. 189. Göttingen: Vanderhoech & Ruprecht, 1991.

——. "Notes on the Formation of Buddhist Sects and the Origins of Mahāyāna." In *German Scholars on India*, edited by the Cultural Dept. of the Embassy of the Federal Republic of Germany, New Delhi, 1:6–18. Varanasi: Chowkhamba Sanskrit Series Office: 1973.

——. "On a Fragment of *Vimānāvadāna*, A Canonical Buddhist Sanskrit Work." In *Buddhist Studies in Honour of I. B. Horner*, edited by L. Cousins et al., 19–25. Dordrecht: D. Reidel, 1974.

Biardeau, Madeleine. "Le sacrifice dans l'Hindouisme." In *Le sacrifice dans l'Inde ancienne*, edited by Madeleine Biardeau and Charles Malamoud, 7–154. Paris: Presses Universitaires de France, 1976.

Bodewitz, H. W. *The Daily Evening and Morning Offering (*Agnihotra*) According to the* Brāhmaṇas. Leiden: E. J. Brill, 1976.

——. *Jaiminīya Brāhmaṇa I, 1–65: Translation and Commentary with a Study, Agnihotra and Prāṇāgnihotra*. Leiden: E. J. Brill, 1973.

——. "Life after Death in the Ṛgvedasaṃhitā." *Wiener Zeitschrift für die Kunde Südasiens und Archiv für indische Philosophie* 38 (1994): 23–41.

——. "Non-Ritual Karman in the Veda." In *Chowkhamba Sanskrit Series Office Centenary Commemoration Volume (1892–1992)*, edited by Sudhakar Malaviya, 221—230. Chowkhamba Sanskrit Series 105. Varanasi: Chowkhamba Sanskrit Series Office, 1993.

——. "Pits, Pitfalls, and the Underworld in the Veda." *Indo-Iranian Journal* 42 (1999): 21—226.

——. "Redeath and its Relation to Rebirth and Release." *Festschrift Paul Thieme: Studien für Indologie und Iranistik* 20 (1996): 27–46.

——. "Yonder World in the Atharvaveda." *Indo-Iranian Journal* 42 (1999): 107–120.

Bodhi, Bhikkhu. "Introduction." In *Dāna: The Practice of Giving, Wheel* 367/369, edited by Bhikkhu Bodhi, 1–3. Kandy: Buddhist Publication Society, 1990.
Bond, George D. "Theravāda Buddhism's Two Formulations of the *Dasa Sīla* and the Ethics of the Gradual Path." In *Pāli Buddhism*, edited by Frank J. Hoffman and Deegalle Mahinda, 17–42. Richmond, Surrey: Curzon, 1996.
Bopearachchi, Elizabeth. "Le don dans le littérature singhalese." In *Donner et recevoir*, edited by Flora Blanchon, 59–69. Paris: Presses de l'Université de Paris-Sorbonne, 1992.
Brekke, Torkel. "Contradiction and the Merit of Giving in Indian Religions." *Numen* 45 (1998): 287—320.
Bronkhorst, Johannes. "Did the Buddha Believe in Karma and Rebirth?" *Journal of the International Association of Buddhist Studies* 21 (1998): 1–20.
——. *The Two Sources of Indian Asceticism.* Schweitzer Asiatische Studien 13. Bern: Peter Lang, 1993.
Brough, John. "Thus Have I Heard . . ." *Bulletin of the School of Oriental and African Studies* 13 (1949—1950): 416–426.
Brown, W. Norman. "The Basis for the Hindu Act of Truth." *Review of Religion* 5 (1940): 36–45.
——. "Duty as Truth in the Rig Veda." In *India Maior: Congratulatory Volume Presented to Jan Gonda*, edited by J. Ensink and P. Gaeffke, 57–67. Leiden: 1972.
——. "The Metaphysics of the Truth Act." In *Mélanges d'Indianisme: à la mémoire de Louis Renou*, 171–7. Paris: Editions E. de Boccard, 1968.
Bruner, Jerome. *Actual Minds, Possible Worlds.* Cambridge, MA: Harvard University Press, 1986.
Burghart, Richard. "Gifts to the Gods: Power, Property and Ceremonial in Nepal." In *Rituals of Royalty: Power and Ceremonial in Traditional Societies*, edited by David Cannadine and Simon Price, 237–270. Cambridge: Cambridge University Press, 1987.
Burkert, Walter, René Girard, and Jonathan Z. Smith. *Violent Origins.* Edited by Robert G. Hamerton-Kelly. Stanford: Stanford University Press, 1987.
Burlingame, Eugene Watson. "The Act of Truth (*Saccakiriya*): a Hindu Spell and its Employment as a Psychic Motif in Hindu Fiction." *Journal of the Royal Asiatic Society*, 1917: 429–468.
Butzenberger, Klaus. "Ancient Indian Conceptions on Man's Destiny after Death." *Berliner Indologische Studien* 9 (1996): 55–118.
Carman, John B. and Frédérique Apffel Marglin, eds. *Purity and Auspiciousness in Indian Society.* Leiden: E. J. Brill, 1985.
Carter, John Ross. "Beyond 'Beyond Good and Evil.'" In *Buddhist Studies in Honour of Hammalava Saddhātissa*, edited by Gatave Dhammapala, Richard Gombrich, and K. R. Norman, 41–55. Nugegoda: Buddhist Research Library Trust, 1984.
——. "The Notion of "Refuge" (*Saraṇa*) in the Theravāda Buddhist Tradition." In *Studies in Pali and Buddhism: A Memorial Volume in Honor of Bhikkhu Jagdish Kashyap*, edited by A. K. Narain, 41–52. Delhi: B. R. Publishing Corporation, 1979.
Collins, Steven. "*Braḥ Māleyyadevattheravatthu.*" *Journal of the Pali Text Society* 18 (1993): 1–17.

——. *Nirvana and other Buddhist felicities: Utopias of the Pali imaginaire*. Cambridge: Cambridge University Press, 1998.

——. "Notes on Some Oral Aspects of Pali Literature." *Indo-Iranian Journal* 35 (1992): 121–135.

——. "On the Very Idea of the Pali Canon." *Journal of the Pali Text Society* 15 (1990): 89—126.

——. *Selfless Persons: Imagery and Thought in* Theravāda *Buddhism*. Cambridge: Cambridge University Press, 1982.

Coomaraswamy, Ananda K. "Headless Magicians; and an Act of Truth." *Journal of the American Oriental Society* 64 (1944): 215–217.

Cort, John E. "The Gift of Food to a Wandering Cow: Lay-Mendicant Interaction among the Jains." *Journal of Asian and African Studies* 34 (1999): 89ff.

Cousins, L. S. "Pali Oral Literature." In *Buddhist Studies, Ancient and Modern*, edited by A. Piatgorsky and P. T. Denwood, 1–11. London: Curzon Press, 1983.

Cutler, Sally Mellick. "The Pāli Apadāna Collection." *Journal of the Pali Text Society* 20 (1994): 1–42.

Dayal, Har. *The Bodhisattva Doctrine in Buddhist Sanskrit Literature*. Kegan and Paul, 1932; reprint, Delhi: Motilal Banarsidass, 1970.

De Jong, J. W. "The Beginnings of Buddhism." *The Eastern Buddhist* 26 (1993): 11–30.

——. *A Brief History of Buddhist Studies in Europe and America*. Tokyo: Kosei Publishing Co., 1997.

De Silva, Lily. "Giving in the Pali Canon." In *Dāna: The Practice of Giving, Wheel* 367/369, edited by Bhikkhu Bodhi, 19–38. Kandy: Buddhist Publication Society, 1990.

——. "*Vedanānupassanā*: On the Management of *Kamma*." *The Sri Lanka Journal of the Humanities* 14 (1988/1990): 171–178.

Denis, Eugène. *La Lokapaññatti et les idées cosmologiques du bouddhisme ancien*. Ph.D. dissertation, Université de Paris IV, 1976.

Dhammaratana, Tampalawela and Édith Parlier. "Aspects du don dans le canon pali." In *Donner et Recevoir*, edited by Flora Blanchon, 51–57. Paris: Presses de l'Université de Paris-Sorbonne, 1992.

Dirks, Nicholas B. *The Hollow Crown: Ethnography of an Indian Kingdom*. Cambridge: Cambridge University Press, 1987.

——. "Political Authority and Structural Change in Early South Indian History." *The Indian Economic and Social History Review* 8 (1976): 125–157.

Dixit, K. K. "The Problems of Ethics and Karma Doctrine as Treated in the *Bhagavatī Sūtra*." *Sambodhi* 2 (1974): 1–13.

Dundas, Paul. *The Jains*. New York: Routledge, 1992.

Durkheim, Émile. *The Elementary Forms of Religious Life*. Translated by Karen E. Fields. New York: The Free Press, 1995.

Dutt, Sukumar. *Early Buddhist Monachism*. Revised edition. Bombay: Asia Publishing House, 1960.

Egge, James R. *Sacrifice and Purification: The Meanings of Religious Giving in Theravāda Buddhism*. Ph.D. diss., University of Chicago, 1998.

Endo, Toshiichi. *Dāna: The Development of Its Concept and Practice*. Colombo: M. D. Gunasena & Co., 1987.

Enomoto Fumio. "On the Annihilation of *Karman* in Early Buddhism." *Transactions of the International Conference of Orientalists in Japan* 34 (1989): 43–55.

Erdosy, George. *Urbanisation in Early Historic India*. Oxford: British Archaeological Reports, 1988.

Falk, Harry. "Vedische Opfer im Pali-Kanon." *Bulletin d'Études indiennes*. 6 (1988): 225–254.

Falk, Nancy Auer. "The Case of the Vanishing Nuns: The Fruits of Ambivalence in Ancient Indian Buddhism." In *Unspoken Worlds: Women's Religious Lives in Non-Western Cultures*, edited by Nancy A. Falk and Rita M. Gross, 207–224. San Francisco: Harper & Row, 1980.

——. "Exemplary Donors of the Pāli Tradition." In *Ethics, Wealth and Salvation: A Study in Buddhist Social Ethics*, edited by Russell F. Sizemore and Donald K. Swearer, 124–144. Columbia, SC: University of South Carolina Press, 1990.

Feer, Léon. "Comment on devient deva." *Journal Asiatique* 3 (1884): 5–41.

——. "Comment on devient preta." *Journal Asiatique* 3 (1884): 109–140.

Filliozat, Jean. "Sur le domain sémantique de *puṇya*." In *Indianisme et Bouddhisme: Mélanges offerts à Msgr. Étienne Lamotte*, 101–116. Louvain-la-Neuve: Institut Orientaliste, 1980.

Findly, Ellison Banks. "Ānanda's Hindrance: Faith (*Saddhā*) in Early Buddhism." *Journal of Indian Philosophy* 20 (1992): 253–273.

Freedman, David Noel, editor-in-chief. *The Anchor Bible Dictionary*. New York: Doubleday, 1992.

Fujita, Kotatsu. "The Doctrinal Characteristics of *Karman* in Early Buddhism." In *Indological and Buddhist Studies: Volume in Honour of Professor J. W. de Jong on his Sixtieth Birthday*, edited by L. A. Hercus et al., 149–159. Canberra: Faculty of Asian Studies, 1982.

Fuller, C. J. *The Camphor Flame: Popular Hinduism and Society in India*. Princeton: Princeton University Press, 1992.

Gehman, Henry S. "*Ādisati, anvādisati, anudisati,* and *uddisati* in the Peta-Vatthu." *Journal of the American Oriental Society* 43 (1923): 410–421.

——. "A Pālism in Buddhist Sanskrit." *Journal of the American Oriental Society* 44 (1924): 73–75.

Geiger, Wilhelm. *A Pāli Grammar*. Translated by Batakrishna Ghosh, and revised and edited by K. R. Norman. Oxford: Pali Text Society, 1994.

——. *Pāli Literature and Language*. Translated by Batakrishna Ghosh. 2d ed. Delhi: Oriental Books Reprint Corporation, 1968.

Gethin, Rupert. *The Buddhist Path to Awakening: A Study of the Bodhi-Pakkhiyā Dhammā*. Leiden: E. J. Brill, 1992.

——. "The *Mātikās*: Memorization, Mindfulness, and the List." In *In the Mirror of Memory*, edited by Janet Gyatso, 149–172. Albany: State University of New York Press, 1992.

Gokhale, Balkrishna Govind. "Early Buddhism and the Brahmanas." In *Studies in the History of Buddhism*, edited by A. K. Narain, 67–77. Delhi: B. R. Publishing Co., 1980.

——. "The Early Buddhist Elite." *Journal of Indian History* 43 (1965): 391–402.

Gold, Ann Grodzins. *Fruitful Journeys: The Ways of Rajasthani Pilgrims*. Berkeley: University of California Press, 1988.

Gómez, Luis O. "Proto-Mādhyamika in the Pāli Canon." *Philosophy East and West* 26 (1976): 137–165.

Gombrich, Richard F. "Ancient Indian Cosmology." In *Ancient Cosmologies*, edited by Carmen Blacker and Michael Loewe, 110–142. George Allen & Unwin, 1975.

——. "Buddhist Karma and Social Control." *Comparative Studies in Society and History* 17 (1975): 212—220.

——. *Buddhist Precept and Practice: Traditional Buddhism in the Rural Highlands of Ceylon*. Delhi: Motilal Banarsidass, 1991. (Second edition of *Precept and Practice: Traditional Buddhism in the Rural Highlands of Ceylon*.) Oxford: Clarendon Press, 1971.)

——. *How Buddhism Began: The Conditioned Genesis of the Early Teachings*. London: Athlone, 1996.

——. "Merit Transference in Sinhalese Buddhism: A Case Study of the Interaction between Doctrine and Practice." *History of Religions* 11 (1971): 203–219.

——. "Notes on the Brahmanical Background to Buddhist Ethics." In *Buddhist Studies in Honour of Hammalava Saddhātissa*, edited by Gatave Dhammapala, Richard Gombrich, and K. R. Norman, 91–102. Nugegoda: Buddhist Research Library Trust, 1984.

——. "On Pain of Retribution." Review of *Karma and Rebirth in Classical Indian Traditions*, edited by Wendy Doniger O'Flaherty. *Times Literary Supplement*, September 4, 1981.

——. "Recovering the Buddha's Message." In *Panels of the VIIth World Sanskrit Conference*, edited by Johannes Bronkhorst, vol. 2: *Earliest Buddhism and Madhyamaka*, edited by David Seyfort Ruegg and Lambert Schmithausen, 5–23. Leiden: E. J. Brill, 1990.

——. *Theravada Buddhism: A Social History from Ancient Benares to Modern Colombo*. London: Routledge, 1988.

Gonda, Jan. *Change and Continuity in Indian Religion*. The Hague: Mouton & Co., 1965.

——. "'Gifts' and 'Giving' in the Ṛgveda.'" In Jan Gonda, *Selected Studies IV*, 122–143. Leiden: E. J. Brill, 1975. Originally published in *Vishveshvarand Indological Journal* 2 (1964): 9–30.

——. *Loka: World and Heaven in the Veda*. *Verhandlingen den Koninklinjke Nederlandse Akademie van Wetenschappen afd. Letterkunde*, n.s. 73, no. 1 (1966).

——. *Les Religions de l'Inde*. Translated by L. Jospin. Paris: Payot, 1979.

——. *The Ritual Sūtras*. Vol. I, fasc. 2 of *A History of Indian Literature*, ed. Jan Gonda. Wiesbaden: Otto Harrassowitz, 1975.

——. *The Savayajñas*. *Verhandlingen den Koninklinjke Nederlandse Akademie van Wetenschappen afd. Letterkunde*, n.s. 71, no. 2 (1965).

——. *Vedic Literature* (Saṃhitās *and* Brāhmaṇas). Vol. I, fasc. 1 of *A History of Indian Literature* ed. Jan Gonda. Wiesbaden: Otto Harrassowitz, 1975.

Griffiths, Paul J. "Buddhist Jhāna: A Form-Critical Study." *Religion* 13 (1983): 55–68.

——. *Indian Buddhist Meditation-Theory: History, Development, and Systematization*. Ph.D. diss., University of Wisconsin, Madison, 1983.

Halbfass, Wilhelm. "Karma, *Apūrva*, and 'Natural' Causes: Observation on the Growth and Limits of the Theory of *Saṃsāra*." In *Karma and Rebirth in Classical Indian Traditions*, edited by Wendy Doniger O'Flaherty, 268–302. Berkeley: University of California Press, 1980.

——. *Tradition and Reflection: Explorations in Indian Thought*. Albany: SUNY Press, 1991.

Hallisey, Charles. "Ethical Particularism in Theravāda Buddhism." *Journal of Buddhist Ethics* 3 (1996): 32–43.

Hamilton, Sue. "The 'External World': Its Status and Relevance in the Pali Nikāyas." *Religion* 29 (1999): 73–90.

——. *Identity and Experience: The Constitution of the Human Being According to Buddhism*. London: Luzac Oriental, 1996.

Hanks, L. M. Jr. "Merit and Power in the Thai Social Order." *American Anthropologist*. 64 (1962): 1247–1261.

Hara, Minoru. "Transfer of Merit." *The Adyar Library Bulletin* 31–32 (1967–68): 382–411.

Harrison, Paul. "Commemoration and Identification in *Buddhānusmṛti*." In *In the Mirror of Memory: Reflections on Mindfulness and Remembrance in Indian and Tibetan Buddhism*, edited by Janet Gyatso, 215–238. Albany: State University of New York Press, 1992.

Heesterman, J. C. *The Broken World of Sacrifice: An Essay in Ancient Indian Ritual*. Chicago: University of Chicago Press, 1993.

——. "Householder and Wanderer." In *Way of Life: King, Householder, Renouncer: Essays in Honor of Louis Dumont*, edited by T. N. Madan, 251–271. New Delhi: Vikas Publishing House, 1982.

——. *The Inner Conflict of Tradition: Essays in Indian Ritual, Kingship, and Society*. Chicago: University of Chicago Press, 1985.

——. "Reflections on the Significance of the *Dákṣiṇā*." *Indo-Iranian Journal* 3 (1959): 241–258.

——. "Vrātya and Sacrifice." *Indo-Iranian Journal* 6 (1962): 1–37.

Hibbets, Maria. "The Ethics of Esteem." *Journal of Buddhist Ethics* 7 (2000): 26–42.

——. "Saving Them from Yourself: An Inquiry into the South Asian Gift of Fearlessness." *Journal of Religious Ethics* 27 (1999): 437–469.

Hiltebeitel, Alf. "Purity and Auspiciousness in the Sanskrit Epics." In *Purity and Auspiciousness in Indian Society*, edited by John B. Carman and Frédèrique Apffel Marglin, 41–54. Leiden: E. J. Brill, 1985.

Hoffman, Frank J. "*Evaṃ Me Sutaṃ*: Oral Tradition in Nikāya Buddhism." In *Texts in Context: Traditional Hermeneutics in South Asia*, edited by Jeffrey R. Timm, 195–219. Albany: State University of New York Press, 1992.

Holt, John C. "Assisting the Dead by Venerating the Living: Merit Transfer in the Early Buddhist Tradition." *Numen* 28 (1981): 1–28.

Hopkins, E. Washburne. "Modifications of the Karma Doctrine." *Journal of the Royal Asiatic Society* 1906: 581–593.

——. "More about the Modifications of the Karma Doctrine." *Journal of the Royal Asiatic Society* 1907: 665–672.

Horsch, Paul. *Die vedische Gāthā- und Śloka-Literatur*. Bern: Francke Verlag, 1966.

——. "Vorstufen der indischen Seelenwanderungslehre." *Asiatische Studien* 25 (1971): 99–157.

Humphrey, Caroline and James Laidlaw. *The Archetypal Actions of Ritual: A Theory of Ritual Illustrated by the Jain Rite of Worship*. Oxford: Clarendon Press: 1994.

Inden, Ronald. "The Ceremony of the Great Gift (*Mahādāna*): Structure and Historical Context in Indian Ritual and Society. In *Asie du Sud: Traditions et Changements*, 131–6. Paris: Études du Centre National de la Recherche Scientifique, 1979.

——. "Ritual, Authority, and Cyclic Time in Hindu Kingship." In *Kingship and Authority in South Asia*, edited by J. F. Richards, 28–73. Madison: University of Wisconsin, 1978.

Jaini, Padmanabh S. "Karma and the Problem of Rebirth in Jainism." In *Karma and Rebirth in Classical Indian Traditions*, edited by Wendy Doniger O'Flaherty, 217—238. Berkeley: University of California Press, 1980.

——. "The Pure and the Auspicious in the Jaina Tradition." *Journal of Developing Societies* 1 (1985): 84–93.

——. "The Sautrāntika Theory of *Bīja*." *Bulletin of the School of Oriental and African Studies* 22 (1959): 236–249.

Jamison, Stephanie W. *The Ravenous Hyenas and the Wounded Sun: Myth and Ritual in Ancient India*. Ithaca, NY: Cornell University Press, 1991.

——. *Sacrificed Wife/Sacrificer's Wife: Women, Ritual, and Hospitality in Ancient India*. New York: Oxford University Press, 1996.

——. "Vedic mení, Avestan maēni, and the power of thwarted exchange." *Festschrift Paul Thieme. Studien zur Indologie und Iranistik* 20 (1996): 187–203.

Jayawickrama, N. A. "A Critical Analysis of the Pāli Sutta Nipāta Illustrating its Gradual Growth: General Observations and Conclusions." *University of Ceylon Review* 9 (1951): 113–124.

——. "The Sutta Nipāta: Its Title and Form." *University of Ceylon Review* 6 (1948): 78–86.

——. "The Sutta Nipāta: Pucchās of the Pārayana Vagga." *University of Ceylon Review* 9 (1951): 61–68.

——. "Sutta Nipāta: Some Suttas from the Aṭṭhaka Vagga." *University of Ceylon Review* 8 (1950): 244–255.

——. "The Vaggas of the Sutta Nipāta." *University of Ceylon Review* 6 (1948): 229—257.

Kaelber, Walter O. "*Tapas* and Purification in Early Hinduism." *Numen* 26 (1979): 192–214.

Kane, P. V. *History of Dharmaśāstra*. 5 vols. Pune: Bhandarkar Oriental Research Institute, 1930–62.

Karunatillake, W. S. "The Religiousness of Buddhists in Sri Lanka through Belief and Practice." In *Religiousness in Sri Lanka*, edited by John Ross Carter, 1–34. Colombo: Marga Institute, 1979.

Keith, Arthur Berriedale. *The Religion and Philosophy of the Vedas and Upanishads*. Harvard Oriental Series, vols. 31 & 32. Cambridge: Harvard University Press, 1925.

Kemper, Steven. "Wealth and Reformation in Sinhalese Buddhist Monasticism." In *Ethics, Wealth and Salvation: A Study in Buddhist Social Ethics*, edited by Russell F. Sizemore and Donald K. Swearer, 152–169. Columbia, SC: University of South Carolina Press, 1990.

Keown, Damien. *The Nature of Buddhist Ethics*. New York: St. Martin's Press, 1992.

Keyes, Charles F. "Buddhist Pilgrimage Centers and the Twelve Year Cycle: Northern Thai Moral Order in Space and Time." *History of Religions* 15 (1975): 71–89.

——. "Economic Action and Buddhist Morality in a Thai Village." *Journal of Asian Studies* 42 (1983): 851–868.

——. "Introduction." In *Karma: An Anthropological Inquiry*, edited by Charles F. Keyes and E. Valentine Daniel. Berkeley: University of California Press, 1983.

——. "Merit-Transference in the Kammic Theory of Popular Theravāda Buddhism." In *Karma: An Anthropological Inquiry*, edited by Charles F. Keyes and E. Valentine Daniel, 261–286. Berkeley: University of California Press, 1983.

——. "Millenialism, Theravāda Buddhism, and Thai Society." *Journal of Asian Studies* 36 (1977): 283–302.

——. "The Power of Merit." *Visakha Puja* BE 2516 (1973): 95–102.

Keyes, Charles F. and E. Valentine Daniel, eds. *Karma: An Anthropological Inquiry*. Berkeley: University of California Press, 1983.

Kierkegaard, Søren. *The Sickness unto Death*. Translated by Edward V. Hong and Edna H. Hong. Princeton: Princeton University Press, 1980.

King, Winston L. *A Thousand Lives Away: Buddhism in Contemporary Burma*. Cambridge, MA: Harvard University Press, 1964.

Klaus, Konrad. *Die altindische Kosmologie: Nach den Brāhmaṇas dargestellt*. Indica et Tibetica: Monographien zu den Sprachen und Literaturen des indo-tibetischen Kulturraumes, Band 9. Bonn: Indica et Tibetica Verlag, 1986.

Knipe, David M. "*Sapiṇḍīkarana*: The Hindu Rite of Entry into Heaven." In *Religious Encounters with Death: Insights from the History and Anthropology of Religions*, edited by Frank E. Reynolds and Earle H. Waugh, 111–124. University Park: Penn State University Press, 1977.

Köhler, Hans-Werbin. Śrad-dhā- *in der vedischen und altbuddhistischen Literatur*. Wiesbaden: Franz Steiner Verlag, 1973.

Krishnan, Y. "Collective Karmas." *East and West* 39 (1989): 179–194.

——. "Karma Vipāka." *Numen* 30 (1983): 199–214.

Laidlaw, James. *Riches and Redemption: Religion, Economy, and Society among the Jains*. Oxford: Clarendon Press, 1995.

Lamotte, Étienne. *History of Indian Buddhism: From the Origins to the Śaka Era*. Translated by Sara Webb-Boin. Louvain-la-Neuve: Institut Orientaliste, 1988.

Lindh, Anders B. "Gāthā – Gītā: A Genre-Study." *Temenos* 28 (1992): 125–144.

Lindtner, Christian. "The Problem of Precanonical Buddhism." *Buddhist Studies Review* 14 (1997): 109–137.

Little, David. "Ethical Analysis and Wealth in Theravāda Buddhism: A Response to Frank Reynolds." In *Ethics, Wealth and Salvation: A Study in Buddhist Social Ethics*, edited by Russell F. Sizemore and Donald K. Swearer, 77—86. Columbia, SC: University of South Carolina Press, 1990.

Long, J. Bruce. "The Concepts of Human Action and Rebirth in the *Mahābhārata*." In *Karma and Rebirth in Classical Indian Traditions*, edited by Wendy Doniger O'Flaherty, 38–60. Berkeley: University of California Press, 1980.

Macy, Joanna R. "Not to Escape, but to Transform: Enlightenment and the Concept of Parināmanā in the *Aṣṭasāhasrikā Prajñāpāramitā*." In *Buddhist Heritage in India and Abroad*, edited by G. Kuppuram and K. Kumudamani, 143–159. Delhi: Sundeep Prakashan, 1992.

Madan, T. N. "Concerning the Categories *Śubha* and *Śuddha* in Hindu Culture: an Exploratory Essay." In *Purity and Auspiciousness in Indian Society*, edited by John B. Carman and Frédérique Apffel Marglin, 11–29. Leiden: E. J. Brill, 1985.

Malalasekere, G. P. "Transference of Merit in Ceylonese Buddhism." *Philosophy East and West* 17:85–90.

Malamoud, Charles. "Terminer le Sacrifice." In *Le Sacrifice dans l'Inde ancienne*, edited by Madeleine Biardeau and Charles Malamoud, 155–204. Paris: Presses Universitaires de France, 1976.

Manné, Joy. "Categories of Sutta in the Pāli Nikāyas and their Implications for Our Appreciation of the Buddhist Teaching and Literature." *Journal of the Pali Text Society* 15 (1990): 30–87.

Marglin, Frédérique Apffel. "Introduction" and "Types of Oppositions in Hindu Culture." In *Purity and Auspiciousness in Indian Society*, edited by John B. Carman and Frédérique Apffel Marglin, 1–10 and 65–83. Leiden: E. J. Brill, 1985.

Matthews, Bruce. "Post-Classical Developments in the Concepts of Karma and Rebirth in Theravāda Buddhism." In *Karma and Rebirth: Post Classical Developments*, edited by Ronald W. Neufeldt, chapter 7, 123–143. Albany: State University of New York Press, 1986.

Mauss, Marcel. *The Gift: The Form and Reason for Exchange in Archaic Societies*. Translated by W. D. Halls. London: Routledge, 1990.

Mayrhofer, Manfred. *Etymologisches Wörterbuch des Altindoarischen*. Heidelberg: Carl Winter Universitätsverlag, 1986–.

McDermott, James Paul. *Development in the Early Buddhist Concept of Kamma/Karma*. New Delhi: Munshiram Manoharlal, 1984.

——. "Is There Group Karma in Theravāda Buddhism?" *Numen* 23 (1976): 67–80.

——. "Karma and Rebirth in Early Buddhism." In *Karma and Rebirth in Classical Indian Traditions*, edited by Wendy Doniger O'Flaherty, 165–192. Berkeley: University of California Press, 1980.

——. "Nibbāna as a Reward for Kamma." *Journal of the American Oriental Society* 93 (1973): 344–347.

——. "*Sādhīna Jātaka*: A Case Against the Transfer of Merit." *Journal of the American Oriental Society* 94 (1974): 385–387.

——. "Undetermined and Indeterminate Kamma." *Indo-Iranian Journal* 19 (1977): 31–35.

Mette, Adelheid. "The Synchronism of the Buddha and the Jina Mahāvīra and the Problem of Chronology in Early Jainism." In *The Dating of the Historical Buddha*, Part 1, edited by Heinz Bechert, 132–137. *Abhandlungen der Akademie der Wissenschaften in Göttingen, Philologisch-Historische Klasse Dritte Folge*, Nr. 189. Göttingen: Vanderhoech & Ruprecht, 1991.

Misra, G. S. P. "Reflections on the Buddhist Doctrine of Karman." *Journal of the Oriental Institute (Baroda)*. 25 (1975): 47–56.

Mitchell, Daniel W. "Karma in Buddhist Thought." In *The Dimensions of Karma*, edited by S. S. Rama Rao Pappu, –93. Delhi: Chanakya, 1987.

Murakami, Shinkan. "Non-desire and Non-possession: The *Mahābhārata* and Buddhism." *Tōhoku Daigaku Bungako-bu Kenkyū Nempō* 29 (1979): 244—248.

Mus, Paul. *Barabuḍur: Esquisse d'une histoire du bouddhisme fondée sur la critique archéologique des textes.* Hanoi: Imprimerie d'Extrême-Orient, 1935.

Nakamura, Hajime. "Common Elements in Early Jain and Buddhist Literature." *Indologica Taurinensia* 11 (1983): 303–330.

——. *Indian Buddhism: A Survey with Bibliographical Notes.* Hirakata, Osaka: KUFS, 1980.

Nash, Manning. *The Golden Road to Modernity: Village Life in Contemporary Burma.* New York: John Wiley & Sons, 1965.

Nath, Vijay. *Dāna: Gift System in Ancient India (c. 600 BC - c. AD 300): A Socio-economic Perspective.* New Delhi: Munshiram Manoharlal, 1987.

Norman, K. R. "Aspects of Early Buddhism." *Panels of the VIIth World Sanskrit Conference*, edited by Johannes Bronkhorst, vol. 2, *Earliest Buddhism and Madhyamaka*, edited by David Seyfort Ruegg and Lambert Schmithausen, 24–35. Leiden: E. J. Brill, 1990.

——. *Collected Papers.* Oxford: Pali Text Society, 1990–.

——. *Pāli Literature.* Vol. VII, fasc. 2 of *A History of Indian Literature*, ed. Jan Gonda. Wiesbaden: Otto Harrassowitz, 1983.

Nyanatiloka. *Buddhist Dictionary: Manual of Buddhist Terms and Doctrines.* Edited by Nyanaponika. 3d ed. Colombo: Frewin & Co., Ltd., 1972.

Oberhammer, Gerhard, ed. *Im Tod gewinnt der Mensch sein Selbst: Das Phänomen des Todes in asiatischer und abendländischer Religionstradition.* Vienna: Verlag der Österreichischen Akademie der Wissenschaften, 1995.

Obeyesekere, Gananath. "The Buddhist Pantheon in Ceylon and its Extensions." In *Anthropological Studies in Theravada Buddhism*, edited by Manning Nash et al., 1–26. Yale University South East Asia Cultural Report Series No. 13, 1966.

——. "The Rebirth Eschatology and its Transformations: A Contribution to the Sociology of Early Buddhism." In *Karma and Rebirth in Classical Indian Traditions*, edited by Wendy Doniger O'Flaherty, 137–164. Berkeley: University of California Press, 1980.

——. "Theodicy, Sin, and Salvation in a Sociology of Buddhism." In *Dialectic in Practical Religion*, edited by E. R. Leach, 7–40. Cambridge: Cambridge University Press, 1968.

Oertel, Hanns. "Extracts from the Jāiminīya-Brāhmaṇa and Upanishad-Brāhmaṇa, Parallel to Passages of the Çatapatha-Brāhmaṇa and Chāndogya-Upanishad." *Journal of the American Oriental Society* 15 (1893): 233–251.

O'Flaherty, Wendy Doniger. *Asceticism and Eroticism in the Mythology of Śiva.* Delhi: Oxford University Press, 1973.

——. "Karma and Rebirth in the Vedas and Purāṇas." In *Karma and Rebirth in Classical Indian Traditions*, edited by Wendy Doniger O'Flaherty, 3–37. Berkeley: University of California Press, 1980.

——. *The Origins of Evil in Hindu Mythology.* Berkeley: University of California Press, 1976.

——. *Tales of Sex and Violence: Folklore, Sacrifice, and Danger in the* Jaiminīya Brāhmaṇa. Chicago: University of Chicago Press, 1985.

——. *Women, Androgynes, and Other Mythical Beasts.* Chicago: University of Chicago Press, 1980.

——, ed. *Karma and Rebirth in Classical Indian Traditions.* Berkeley: University of California Press, 1980.

Oguibénine, Boris. "La dakṣiṇā dans le Ṛgveda et le transfert de mérite dans le Bouddhisme." In *Indological and Buddhist Studies: Volume in Honour of Professor J. W. de Jong on his Sixtieth Birthday,* edited by L. A. Hercus et al., 393–414. Canberra: Faculty of Asian Studies, 1982.

Olivelle, Patrick. *The Āśrama System: The History and Hermeneutics of a Religious Institution.* New York: Oxford University Press, 1993.

Pande, Govind Chandra. *Studies in the Origins of Buddhism.* Allahabad: University of Allahabad, 1957.

Paranavitana, Senarat. *Inscriptions of Ceylon.* [Colombo]: Department of Archaeology, 1970–.

Parry, Jonathan P. *Death in Banaras.* Cambridge: Cambridge University Press, 1994.

——. "*The Gift,* the Indian Gift, and the 'Indian Gift.'" *Man* (n.s.) 21 (1986): 453–473.

——. "The Hindu Lexicographer? A Note on Auspiciousness and Purity." *Contributions to Indian Sociology* (n.s.) 25 (1991): 277–285.

——. "On the Moral Perils of Exchange." In *Money and the Morality of Exchange,* edited by J. Parry and M. Bloch, 64–93. Cambridge: Cambridge University Press, 1989.

Parry, Jonathan and Maurice Bloch. "Introduction: Money and the Morality of Exchange." In *Money and the Morality of Exchange,* edited by J. Parry and M. Bloch, 1–32. Cambridge: Cambridge University Press, 1989.

Pollock, Sheldon. "From Discourse of Ritual to Discourse of Power in Sanskrit Culture." *Journal of Ritual Studies* 4 (1990): 315–345.

Potter, Karl H. "The Karma Theory and its Interpretation in Some Indian Philosophical Systems." In *Karma and Rebirth in Classical Indian Traditions,* edited by Wendy Doniger O'Flaherty, 241–267. Berkeley: University of California Press, 1980.

——. *Presuppositions of India's Philosophies.* Delhi: Motilal Banarsidass, 1991.

Premasiri, P. D. "Interpretation of Two Principal Ethical Terms in Early Buddhism." *Sri Lanka Journal of the Humanities* 2 (1976): 63–74.

Przyluski, Jean. *The Legend of Emperor Aśoka in Indian and Chinese Texts.* Translated by Dilip Kumar Biswas. Calcutta: Firma K. L. Mukhopadhyay, 1967.

Raheja, Gloria Goodwin. "Caste Ideologies, Protest and the Power of the Dominant Caste: A Reply to Gregory and Heesterman." *Social Analysis* 34 (1993): 17—32.

——. "India: Caste, Kingship, and Dominance Reconsidered." *Annual Review of Anthropology* 17 (1988): 497–522.

——. *The Poison in the Gift: Ritual, Prestation, and the Dominant Caste in a North Indian Village.* Chicago: University of Chicago Press, 1988.

Reynolds, Frank E. "Ethics and Wealth in Theravāda Buddhism: A Study in Comparative Religious Ethics." In *Ethics, Wealth and Salvation: A Study in Buddhist Social Ethics*, edited by Russell F. Sizemore and Donald K. Swearer, 59—76. Columbia, SC: University of South Carolina Press, 1990.

Rhys Davids, T. W., and William Stede. *The Pali Text Society's Pali-English Dictionary*. London: Pali Text Society, 1921–1925.

Rocher, Ludo. "Karma and Rebirth in the Dharmaśāstras." In *Karma and Rebirth in Classical Indian Traditions*, edited by Wendy Doniger O'Flaherty, 61—89. Berkeley: University of California Press, 1980.

Saddhatissa, Hammalawa. *Buddhist Ethics*. Third edition. Boston: Wisdom Publications, 1997.

Scherman, Lucian. *Materialen zur Geschichte der indischen Visionslitteratur*. Leipzig: A. Twietmeyer, 1892.

Schmithausen, Lambert. "An Attempt to Estimate the Distance in Time between Aśoka and the Buddha in Terms of Doctrinal History." In *The Dating of the Historical Buddha*, Part 1, edited by Heinz Bechert, 110–147. *Abhandlungen der Akademie der Wissenschaften in Göttingen, Philologisch-Historische Klasse Dritte Folge*, Nr. 189. Göttingen: Vanderhoech & Ruprecht, 1991.

——. "Critical Response." In *Karma and Rebirth: Post Classical Developments*, edited by Ronald W. Neufeldt, chapter 12, 203–230. Albany: State University of New York, 1986.

——. "On Some Aspects of Descriptions or Theories of 'Liberating Insight' and 'Enlightenment' in Early Buddhism." In *Studien zum Jainismus und Buddhismus: Gedenkenschrift für Ludwig Alsdorf*, edited by Klaus Bruhn and Albrecht Wezler, 199–250. Wiesbaden: Franz Steiner Verlag GmbH, 1981.

——. "On the Problem of the Relation of Spiritual Practice and Philosophical Theory in Buddhism." In *German Scholars on India*, edited by the Cultural Dept. of the Embassy of the Federal Republic of Germany, New Delhi, 2:235–250. Bombay: Nachiketa Publications, 1976.

——. "Preface" to *Panels of the VIIth World Sanskrit Conference*, edited by Johannes Bronkhorst, vol. 2: *Earliest Buddhism and Madhyamaka*, edited by David Seyfort Ruegg and Lambert Schmithausen, 1–4. Leiden: E. J. Brill, 1990.

——. Review of *The Vedic Origins of Karma*, by Herman W. Tull. In *Indo-Iranian Journal* 37 (1994): 151–158.

Schopen, Gregory. "Archaeology and Protestant Presuppositions in the Study of Indian Buddhism." *History of Religions*: 31 (1991): 1–23.

——. *Bones, Stones, and Buddhist Monks: Collected Papers on the Archaeology, Epigraphy, and Texts of Monastic Buddhism in India*. Honolulu: University of Hawai'i Press, 1997.

——. "Burial *'Ad Sanctos'* and the Physical Presence of the Buddha in Early Indian Buddhism: A Study in the Archaeology of Religions." *Religion* 17 (1987): 193–225.

——. "Mahāyāna in Indian Inscriptions." *Indo-Iranian Journal* 21 (1979): 1–19.

——. "Monastic Law Meets the Real World: A Monk's Continuing Right to Inherit Family Property in Classical India." *History of Religions*: 35 (1995): 101–123.

——. "The Monastic Ownership of Servants or Slaves: Local and Legal Factors in the Redactional History of Two *Vinayas*." *Journal of the International Association of Buddhist Studies* 17 (1994): 145–173.

——. "An Old Inscription from Amarāvatī and the Cult of the Local Monastic Dead in Indian Buddhist Monasteries." *Journal of the International Association of Buddhist Studies* 14 (1991): 281–329.

——. "On Avoiding Ghosts and Social Censure: Monastic Funerals in the Mūlasarvāstivāda-Vinaya." *Journal of Indian Philosophy* 20 (1992): 1–39.

——. "On Monks, Nuns, and 'Vulgar" Practices: The Introduction of the Image Cult into Indian Buddhism." *Artibus Asiae* 49 (1988/1989): 153–168.

——. "The Ritual Obligations and Donor Roles of Monks in the Pāli Vinaya." *Journal of the Pali Text Society* 16 (1992): 87–107.

——. "Ritual Rights and Bones of Contention: More on Monastic Funerals and Relics in the *Mūlasarvāstivāda-vinaya*. *Journal of Indian Philosophy* 22 (1994): 31–80.

——. "The Suppression of Nuns and the Ritual Murder of their Special Dead in Two Buddhist Monastic Texts." *Journal of Indian Philosophy* 24 (1996): 563—592.

——. "Two Problems in the History of Indian Buddhism: The Layman/Monk Distinction and the Doctrine of the Transference of Merit." *Studien zur Indologie und Iranistik* 10 (1987): 9–47.

Schubring, Walther. *The Doctrine of the Jains: Described after the Old Sources.* Translation of *Die Lehre Jainas*, revised edition, by Wolfgang Beurlen. Delhi: Motilal Banarsidass, 1962.

Shulman, David Dean. *The King and the Clown in South Indian Myth and Poetry.* Princeton: Princeton University Press, 1985.

——. "Kingship and Prestation in South Indian Myth and Epic." *Asian and African Studies* 19 (1985): 93–117.

Silber, Ilana Friedrich. "Gift-giving in the Great Traditions: The Case of Donations to Monasteries in the Medieval West." *Archives européennes de sociologie* 36 (1995): 209–243.

Sizemore, Russell F., and Donald K. Swearer. *Ethics, Wealth and Salvation: A Study in Buddhist Social Ethics.* Columbia, SC: University of South Carolina Press, 1990.

Smith, Brian K. *Classifying the Universe: The Ancient Indian* Varṇa *System and the Origins of Caste.* New York: Oxford University Press, 1994.

Smith, William Robertson. *Lectures on the Religions of the Semites: The Fundamental Institutions.* 3d ed. 1927; reprint, [New York:] Ktav Publishing House, 1969.

Southwold, Martin. *Buddhism in Life: The Anthropological Study of Religion and the Sinhalese Practice of Buddhism.* Manchester, U. K.: Manchester University Press, 1983.

Spiro, Melford E. *Buddhism and Society: A Great Tradition and Its Burmese Vicissitudes.* Second edition. Berkeley: University of California Press, 1982.

Staal, Frits. *Agni: The Vedic Ritual of the Fire Altar.* 2 vols. Berkeley: Asian Humanities Press, 1983.

——. "The Meaninglessness of Ritual." *Numen* 26 (1979): 2–22.

Stede, Wilhelm. *Über das Peta Vatthu.* Inaugural diss., University of Leipzig, 1914. [=*Die Gespenstergeschichten des Peta Vatthu*, Leipzig: Otto Harassowitz.]

Sternbach, Ludwik. *Subhāṣita, Gnomic and Didactic Literature.* Vol. IV, Part 1 of *A History of Indian Literature* ed. Jan Gonda. Wiesbaden: Otto Harrassowitz, 1974.

Strenski, Ivan. "On Generalized Exchange and the Domestication of the *Saṅgha.*" *Man* (n.s.) 18 (1983): 463–477.

Strong, John S. *The Legend of King Aśoka: A Study and Translation of the* Aśokāvadāna. Princeton: Princeton University Press, 1983.

——. *Making Merit in the* Aśokāvadāna*: A Study of Buddhist Acts of Offering in the Post-*parinirvāṇa *Age.* Ph.D. diss., University of Chicago, 1977.

——. "Rich Man, Poor Man, *Bhikkhu*, King: Aśoka's Great Quinquennial Festival and the Nature of *Dāna.*" In *Ethics, Wealth and Salvation: A Study in Buddhist Social Ethics*, edited by Russell F. Sizemore and Donald K. Swearer, 107—123. Columbia, SC: University of South Carolina Press, 1990.

——. "The Transforming Gift: An Analysis of Devotional Acts of Offering in Buddhist Avadāna Literature." *History of Religions* 18 (1979): 221–237.

Takahara, Shin-ichi. "Puṇya in the Mahāvastu." *Indogakyu Bukkyōgaku Kenkyū* 18: 433–440 (=9–15).

Tambiah, Stanley J. *Buddhism and the Spirit Cults in North-east Thailand.* London: Cambridge University Press, 1970.

——. *The Buddhist saints of the forest and the cult of amulets.* Cambridge: Cambridge University Press, 1984.

——. "The Ideology of Merit and the Social Correlates of Buddhism in a Thai Village." In *Dialectic in Practical Religion*, edited by E. R. Leach, 41–121. Cambridge: Cambridge University Press, 1968.

——. "A Performative Approach to Ritual." *Proceedings of the British Academy* 65 (1981): 113–169.

——. "Purity and Auspiciousness at the Edge of the Hindu Context – in Theravāda Buddhist Societies." In *Purity and Auspiciousness in Indian Society*, edited by John B. Carman and Frédérique Apffel Marglin, 94–108. Leiden: E. J. Brill, 1985.

Teiser, Stephen F. *The Ghost Festival in Medieval China.* Princeton: Princeton University Press, 1988.

Thapar, Romila. "The householder and the renouncer in Brahmanical and Buddhist traditions." In *Way of Life: King, Householder, Renouncer: Essays in Honor of Louis Dumont*, edited by T. N. Madan, 273–298. New Delhi: Vikas Publishing House, 1982.

——. "Sacrifice, Surplus, and the Soul." *History of Religions* 33 (1994): 305–324.

Thompson, George. "On Truth-Acts in Vedic." *Indo-Iranian Journal* 41 (1998): 125–153.

Trainor, Kevin. *Relics, Ritual, and Representation in Buddhism: Rematerializing the Sri Lankan Theravāda tradition.* Cambridge: Cambridge University Press, 1997.

Trautmann, Thomas R. *Aryans and British India.* Berkeley: University of California Press, 1997.

——. *Dravidian Kinship*. Cambridge: Cambridge University Press, 1981.

Trenckner, Vilhelm. et al. *A Critical Pāli Dictionary*. Copenhagen: The Royal Danish Academy of Sciences and Letters, 1924–.

Tull, Herman W. *The Vedic Origins of Karma: Cosmos as Man in Ancient Indian Myth and Ritual*. Albany: State University of New York, 1989.

Van Baal, J. "Offering, Sacrifice, and Gift." *Numen* 23 (1976): 161–178.

Vetter, Tilmann. *The Ideas and Meditative Practices of Early Buddhism*. Leiden: E.J. Brill, 1988.

Von Fürer-Haimendorf, Christoph. *Morals and Merit: A Study of Values and Social Controls in South Asian Societies*. Chicago: University of Chicago, 1967.

Von Hinüber, Oskar. *A Handbook of Pāli Literature*. Berlin: Walter de Gruyter, 1996.

Walters, Jonathan S. "The Buddha's Bad Karma: A Problem in the History of Theravāda Buddhism." *Numen* 37 (1990): 70–95.

——. "Gotamī's Story." In *Buddhism in Practice*, edited by Donald S. Lopez, Jr., 113—138. Princeton: Princeton University Press, 1995.

——. "Mahāsena at the Mahāvihāra: On the Interpretation and Politics of History in Pre-Colonial Sri Lanka." In *Invoking the Past: The Uses of History in South Asia*, edited by Daud Ali, 322–366. New Delhi: Oxford University Press, 1999.

——. "Mahāyāna Theravāda and the Origins of the Mahāvihāra." *Sri Lanka Journal of the Humanities* 23 (1997): 100–119.

——. "Stūpa, Story and Empire: Constructions of the Buddha Biography in Early Post-Aśokan India." In *Sacred Biography in the Buddhist Traditions of South and Southeast Asia*, edited by Juliane Schober, 160—192. Honolulu: University of Hawai'i Press, 1997.

——. "Suttas as History: Four Approaches to the *Sermon on the Noble Quest* (Ariyapariyesanasutta)." *History of Religions* 38 (1999): 247–284.

——. "A Voice From the Silence: The Buddha's Mother's Story." *History of Religions* 33 (1994): 358–379.

Warder, A. K. *Introduction to Pali*. Third edition. Oxford: Pali Text Society, 1991.

——. *Pali Metre: A Contribution to the History of Indian Literature*. London: Pali Text Society, 1967.

Wayman, Alex. "The Hindu-Buddhist Rite of Truth – An Interpretation." In *Studies in Indian Linguistics [Professor M. B. Emeneau Ṣaṣṭipūrti Volume]*, edited by Bhadrivaju Krishnamurti, 365–9. Poona: 1968.

White, David Gordon. "*Dakkhiṇa* and *Agnicayana*: An Extended Application of Paul Mus' Typology." *History of Religions* 26 (1986): 188–213.

Wijayaratna, Mohan. *Buddhist Monastic Life: According to the Texts of the Theravāda Tradition*. Translated by Claude Grangier and Steven Collins. Cambridge: Cambridge University Press, 1990.

Willis, Janice D. "Nuns and Benefactresses: The Role of Women in the Development of Buddhism." In *Women, Religion, and Social Change*, edited by Yvonne Yazbeck Haddad and Ellison Banks Findly, 59–85. Albany: State University of New York, 1985.

Winternitz, Moriz. *A History of Indian Literature*. Translated by S. Ketkar, and revised by the author. 1931; reprint, New York: Russell and Russell, 1971.

Witzel, Michael. "The Oldest Form of the Idea of Rebirth." In *Proceedings of the 31st International Congress of Human Sciences in Asia and North Africa Tokyo-Kyoto 1983*, edited by T. Yamamoto, 145–146. Tokyo: 1984.

——. "Sur le chemin du ciel." *Bulletin d'Études indiennes* 2 (1984): 213–279.

Woodward, F. L. "The Buddhist Doctrine of Reversible Merit." *The Buddhist Review* 6 (1914): 38–50.

Woodward, Frank Lee, E. M. Hare, et al. *Pāli Tipiṭakaṁ Concordance*. Oxford: Pali Text Society, 1991–.

Yerkes, Royden Keith. *Sacrifice in Greek and Roman Religions and Early Judaism*. London: Adam and Charles Black, 1953.

INDEX